RELIGION FOR MANKIND

RELIGION FOR MANKIND

by

HORACE HOLLEY

BAHÁ'Í PUBLISHING TRUST
Wilmette, Illinois

Printed in Great Britain

"*I believe that at this very hour the great revolution is beginning which has been preparing for two thousand years in the religious world—the revolution which will substitute for corrupted religion, and the system of domination which proceeds therefrom, the true religion, the basis of equality between men, and of the true liberty to which all beings endowed with reason aspire.*" TOLSTOY.

PREFACE TO THE 1966 EDITION

AS HORACE HOLLEY himself said in his Introduction to this collection of some of his writings, first published in this form in 1956, his life for the past forty-seven years had been "a series of efforts to find out what the Bahá'í World Faith is, what it means, and how it functions."

Most of these essays were written during the period 1921–1957, when Shoghi Effendi Rabbani was Guardian of the Faith at its World Centre in Haifa, Israel, in accordance with his appointment in the Will and Testament of his grandfather, 'Abdu'l-Bahá. After Shoghi Effendi's death on November 4, 1957, without issue, his plans were carried forward by the body of the Hands of the Cause of God whom he had appointed, in their capacity as "Chief Stewards" of Bahá'u'lláh's embryonic World Order, until it became possible for the fifty-six National Spiritual Assemblies of the Bahá'í world to convene in Haifa for the election of the first Universal House of Justice, on April 21, 1963. This supreme legislative body, instituted by Bahá'u'lláh, directs the affairs of the world community of His followers and under its guidance His Faith, now one hundred and twenty-three years old, is spreading to every part of the planet. As this book goes to press, there are Bahá'ís in one hundred and twenty-four independent nations and in over one hundred and sixty significant territories and islands, while the literature of the Faith has been translated into three hundred and seventy-one languages. The number of localities where Bahá'ís reside exceeds twenty-one thousand and there are seventy National Spiritual Assemblies.

Horace Holley died on July 12, 1960, before many of these developments had taken place. It will now be seen that some of the events he anticipated, from his reading of the Will and Testament of 'Abdu'l-Bahá and the writings of the Guardian, had another outcome, but he would have been the first to acclaim the birth and support the authority of the Universal House of Justice. The enduring value of his thought lies in its spirit of search and devotion to the Word of God in this age, which makes these essays a constant inspiration to any serious student of the Bahá'í Faith.

For the sake of preserving the integrity of the author's work, no alterations in his text have been introduced, but the reader will be able to appreciate, by reference to this editorial note, the continuing evolution and dynamic growth of the Faith of Bahá'u'lláh since 1956.

CONTENTS

CONTENTS (*continued*)

ILLUSTRATION

The Bahá'í Temple, Wilmette, Illinois,

facing page 179

INTRODUCTION

FORTY-SEVEN years ago while on board ship a book was lent me, by a passenger, entitled *Abbas Effendi*.

That was my first encounter with the Faith of Bahá'u'lláh. The wisdom, the universality of spirit and the profound love expressed in 'Abdu'l-Bahá, persecuted leader of a new religion, captivated me. He stood apart from the epic heroes and thinkers of history and brought a new dimension to my inexperienced, naïve liberal culture. Without knowing what it meant I had become a Bahá'í.

The pattern of life since then has been a series of efforts to find out what the Bahá'í World Faith is, what it means, and how it functions. The present work represents a collection of articles written during these forty-seven years as explorations of this supreme Reality offered modern man in his most desperate era.

At first it seemed possible to encompass the Revelation of Bahá'u'lláh by reducing it to a formula or confining it within a well-turned phrase. Gradually my ventures proved to me that I myself was to be encompassed, re-oriented, remoulded in all the realms of being. For religion in its purity reveals God, and only God can reveal man to himself.

Nothing could be more absorbing than the effort to discover the sources of history and cultures in the revealed will of God. Nothing could induce greater reverence than the realization that all the Prophets are successive manifestations of one Being, intermediary between God and man. Nothing could be more dramatic than to perceive the oneness of humanity which has become the essential fact of human existence today. Nothing could be more soul-satisfying than to become one member of a world-wide community devoted to the promotion of the majestic and creative principles associated with the mission of Bahá'u'lláh.

Fortunate above fortune itself was the early privilege of meeting 'Abdu'l-Bahá in Thonon, on Lake Geneva, and of hearing many of His intimate daily talks in Paris. Here seemed to be throbbing the very heart of a new and regenerated mankind, conscious at last of its heritage from God and its mission to establish a heaven upon earth. Later, in America, association with the Bahá'í community enabled me to witness not only the spread of interest in the Faith but the construction through all its stages of the Bahá'í House of Worship and the functioning of Spiritual Assemblies as institutions reflecting the application of Bahá'í principles to community life. Then, too, in public addresses and Bahá'í summer school teaching service I could appreciate the importance of attaining a deeper and orderly understanding of the Faith.

Thus the exploration pursued many paths; at first a literary effort, later the study of human relations, brief flights into mysticism and even concern with the nature of institutional functions in terms of constitution and by-law.

The outlets for these brief writings have for the most part been Bahá'í organs—magazine, news bulletin and year book, as the community became more highly articulate and more responsible for mission efforts to other lands.

Finally it was my privilege to discover the Bahá'í community itself, as it has developed in East and West, through attendance at conferences held in Kampala, Chicago, Stockholm and New Delhi during 1953. There the great variety of racial and cultural types gathered in unity, peace and constructive purpose. That same miraculous year closed with a pilgrimage to the Bahá'í World Centre in Haifa, Israel, where I remained several days, visiting the Bahá'í Shrines, Holy Places and Gardens, and felt the power of an advancing Faith express itself through the Guardian, Shoghi Effendi Rabbani.

Thus the spirit of investigation brought prodigious reward beyond its desert. Now, as others in their turn arise to seek a new Spirit, a new Guidance in this troubled age, may they find a few trails blazed and at least a faint path marked for them leading from the world of Self toward the world of Revelation.

Wilmette, Illinois   HORACE HOLLEY
February 16, 1956

PART I

THE NEED FOR RELIGION

THE HUMAN SITUATION

THE SWIFT movement of world events from 1919 to 1956 has brought humanity to that stage in the destruction of a long historic cycle when inner incompatibility, prejudice, fear and ambition seize upon the instruments of civilization and employ the terms of political and economic policy in order to render to violence its supreme expression. The trend has become fixed and irrevocable. Failing to yield itself to the divine Will, human will has become victim to that frenzy which is the more sinister because it is no longer primitive excitement but the crystallization of implacable formulas of collective power. The individual consciousness is not scaled to such vast areas of experience. Spiritually little men raise up artificial formulas to serve as substitutes for the essential truths uttered by the Prophet as He walks among men.

The condition was defined by these words in a cablegram from Shoghi Effendi received in America August 30, 1939; "Shades (of) night, descending (upon) imperilled humanity, inexorably deepening." Dark, encircling night, witnessing the setting of all the illumined heavenly bodies which had brought light to mankind in the past, hopeless of any new dawn, the state in which man learns that he must confront his own ignorance and his own evil !

What more can the civilized man do for himself and for others when the ends, the issues and the plans of existence have been seized from his grasp by Caesar and his legions? What more can the loyal follower of a sectarian creed accomplish for himself, his church or his neighbours when the ancestral world which the creed might have fitted is utterly abandoned, an empty house fallen to decay? How long can the stronger, cleverer few hope to fish in troubled waters when the hurricane engulfs even the dry land and dashes ships of steel against houses of stone? " (The) long-predicted world-encircling conflagration, essential pre-requisite (to) world unification, (is) inexorably moving to its appointed climax," Shoghi Effendi cabled a few months later, in 1940.

Immersed in such a vast movement of destiny, knowing that in this crisis there is no escape by migration, discovery, even by conquest and seizure, the Bahá'í at moments turns back to significant pictures by which human feeling attempts to grasp the meaning of times, people and civilizations. One of these pictures reveals the image of an inhuman god, enthroned by a powerful priesthood high above the people, his belly a smoking fire, his worship the sacrifice of children torn from their mothers' arms. Another uncovers the rising waters of the great flood, inch by inch submerging every safety and every stronghold which mankind has built for protection against its foes. One sees, finally, the Figure of the Holy One walking on earth, asserting truth and love against every human argument and condition, the miracle of history, shepherding the lowly and sincere into His Kingdom, judging and condemning the cruel, the truthless, the deniers.

Never in all recorded time has a destined destruction of civilization been stayed by any of the institutions, secular or religious, through which the civilization has developed to the degree of external glory and inner decay. All that has fed upon the civilization and exploited the weakness of its peoples, all that has attained influence and power for its own ends, all that depends directly or indirectly upon its injustice, goes down with the collapse of the civilization as parasites go down with the dying tree. For wars and revolutions to come, there must be a succession of awful prior defeats in the world of the soul. There must be abdications of truth and righteousness, there must be prostitutions of public privilege and power, there must be accommodations entered into with despoilers of the people. One by one the mighty walls raised by the people of faith must be undermined by creed, ceremony and policy before the hosts of the destroyers can enter the city gates. The work of evil goes on unchecked and unnoticed when leaders are busy in disputes concerning the priorities of institutional religion. At last the process culminates in necessity to uphold immoral public policy in the guise of programmes for crisis. At last, having abandoned voluntary effort to remain true to the Faith of God, it becomes imperative for the multitudes to perform what their faith had originally condemned. Definitions of necessity are a last vain effort of man to remain rational when he has betrayed the true aim and function of reason.

No concentration of social force nor combination of moribund institutions can restore the youthful vigour and integrity that have been lost. The spirit creates the social institutions needed for accomplishing tasks concerned with the development of one historic era. When the tool has done its work, and different instruments are needed, the institutions are destroyed by that same spirit, which then is engaged in creating new and more effective tools. But faith is the capacity to live positively in and through conditions which to the denier seem to be utterly irreconcilable and mutually exclusive. The beginnings and the ends of all things on earth are matters of faith. The tenderest love which the Prophet can convey, and the violence of war itself, can to the man of faith be one mystery.

The outcome of the trend when the power of destruction is manifest discloses the true nature of the prevalent human qualities and attitudes. Destruction is never merely the expression of one evil party in relation to another innocent party, for the outcome rests upon prior indifference and non-action as much as upon explosive ambition. The passive unwillingness of a great body of cultured, humane and civilized people in many countries to exert themselves sufficiently to establish either justice for their own poor or collective security for all nations, weak or powerful, provided the opportunity for the active forces to work. Those who build an anvil may deny having built the hammer, but in action the anvil and the hammer are one instrument and one function. That is why, in a time like the present, there can be so much apparent good and so much innocence, such wonderful virtues and such heroic suffering. Praiseworthy in relation to ethical standards of the past, they nevertheless did not suffice to stay the hand of the great destroyers. The eventual outcome of events is their condemnation.

But destruction itself is part of that larger order whose dynamic form is growth. The Bahá'ís find in their Faith complete assurance that this outer darkness will end and the light of spiritual knowledge cover the earth. By the elimination of the social patterns, which have become agencies of destruction, and the refutation of the human loyalties which serve to organize and perpetuate prejudice of race, creed, class and nation, the creative spirit sent down through Bahá'u'lláh will gradually disclose its one world pattern and establish it with the authority of truth and discipline in the hearts of men.

THE DIVINE TEACHER

A GALILEAN shepherd or fisherman, whom good fortune or the sure intuition of divine curiosity had permitted to hear the Sermon on the Mount, on returning to his neighbours filled with intense joy and conviction, might conceivably have told them of this teaching without mentioning the Christ who uttered it; but however thoroughly he understood the new gospel, however clearly he repeated it in his native village, the completeness and power of his story would have been fatally broken without an expressed personal attitude towards the Prophet, and a lifelong, lifedeep consciousness of the divine-human presence. For the Prophet's relation to his teaching utterly transcends its mere formulation into written or spoken words. He is not merely the creator of a new body of spiritual truth, in the manner that a poet creates a new interpretation of life in terms of a dramatic or epic reaction. Homer attains personality through the Iliad; Shakespeare's presence defines itself in the presence of his characters; but a revelation exists only to the extent that its Prophet continues to exist in the consciousness of men, and apart from its existence in human consciousness it has no being. For a revelation is essentially personality, human life, character, destiny. Printed, it remains only a philosophy or dream until, somehow, by an overwhelming, passionate desire for spiritual excellence, the Prophet Himself is felt as a living, immediate presence and being, when the words leap out as from moving lips, and become ever afterward *His* words, wherever, however met. No man, it can be stated, ever actually found Christ in His message, but always His message in the Christ.

The secret of this lies in the fact that the spiritual life, as we understand and desire it, *is* Christ. The two have become identified, and in the person of the man Jesus the spiritual life has its eternal type and reality. The spiritual life, we must realize, is the expression of an inner activity which renders the individual a perfect harmony. All morality, all virtue, all spiritual conduct derive *from* the individual, as leaves derive from the activity of a tree. Without inner balance and unity, there can be no morality, virtue, nor spiritual conduct, or, as the personality is partly and incompletely spiritual, life expresses itself in spasmodic and fragmentary morality and action. Christ the Prophet, and Christ the inner balance, are a perfect whole— *a man*. The rest of the world are only parts of a perfect whole and fractions of men. But this perfection of manhood, the conscious or unconscious passion of every life, can never be realized apart from its perfect type. Thus, in proportion as men have from time to time recovered His presence as an actual, palpable existence in their conscious souls, they have recovered for themselves the manhood he expressed to the world. At other times, when the presence is lost, the type of perfect manhood disappears and men become unable to rise above their weak and sundered natures. They become desperately virtuous without sympathy, moral without joy, or theological without vision—subject always to disastrous readjustments, plunging them into frank bestiality or critical atheism. The Prophet, then, has this supremely important relationship to the world: He is the eternal point of recovery for the vision of self, and in the Prophet's station all men exist potentially perfect. No other man can effect this recovery—perfection is unique for the civilization it represents—and for us, accordingly, the ideal of human nature has been for ever set apart and sanctified in the person of the Jew, Jesus Christ.

For all that the Prophet was human nature made perfect, and for all that men in every age, of all classes and kinds, have recovered their own innate perfection in Him, yet Christianity, as a social order, is completely, conspicuously a failure. It has worked out for individuals, but not for society. Why should that be? Why should it be that the Church, in the vigour of its youth, could not retain its unity, but split into Roman and

Greek? Why is it that this Holy Catholic Church is neither holy nor catholic? Why is it that under the very shadow of the Cross, the national instinct of Europe developed into an over-whelming racial egotism and State selfishness? While Europeans all professed themselves Christians, why did they divide themselves into Germans, Italians, French? Why is the national government today, even in Catholic countries, far stronger and more popular than the ecclesiastical organization? The facile reply to this indictment, throwing the fault upon human nature itself, or even upon "external irresistible forces," involves the deduction that either the Christian ideal is essentially impracticable and obsolete, or that religion itself really has no concern with daily life. But Christianity has always worked out for individuals with undiminished success. *Its failure evidently consists in its lack of a social control.*

Christianity, indeed, as all dimly recognize, is religion in terms of the individual, not in terms of society. To understand the distinction fully, we must go back to Christ's ministry and study its method. He met people singly, in groups, or in assembled multitudes. But the groups and the multitudes were only the individual man and woman multiplied. That is, the multitude who heard the Sermon on the Mount came and heard it in their simple capacity of human beings. Like any casual multitude which our civilization contributes to a public speech or exhibition, they threw aside for the time their accidental class distinctions, their political opinions and connections, their trades and professions, and entered heartily into the spirit of the occasion. The same man-to-man unity and simplicity takes place today, *under one condition*, at every public meeting, whether it be the church, the theatre, or the athletic field, and that condition is that the occasion offer interest enough to divest the individual of his accidental social attributes. Christ's conversations and addresses offered this interest in the most abundant measure. His personality possessed, *and still possesses*, the unique property of desocializing the individual and making him, for the time being, an elemental and eternal soul. He addressed himself to that elemental and eternal soul-thing inherent in every man and woman, summoning it from its inactive immaturity or controlling it in its often violent and misdirected maturity—always and for ever devoting himself to the task of intensifying the spiritual activity of men. He found human nature a misunderstood, uncorrelated form of existence, and he gave our civilization the type of personality at its best. But it is only for the time that the individual man and woman can be desocialized. When the sermon is spoken, the drama played, the multitude separates, each man his own way to his own duty. Little by little the charm is broken; slowly but surely the fisherman finds himself a fisherman once more, the banker becomes the banker, the democrat the democrat, the philosopher the philosopher, and the fool the fool. Within less than a day the common social necessity has seized inexorably upon each man and woman, and all fall back into their former races, classes, occupations, and temperaments.

Yet all alike may carry away the Christ-given vision of their own perfection with the desire to attain that perfection in terms of daily life. But what happens? What *did* happen, historically? The individual found that the new gospel taught him precisely his proper attitude toward every other individual, but it said absolutely nothing as to his proper attitude toward other men and women as society. The Christian thus found, and finds today, that his religion succeeds wherever he deals with individuals, but fails wherever he deals with numbers. He is equipped to treat properly his father, his mother, his brother and sister, his wife, his children, his servants and his neighbours—in other words, he is equipped for life in the simplest of all societies; but in any society even by a little more extended and complex, he must depend upon the experience of men. That is, *he goes to religion to solve his personal relations, but he goes to science to solve his social relations.* When it comes to a matter of law-making, the beatitudes are less useful than a child's primer of economics; and the Golden Rule is mute in the presence of the vote. We have in Christianity, then, a man-to-God and a man-to-man revelation, but not a man-to-men revelation, by reason of Christ's method of ministry. For our modern life, therefore, Christianity is not only incidentally or accidentally inadequate; it is inherently, absolutely, and permanently inadequate. It does not fail to work in the same way that a child's tin sword would fail to work in a desperate battle—it fails to work as the microscope fails to work when directed against the stars. The focus lies in the individual consciousness, while the whole world travails for a religion whose focus is projected into the consciousness of society.

If any doubt of these conclusions exists, we have only to consider the case of Tolstoy. Tolstoy was so great a man that by his individual spiritual efforts he recovered the soul of a departed age. The "Bible times," with their tremendous background and atmosphere palpitant with divine things, seemed to return as the environment of his life, and through one personality to be imposed upon our modern civilization. The Hebrew tradition, created in the Eden of some ancient popular joy, thrust into unhappiness for disobedience to the spiritual impulse; populating the earth; accumulating the dynamic experience of Cain, Noah, Abraham, Job; enriched by the visions of Ezekiel and Isaiah; socialized and civilized by the Mosaic law; consummated in the revelations of Christ and Muḥammad; vitalized thereby with eternal authority and power, but diverted into the consciousness of two hostile races; for us continuing through the Apostles, the evangelists, and martyrs, to the doctors and mystics of the Roman Church; broken again into two hostile currents by the Reformation; now feebly and ineffectually diffused through our social consciousness by the rills of a thousand sects—that tradition, the world's most imposing synthesis of socialized spiritual experience, flashed like an archangel's sword in this man's hand, and clove in two the rotten shield of civilization. He tried the world by the eternal test of personal experience, and found beneath its heavy vestments a heart dried by grief or fouled by joyless passion. He held Europe before the divine, searching

mirror of the soul, and Europe leered back a harlot and a knave.
Tolstoy is apostolic. Our dialects have no word for him—we
must make use of the speech of peoples who walked with God.
King David, who was also Warrior-David and Poet-David,
could understand this Russian better than the Russians; Job and
St. Peter are nearer akin to his nature than his own children.
But what was the effect upon society of this greatest of
Christians? What did the Christian ideal accomplish through
this best of modern believers? Tolstoy's influence is a ferment
whose activity has only just begun. Nevertheless, judging his
life by its effects upon social abuse—upon the really fundamental, inherent injustice of society—it is fair to say that the
governor of Tolstoy's province, or the mayor of any western
city, could accomplish more public benefit in six months than
Tolstoy brought about in a lifetime. Moreover, the governor
or mayor could do so without possessing more than a fraction
of Tolstoy's personal spirituality, and without paying the
penalty of his mental pain. Why? Because the public official has
under his hands a few levers which control the operation of the
social machine—because he can affect a multitude of people of
both sexes, all ages, classes, religions, intellects, and temperaments, without coming into direct contact with a single one, or
being diverted from his purposes by maddening personal
questions; while Tolstoy, working *apart* from the social organization, had to influence people one by one, through his
example, his conversation, his literature and his daily acts. That
is, he dealt with the world as if it were merely an extensive but
homogeneous group, like a Highland clan or an African village.
He used the microscope of personal salvation instead of the
telescope of social salvation. His life, therefore, was shut off
from all other lives by an invisible but impassable line; he was
a lone patriarch, an austere apostle moving among his fellow
men, loving all, consecrated to the service of all, yet unable to
do more than clothe a few naked, visit a few sick, and comfort
a few broken-hearted.

Yet this merely implies inadaptability of the Christian

revelation to modern conditions; it does not expose any weakness in Christianity when working in its own sphere. The microscope is not to be broken because it will not reveal the stars. No. Christianity remains a perfect revelation for the personal life. It is not an old, romantic dream, a hopeless effort to spiritualize men, an almost abandoned faith in God and heaven. Nor is religion merely a function of primitive races and homogeneous peoples, a refuge from the world and a cloistered immunity from war, taxes, and children; but if really divine, it is evolutional, and will show itself more administrative than government, more authoritative than economics. Can it be so?

It is very evident that we need a religion in terms of society —a revelation, that is, which will not attempt to displace and deny the essential truth of Christianity, but fulfil it for the modern world. We need, in other words, the additional lens which transforms the microscope into an instrument for long distances. This religion must not be a new religion, in the sense of being an exotic, but a renewal of the existing religions and their translation into a modern code and gospel. Broadly speaking, it must be an identification of social science with individual initiative and spiritual passion. The religious personality must express itself socially, in public service, allying itself with every available instrument for reform. The old passion for self-salvation must be recovered, invigorated, and intensified by every possible means, but diverted, *once for all*, into the channel of human service. Self-salvation as a traditional psychology must be absolutely stamped from the human consciousness; as an end for religious organization it must be fought as the true enemy of welfare, the only successful opponent of the very self-spiritualization it is supposed to bring about. The whole wretched tradition of "self" and "heaven" must be re-interpreted and re-expressed. From the servant-maid who betrays her instincts to a priest lurking in his dark confessional, to the Hamlet who laments his weakness to the stars, the modern world is infected by a diabolical perversion of

Christ's teaching. Instead of turning inward to that fatal mal-adjustment by which most men and women at some period of their lives are rendered miserable and erring, instead of magnifying our evil by concentrating upon its power to affect our lives, we must resolutely turn all hope and interest outward, fixing our thoughts on any external—a friend, a great social movement, or *God*—endeavouring by prayer and activity to put ourselves into the stream of faith and enthusiasm constantly flowing across the world. For the joyous and "free" man—that is, the man who has found *salvation*—is he whose consciousness has burst the bonds of self and become identified with an outside thing. For him "self" no longer exists; and by entering his new state of self-forgetfulness he transfers his spiritual habitation, as it were, from a low, mean, smoke-oppressed city to the vision-lapped mountain of God.

But I need no more than suggest the new theology, which has already achieved the attention of modern minds. We are concerned here rather with the origins of the religious movement which alone can bring about the consummation we have learned so devoutly to desire. It exists as the best aspiration of earnest men, and as an aspiration it has long existed. So also the aspiration for a divine manhood and womanhood existed in the racial consciousness long before the birth of Christ. We yearn for a divine social order as the Hebrews yearned for a divine personality; but our passion is not at all a sign that we have transferred our faith from the soul to the machine. It indicates rather, as every man's experience too clearly shows, that personality depends vitally upon the social environment, and therefore that in order to obtain men we must first obtain means. An English clergyman voiced the common opinion when he said that it is unfair to expect a man to meditate on heaven while he owes the butcher; but we must not overlook the fact that our civilization renders it equally unfair to the butcher. All the Prophets since Christ have pointed the popular consciousness toward social salvation; and the popular instinct, sometimes daring to believe in the second coming of Christ, believes that His modern message will contain hope for this world as well as the next.

At all events, we are certain that religion cannot be re-established except through the medium of a Prophet, a "Messiah." As all the elements that enter into a perfect personality had to be united in one being and expressed in one life in order to set before every man and woman the type of his or her perfection, so must the elements of the perfect social order be gathered and synthesized in one mind in order to set before each social concomitant the type of its own perfection. Before we can accomplish anything with village, city, province, and nation, we must know what the ideal village, city, province and nation are—which in each case involves a knowledge of what a perfect *humanity* would be—or, better still (since every social organization is in a continual state of flux, and perfection in each must consist of a sliding scale of attainment, a balance undisturbed by mere change in number of population or size of community)— better still, we must know what each person's attitude and course of action must be in order to release the evolutional tendencies toward attainment in the social order. For since society is an increasingly complex system of men, women, and children, its structure automatically undergoes constant re-adjustment to the changing attitude and activity of its members. The Prophet of society, accordingly, must first possess the divine personality of the Christ, and then express this personality in terms of social unity. That is, He must take to Himself the relation of all men and women to their environments, *throughout the whole extent of that relation*, from its immediate contact with the town organization to its remote, yet equally important contact with State, with other States, and with other races; and uniting all these complex, mutually opposing, and stultifying relations into one harmonious synthesis by the creative vision of His own soul, give them all out again to the world as an ideal social relationship in which every man, woman and child can find his own proper attitude and activity clearly, eternally expressed. And this ideal type must be able to serve for every nation alike, every race alike, and every religion alike. It must be more English than Magna Charta, more American than the Constitution, more Catholic than Catholicism. It must be a *universal* synthesis, that is, to ensure the right evolutionary adjustment in the individual relationship derived therefrom. By universal is not meant uniform, but that synthetic comprehensiveness which permits to every personality the sanctity of its differentiation, and to every race the sanctity of its peculiar temperament.

The Prophet, then, must be the world's saviour; not the representative of any nation, race, or class. He must possess the unimpeachable authority of the divine personality and the universal soul. He must actually *be* that human unity of which all other men and women are the essential parts. By that power of absolute self-effacement which only the Divine Personality acquires, He must send out His soul to all places and peoples, infusing His divinity like an essence throughout the world, gathering as upon one sensitive plate the experience of every man and woman; then within His intelligence refining from all, the ideal, typical experience in which we may discover our own lives potentially perfect. No less a result will serve; for we have already seen how national, racial, and ecclesiastical egotism, far from ensuring superiority or even safety to the nation, the race or the religion, necessarily surrounds it with implacable foes and an inevitable fate. The continued existence of any social fragment, in other words, depends upon the unity and co-operation of the whole society. The method by which this Prophet would express his message, accordingly, would differ from the method of Christ. Reacting from society as a perfect organization instead of from the individual man or woman as a perfect personality, He would direct His teaching so as to concern our social rather than our personal relations. Re-establishing the authority of all existing authentic revelations, He would not be confined to their mere repetition nor even to their comparison and reconciliation. The modern Prophet, therefore, on taking up the task differentiating Him from all previous Prophets—the task of *extending* Christianity, Muhammadanism, Buddhism, Hinduism, to their evolutionally logical consummation—could not secure His purpose by the spoken word and the sermon alone. The spoken word is limited by the capacity of the hearers and the opportunity of the occasion; but the written word suffers no limitation, since it is available to all men at all times. The *Newest* Testament, that is, would be written by the Prophet Himself.

Without such a Prophet, we know only too thoroughly the helplessness of the world. Liberalizing influences are everywhere at work, but at most these can only raise existing institutions to a higher efficiency, each within its own compass; they cannot transform the purpose for which each institution was originally founded, aligning it with the modern vision, nor can they co-ordinate them. Only the synthesis of all influences into one definite movement can free men and women from this tangle of things. Yet, as we have seen, the Prophet would bring no message essentially new, in the sense that it was unheard of. His message would consist of all the aspirations of East as well as West, of women as well as men. Its newness, therefore, would appear in its supreme capacity to assimilate spiritual passion and social science into one human synthesis. No man could receive such a message and say that he himself had already thought and desired its whole content; yet all men could hear it and say that it realized their highest personal and social ideal. In Him the true Christian would be compelled to recognize the Christ personality, and in Him the atheistic humanitarian must acknowledge a social zeal and wisdom deeper than his own. Resistance to Him, and hatred of his followers, could derive only from obvious and despicable motives; prejudice, ignorance, selfishness, snobbery, bigotry. Discounting the temporary opposition of privileged or official classes fearing for their own private prosperity, we can admit one fertile cause of obstruction in the very general characteristic of men, which after centuries of social development, after we have all learned not too grudgingly to share our food, our education, and our vote, still makes us painfully loath to share our God.

But this raises the question of the relationship between such a Prophet and Christ, Muḥammad, Buddha, and Zoroaster. The orthodox of all communities believe that God and His Prophet are a natural and inalterable duality; and that the existence of any other Prophet is a challenge to the constancy of the Creator. Very happily, it does challenge our conception of His constancy in its especial consideration for any particular race. Each people has had its Prophet; but the message of all has been essentially the same—the possibility of a perfect personality for every man and woman. The new Prophet would fulfil all the Prophets accordingly, by His interpretation of personality in terms of social service. Once admitting the existence of an authentic revelation to every race, we realize that each people has produced not one Prophet only, but a succession of Prophets, the later revealing ever more and loftier truth; and that this fact depends upon a race's increasing capacity to absorb teaching. The relationship of a modern Prophet, such as we have imagined, to Christ or to Muḥammad, may well be expressed in the poetic figure of the East, as the full moon rising on the fourteenth night, which, while the same planet as the new moon, can reflect more light than the new moon by virtue of its more advantageous position.

If such a Prophet should appear, His effect upon the ordinary man and woman would be immediate and immense. As religious natures who felt sorrow at their inability to become more than amateur, occasional, self-conscious, and inefficient social workers, he would give them an activity which increased their spirituality at the same time that it accomplished results in human lives; as practical natures devoted to some social or political reform without benefitting by spiritual powers in themselves or in others, He would set them an ideal which increased their public efficiency at the same time that it initiated their spiritual evolution; and as for the majority, who are neither very spiritual nor very public-minded, He would rouse

c

their lives from negative adjustment to environmental pressure as by the bugle of defensive war. For His supreme influence would consist in restoring the individual conscience to its proper relationship toward self and others. To those confined in the dark prison of sickness or indifference, He would fling the keys of joyful, invigorating freedom; and the over-conscientious He would release from their atlas-burden of the world's wrong. For, after all, the individual is limited as to his social usefulness, and consequently as to his responsibility. Whatever he can accomplish must be done outside the regular course of business, yet inside the compass of the twenty-four hours. Yet the new revelation would provide him with an attitude which automatically, by the *momentum of social evolution*, must turn all his activity into public service, thus preserving his self-respect without hardening his sensibility, and releasing his natural impulses toward joy without insulting the unfortunate and weak. The ordinary person is not only a temperament, which is a limitation in itself, but also a member of one class, one nation, one religion, and one race. These limitations are inherent and eternal, but the new teaching would turn the limitation of temperament into the opportunity of personality, and would provide every social position with a straight path toward human unity and co-operation. As every being can learn his own perfection in the station of Christ, so could the world learn its unity in the station of the new Prophet; which once given mankind could never be lost, but would serve every environment and every age as the point of recovery for its perfect relationship to the whole human society.

ELEMENTS OF WORLD RELIGION

A N IMPORTANT cause of the confusion so prevalent in our thinking today is the breakdown of the conditions under which, throughout a long historical period, the various types of human society gradually developed. Most of us continue to think and feel in accordance with certain assumptions which were sound and true for our ancestors, but which now no longer apply. Our strength as individuals and families has in the past derived from the assumption that our own society, whether race or nation, possessed the integrity of an independent body of human beings able to determine their own scale of values and principles of conduct without interference from any other social body. In other words, each society has in the past been sufficiently isolated from other societies to develop its own special character.

What has happened to our time is the termination of this isolation, so swiftly and unexpectedly that we still act as though we were independent, whereas the truth is that the peoples of the world in all important matters have become mutually involved and interdependent.

What this means to each of us is something too new and apparently too complicated to define in any simple, convenient formula. We can, however, begin to grasp at least part of its meaning if we consider a few examples and use them to measure how vast has been the change.

First, consider the question of language. Every human society has employed its own particular kind of speech. A common language has been the very life-blood infusing vitality into the social group. By it the group, large or small, has developed capacity to act together as a community. By language each people has preserved its special traditions, developed a special culture, provided the individual mind and feeling with a natural arena in which it could find useful and satisfying expression. Language has been a sign of the kinship relating men to their fellows. The outer boundary of any language in the past marked the extent to which kinship had been evolved. Foreignness of language, in the same way, indicated foreignness of outlook, culture, government and physical type.

As long as societies could continue to develop in some degree of isolation from each other, human speech could remain a one-language experience. With the breakdown of that isolation in our time, we have an interdependent, interpenetrating mass of traditional societies whose members are for the most part unable to communicate across the frontiers of the vast number of languages they have brought from the past.

Telephone, telegraph and radio have developed in a multi-language world. They have created the means of universal communication, but there is no language of mankind. Our languages are the organs of race or nation alone. Can we even use the concept "mankind" for human beings who cannot participate in the common experience of mental communication?

What is the solution of this basic problem of our age? Shall we seek to prove that one of the great living languages is so much superior to all others that it should be made the official "world language"? Or would it be preferable to employ some artificial language, and have it adopted as a universal auxiliary tongue and taught in schools throughout the world? These questions are raised, not to be answered here, but to provide a concrete illustration of the unprecedented kind of problem faced by people today. We cannot retreat into that simpler past where one's racial tongue served every purpose of social communication; we cannot control the vast pressures which have destroyed the old patterns; and we have no power to bring about a solution of the language problem soon enough to help the people solve other pressing problems of our time.

The question of a world language is at least simple enough for a child to grasp. We can define it, even if we do not hold its solution in our hands today.

Not in the least simple, however, is the question of race. What we term "race" is the outcome of the operation of a long historical process. It is one of the most powerful forms of kinship that has existed in the life of man. Around the central and sacred institution of family, the social unity of race gradually evolved. A race suggests a larger family. It has a physical homogeneity, reinforcing all other bonds which have brought people together in one common community. It was through race that language evolved; through race the feeling of loyalty gradually enlarged the individual's ethical sense; through race the supreme experiences of poetry and art were unfolded. By race, also, the foundations of economic method were laid. Under no other conditions could humanity even have survived, let alone developed, than by the social grouping we call race. So profound has been its kinship that loyalty to one's race became instinctive, as if race were the final and unchanging meaning of mankind to the individual.

But race is not an eternal arrangement. The development of races resulted from the state of isolation. On an island, or between rivers or mountains, or along the shore, groups of people found means for survival. Their environment was like a box enclosing them within some one area and submitting them to a process of mutualization, the end-term of which, if it continued long enough, was a race. Taking the world as a whole there were hundreds and thousands of boxes, of different shapes and sizes, which served as race-making agencies in the past. Differences of climate, food, economic activity and other factors made the races physically, culturally and morally unlike. Their unlikeness meant little as long as they developed separately, but now the boxes are broken and the human contents have spilled out, and humanity today is the mixture and intermingling of countless little peoples who seem to have nothing in common—neither language, nor government, nor economic standards, nor ethics, nor worship—nothing in common except the crucial and inescapable problem of survival through unity or destruction through struggle.

Exactly as in the case of the languages, the races have been brought together in the one great social arena which the world has become. The question is, do we recognize a "superior" race, one to which all other peoples must yield priority and from which they must receive rule and direction; or are all the races equally valid and equally required to recognize all other races as branches of the same great human family? If equal, what are the ethical and economic and political terms they must agree upon as the very minimum condition of harmony?

For the first time, actually, we are concerned with mankind and not merely with those provincial and temporary human groupings we call races or nations, and there is not much time left, if any, to decide whether mankind is an explosive chemical combination of diverse, antagonistic peoples, or whether each of these diverse peoples must not become subject to the higher needs of mankind.

As a matter of fact, the conditions favourable to race-development came to an end with the rise of modern nationalism. The nation is a multi-racial society, and the first step toward the adjustment of races to mankind has been the adjustment of races to each other within the nation. The kinship of political union has displaced the kinship of racial union in our modern world. Kinship has enlarged to citizenship—one of the most vital changes ever made by mankind. It represents the step from instinct to reason in the socialization of human beings.

Our third example, therefore, is the nation. Nation-building has also been a process dependent on isolation, but the isolation has been less a matter of mountains and other natural barriers than of the fortified frontier defended by an armed state. Within its frontiers the modern nation has undergone two different stages of evolution; first, the establishment of a political structure able to unify or dominate the participating racial stocks hitherto competitive, able likewise to work out a national culture and economy better fitted than the previous racial cultures to provide the individual with a satisfactory life; and second, the establishment of some type of working arrangement with other nations—a stage which has come to a climax in our days.

The physical settlement of the earth in modern times brought the race-making phase of social evolution to an end. Now the scientific exploitation of nature has similarly ended the nation-building phase because it has abolished the armed frontier. The larger and stronger box we call "nationalism" no longer contains within one self-centred society all the means to satisfy the requirements of its body of citizens. To attain security of person and property and to attain the means of his full development, modern man requires a world economy and a world order.

Thus, for the third time, we have briefly traced the change which has overtaken human life in our day. Language, race, nation—these three examples alike reveal that what was done in the past under conditions of isolation must be redone today under the pressure of proximity and intermingling and inter-dependence. It comes down to this: that man to meet certain situations produces a tool in the form of a social group. This tool gradually becomes efficient. It enables man to solve problems otherwise impossible. But life itself is God-directed and not man-controlled and hence the stream runs on, the situations change, and the tool no longer serves. Does this mean that the new problems are insuperable, or that the tool must be discarded and a new and more effective instrument fashioned? What is sacred, the tool of social instrument, or man's capacity to solve problems and develop the latent powers with which his Creator has endowed him?

Now, when races were combined within the same nation, the race was not destroyed; it was fulfilled. It served as stepping-stone to a new and greater unity. The paramount needs of world order today do not mean the destruction of nations, but their fulfilment as partners in the creation of the agencies of brotherhood and peace. Not world order but lack of it is the canker gnawing the flesh of every nation today.

Are there a few legitimate conclusions acceptable to all men of good will? The members of the Bahá'í Faith have conviction and assurance that agreement can exist on certain ethical principles.

1. The eternal path of true religion leads to the attainment of the brotherhood of all mankind.

2. Brotherhood is only a theory and a hope unless it is given foundation in a constitutional society.

3. History has recorded the successive development of the principle of brotherhood in terms of larger communities and more equitable societies.

4. World unity has become the goal of moral and political effort today and the only hope of human survival on ethical terms.

5. The value of a race, nation, class or creed in our desperate crisis is determined by the degree to which it seeks to contribute to world brotherhood and world order.

6. Loyalty to mankind has become the sign of devotion to God.

Two years before the first World War the Bahá'í leader, 'Abdu'l-Bahá, spoke these words at a public gathering in America:—

"Today the world of humanity is walking in darkness because it is out of touch with the world of God. That is why we do not see the signs of God in the hearts of men. The power of the Holy Spirit has no influence. When a divine spiritual illumination becomes manifest in the world of humanity, when divine instruction and guidance appear, then enlightenment follows, a new spirit is realized within, a new power descends and a new life is given. It is like the birth from the animal kingdom into the kingdom of man. When man acquires these virtues the oneness of the world of humanity will be revealed, the banner of international peace will be upraised, equality between all mankind will be realized and the Orient and Occident will become one. Then will the justice of God become manifest, all humanity will appear as the members of one family and every member of that family will be consecrated to co-operation and mutual assistance."

In humility, not in pride, through co-operation and not through struggle for victory, man has in all ages acquired capacity to understand the social and spiritual conditions in which the great epochs and cycles have evolved. Today we stand in the early stages of the greatest epoch of all—the era of humanity, peace and enlightenment.

PART II

THE NEW DISPENSATION

ESSENTIAL BAHÁ'Í TEACHINGS

BAHÁ'Í: NAME OF A WORLD FAITH

BAHÁ'Í is the up-to-date name of the World Faith which in barely one hundred years has spread to two hundred and forty seven countries, translated its sacred literature into one hundred and ninety languages, and brought into spiritual fellowship a host of persons who had been estranged by prejudice of race, class and creed.[1] A point of unity, a centre of agreement, a basis of reconciliation for the diverse peoples of mankind!

The word *Bahá'í* means *glory*. A Bahá'í is one who accepts the Faith founded by Bahá'u'lláh, whose name means *Glory of God*. His Faith brings a mighty renewal of hope in the triumph of righteousness on earth; it quickens the spirit of understanding which binds the soul to God; it offers a source of pure and undefiled spiritual knowledge; it rekindles the flame of devotion and love which are the true happiness of man.

"O Son of Man!" the Prophet reveals, *"I loved thy creation, hence I created thee. Wherefore, do thou love Me, that I may name thy name and fill thy soul with the spirit of life."*

When you hear or see the name *Bahá'í*, think of it as a signpost pointing you along the safe highway leading through the turmoil, the suffering, the chaos and the upheavals of this day to the haven of certitude and peace. The Bahá'í Faith offers each of us a glorious gift—perfect trust in the fulfilment of the Creator's promise to mankind. Have we turned away from that promise as an illusion of the childhood of the human race? Have we abandoned even the idea of a Divine promise as a superstition which will not endure the test of modern science? Have we lost hope in the coming of justice because creeds and sects have disagreed? Do we feel discouraged because strife, prejudice and materialism have so far brought every mighty people and proud civilization to eclipse?

[1] See Preface.

There is a clear Bahá'í answer to these arguments of doubt and unbelief.

It is that for every *Divine* promise there has been a *time* and also a *way* of fulfilment. To attain to assurance of this supreme spiritual mystery is the greatest privilege bestowed upon human beings.

Time and way of fulfilment: The *time* is whenever the Manifestation of God, the holy Prophet and Messenger, comes to earth, age after age, to revive faith, restore the Divine law, and to enlarge the foundation of civilization. The *way* is through the living spirit of faith, sacrifice, unity and understanding which He inspires among men. From earliest times, revealed religion has demonstrated the validity of God's promise, for through its power, and its power alone, has civilization been re-created out of wreckage and destruction.

"Every one of them," says Bahá'u'lláh of the Prophets, "is the way of God that connecteth this world with the realms above, and the Standard of His Truth unto every one in the kingdoms of earth and heaven. They are the Manifestations of God amidst men, the evidences of His truth and the signs of His glory." "The fundamental purpose animating the Faith of God and His Religion is to safeguard the interests and promote the unity of the human race," the Bahá'í teachings declare, "and to foster the spirit of love and fellowship amongst men." "There can be no doubt whatever that the peoples of the world, of whatever race or religion, derive their inspiration from one heavenly Source, and are the subjects of one God."

Our very time, the Bahá'í believes, is the Promised Day of the gathering together of the long-scattered peoples and their welding together, in the flame of a common agony, into one organic union, one race, one faith, one mankind. Our worldwide suffering is the outer sign that the limitations of the past, the separations, the prejudices, are one by one being overthrown by the force of the truth that man is one. "The whole human race hath longed for this Day," Bahá'u'lláh has said, "that perchance it may fulfil that which well beseemeth its station, and is worthy of its destiny."

II. WHAT ARE THE BAHÁ'Í PRINCIPLES?

"Heavenly teachings applicable to the advancement in human conditions have been revealed in this merciful age," the Bahá'í Faith declares. "This reformation and renewal of the fundamental reality of religion constitute the true and out-working spirit of modernism, the unmistakable light of the world, the manifest effulgence of the Word of God, the divine remedy for all human ailments and the bounty of eternal life to all mankind."

Why are new truths and spiritual principles necessary? Because our characters and our virtues reflect the needs and conditions of an age that has passed away. Human beings have become adapted to life in relatively small, self-sustaining and independent societies. Our outlook and our habits were formed when no one had to consider what people might be doing or planning in other parts of the world. Therefore humanity is today in dire need of a broadening of outlook, a clarification of vision and a re-education in ideas and habits, so that we can master the problems of a civilization that has suddenly expanded to include the whole world. Science has created this new and greater world, but men's emotions are still trying to lag behind in the village of yesterday.

The Bahá'í principles are world principles. They produce men and women who can rise above prejudice of race, class and creed and meet the tasks which destiny has set for us in this new age. They are the first lessons we are to learn in order to develop our latent powers and resources as members of a human race which has come to its hour of supreme destiny.

Ponder the significance of these principles, for they offer our souls and minds the tools they must have in order to solve the problems of our time.

There are thirteen of these principles in the following summary:

"The oneness of the world of humanity.

The protection and guidance of the Holy Spirit.

The foundation of all religion is one.

Religion must be the cause of unity.
Religion must accord with science and reason.
Independent investigation of truth.
Equality between men and women.
The abandonment of all prejudices among mankind.
Universal peace.
Universal education.
A universal auxiliary language.
Solution of the economic problem.
An international Tribunal."

What is the source of these principles?

The Bahá'í teachings declare that spiritual truth is revealed to man by the Manifestation of God, and to attain it we must have faith in its divine source and origin. To accept spiritual truth we must practise it in our lives, for passive belief is a form of denial and not a proof of acceptance. The new life offered to us by the Bahá'í Faith calls for heroic action and true understanding. In essence, the Bahá'í principles mean that human nature can and will be regenerated, and this inner change of spirit is what distinguishes revealed truth from philosophy, policy or partisan programme.

The Bahá'í answer to the problem of transmuting world chaos into world order sounds both warning and assurance. "People are holding to the counterfeit and imitation, negligent of the reality which unifies, so they are bereft and deprived of the radiance of religion. . . . The world of humanity is walking in darkness because it is out of touch with the world of God. . . . When a divine, spiritual illumination becomes manifest . . . when divine instruction and guidance appear, then enlightenment follows, a new spirit is realized within, a new power descends and a new life is given. It is like the birth from the animal kingdom into the kingdom of man."

It is yesterday's limited and divided world which is being purified and reshaped on the anvil of universal war. Tomorrow's world is to arise when this process is complete—a world which answers to the ancient promises of religion in all races and to the deepest hopes in the hearts of all peoples of earth. The sufferings through which we pass are no mere historical incident but a manifestation of the Will of God. Therefore the victory of truth is assured, but the path is the path of sacrifice until we become worthy to serve the cause of truth. "Unity is the expression of the loving power of God," 'Abdu'l-Bahá has said.

III. THE BAHÁ'Í CONCEPT OF MAN

"O Son of Man! My first counsel is this: Possess a pure, kindly and radiant heart, that thine may be a sovereignty ancient, imperishable and everlasting."

These words of Bahá'u'lláh summon us to seek and find a true understanding of our own beings. They create a place of peace where for these few moments we may open our souls to new light, new truth and new life. For Bahá'u'lláh continues this majestic theme of man's spiritual nature and his victory over death and hate and fear:

"O Son of Man! I loved thy creation, hence I created thee. Wherefore, do thou love Me, that I may name thy name and fill thy soul with the spirit of life."

"O Son of Spirit! Noble have I created thee, yet thou hast abased thyself. Rise then unto that for which thou wast created . . . Wherefore, free thyself from the veils of idle fancies and enter into My court, that thou mayest be fit for everlasting life and worthy to meet Me. Thus may death not come upon thee, neither weariness nor trouble."

Age after age the Creator speaks through the words of His Manifestations, establishing on earth a Source of love and truth and law—a wellspring where the sincere soul may find comfort and strength. Centuries have passed since the Messenger walked among men to be their quickener, their educator and their guide. The souls of men have become darkened, devoid of assurance in immortality, uncertain of the path, and unconscious of the social laws and principles which fulfil God's purpose on earth. Hence the gradual development of problems between race, class, nation and creed, incapable, to all seeming, of solution through peaceful means. For peace has left the human heart, and when peace leaves the heart, conflict becomes the principle of existence.

Now the Manifestation has returned to earth for the renewal of the spiritual life, and in the words of Bahá'u'lláh we find the consolation, the courage, and the meaning, without which our lives become a burden and a torment.

"O Son of Spirit! The spirit of holiness beareth unto thee the joyful tidings of reunion; wherefore dost thou grieve? The spirit of power confirmeth thee in His cause; why dost thou veil thyself? The light of His countenance doth lead thee; how canst thou go astray?"

The Bahá'í teachings also have a less mystical explanation of the reality of man:

"Man is intelligent, instinctively and consciously intelligent; nature is not . . . . . Man is the discoverer of the mysteries of nature; nature is not conscious of these mysteries herself. It is evident therefore that man is dual in aspect; as an animal he is subject to nature, but in his spiritual or conscious being he transcends the world of material existence. His spiritual powers being nobler and higher, they possess virtues of which nature intrinsically has no evidence; therefore they triumph over natural conditions. . . . Therefore you must thank God that He has bestowed upon you the blessing of life and existence in the human kingdom. Strive diligently to acquire virtues befitting your degree and station. . . . Ascend to the zenith of an existence which is never beclouded by the fears and forebodings of non-existence."

Man's soul, like the fruitful tree, appears first in the condition of the seed. That is why the materialists deny spiritual reality—they look at the small, hard husk of the seed and feel that the tree can never develop from it. They look upon physical personality and condemn as unscientific the faith that supernatural powers and immortal being are latent and concealed within. That is why the Manifestation of God returns to the world in its hour of doubt and denial. He is the Divine

D

Gardener who cultivates the soul of man, guiding its development until the fruitful tree of faith and assurance stands in the
paradise of the love of God. "The purpose of the creation of
man is the attainment of the supreme virtues of humanity
through descent of the heavenly bestowals."

IV. RELIGIOUS UNITY

The crucial task of this age is to establish co-operation as the
fundamental law of human life. Power must be found to create
world unity or the nations perish.

We have seen the principle of strife and competition develop
down the ages from tribe to city, and from city to nation, until
now the world is overwhelmed by war. In modern times, when
the nations were not in conflict, class and race dissension arose
to imperil the structure of civilization. The condition we call
"peace" has not been peace but preparation for renewal of
violence. No moral or ethical force existing in the past has been
able to prevent this development of strife nor transmute the
agencies of civilization into instruments for the promotion of
the law of God.

Why could not the nineteenth century, with all its knowledge and culture, attain the goal of universal peace? Because,
as the Bahá'í Faith steadfastly upholds, mankind was fatally
divided in its allegiance to its divine Creator. Without unity of
faith and agreement on the spiritual teachings which set forth
the purpose of human life, the aim of our existence, the laws
and principles which come from God and which must be
obeyed by governments as well as by peoples and races, there
can be no political nor economic unity. Spiritual unity is the
source and cause of all true co-operation among men. Singleness of faith is the gate which stands between the age of war and
the age of peace, between a war-torn humanity and a humanity
which has attained the blessings of God.

But just what is religious unity? The Bahá'í teachings illumine this vital question with calm radiant light. Religious unity
is union in acceptance of and obedience to the prophet and

messenger whom God sends to each age. Religious unity is union in the spirit and in the law of God. The worldly conception of tolerance between conflicting creeds and sects is not unity—it is merely agreement to disagree. In such an attitude there is no true conception of brotherhood among men nor oneness of divine Truth.

Bahá'u'lláh utters the true call to unity in these words: "O contending peoples and kindreds of the earth! Set your faces towards unity, and let the radiance of its light shine upon you. Gather ye together, and for the sake of God resolve to root out whatever is the source of contention amongst you. Then will the effulgence of the world's great Luminary envelop the whole earth, and its inhabitants become the citizens of one city, and the occupants of one and the same throne. . . . There can be no doubt whatever that the peoples of the world, of whatever race or religion, derive their inspiration from one heavenly Source, and are the subjects of one God."

This mysterious connection between spiritual truth and world unity was set forth by Bahá'u'lláh more than eighty years ago in this statement: "That which the Lord hath ordained as the sovereign remedy and mightiest instrument for the healing of all the world is the union of all its peoples in one universal Cause, one common Faith. This can in no wise be achieved except through the power of a skilled an all-powerful and inspired Physician." [1]

The Bahá'í teachings have given the world an entirely new perspective on the history of religion. The Bahá'í looks upon each successive Revelation as an added chapter in the Divine Book. The Bahá'í acknowledges that all the prophets and messengers came from the one God and were one in spirit and in purpose. Each prophet has renewed the spirit of faith, and revealed a greater degree of truth to meet the needs of an evolving race. Again we turn to Bahá'u'lláh for the essence of the matter: "Know thou assuredly that the essence of all the Prophets of God is one and the same. Their unity is absolute. God, the

[1] Letter to Queen Victoria, written about 1870.

Creator, saith—there is no distinction whatsoever among the
Bearers of My Message. They all have but one purpose; their
secret is the same secret. To prefer one in honour to another, to
exalt certain ones above the rest, is in no wise to be permitted."[1]

Thus it becomes clear that the basis of universal spiritual
agreement has been firmly laid, since the followers of each
Prophet are required to recognize that all other Prophets were
divinely inspired. The contention and dispute about matters of
truth and conscience has been annulled. The substitution of
man-made creeds and philosophies for Revelation has been
forbidden. The eternal path to God has been cleared of the
debris which for so long has hidden the Way. "The Prophets of
God should be regarded as Physicians whose task is to foster the
well-being of the world and its peoples, that, through the spirit
of oneness, They may heal the sickness of a divided humanity."

V. The Oneness of Mankind

In this great age of the maturity of mankind, the very essence
of spiritual truth has been revealed in the teachings of Bahá'u'-
lláh. Former times, because of limited conditions, could only
realize as prophetic hope what today has become the fundamental principle of human existence. Yesterday our life was the
life of race, or class or nation; today our life has become dependent upon the consummation of the unity of all mankind.

Step by step the successive faiths disclosed the coming of a
kingdom of righteousness and peace. Bahá'u'lláh's declaration
of the oneness of mankind signalized that this our day and age
will realize the divine assurance of victory.

Bahá'u'lláh declared: "The utterance of God is a lamp whose
light is these words—Ye are the fruits of one tree, and the leaves
of one branch. Deal ye one with another with the utmost love
and harmony, with friendliness and fellowship. He Who is the
Day Star of Truth beareth Me witness! So powerful is the light
of unity that it can illumine the whole earth."

"In this way," the Bahá'í teachings explain, "His Holiness

[1] Kitáb-i-Iqán.

Bahá'u'lláh expressed the oneness of mankind, whereas in all religious teachings of the past, the human world has been represented as divided into two parts, one known as the people of the Book of God, or the 'pure tree' and the other the people of infidelity and error or the 'evil tree.' The former were considered as belonging to the faithful and the others to the hosts of the irreligious and infidel; one part of humanity the recipients of divine mercy and the other the object of the wrath of their Creator. His Holiness Bahá'u'lláh removed this by proclaiming the oneness of the world of humanity and this principle is specialized in His teachings for He has submerged all mankind in the sea of Divine generosity."

But the Bahá'í teachings likewise warn that spiritual truth, once revealed, cannot be evaded nor annulled by human device. "Humanity has, alas, with increasing insistence, preferred, instead of acknowledging and adoring the Spirit of God as embodied in His religion in this day, to worship those false idols, untruths and half-truths, which are obscuring its religions, corrupting its spiritual life, convulsing its political institutions, corroding its social fabric, and shattering its economic structure . . . The chief idols in the desecrated temple of mankind are none other than the triple gods of Nationalism, Racialism and Communism, at whose altars governments and peoples . . . are, in various forms and in different degrees, now worshipping.

"The theories and policies, so unsound, so pernicious, which deify the state and exalt the nation above mankind, which seek to subordinate the sister races of the world to one single race, which discriminate between the black and the white, and which tolerate the dominance of one privileged class over all others—these are the dark, the false, the crooked doctrines for which any man or people who believes in them or acts upon them, must, sooner or later, incur the wrath and chastisement of God."

All our conceptions of life have been plunged into the cauldron of world conflict, but what will emerge is the pure gold of truth, free from the dross of traditional pride and prejudice which has set one people against another in all generations of past history. Those who can realize the oneness of mankind in this hour have attained the strong foundation of assurance which nothing can impair.

There is no need for human imagination or dogma when we have such sublime utterances as these words of Bahá'u'lláh: "O Children of Men! Know ye not why We created you all from the same dust? That no one should exalt himself over the other. Ponder at all times in your hearts how ye were created. Since We have created you all from the same substance it is incumbent on you to be even as one soul, to walk with the same feet, eat with the same mouth and dwell in the same land, that from your inmost being, by your deeds and actions, the signs of oneness and the essence of detachment may be made manifest."

Just as the coming of the physical springtime is revealed by the appearance of the new leaves and buds, so the spiritual springtime of the new Prophet becomes manifest in new truths which stir the heart of mankind. "The gift of God to this enlightened age," the Bahá'í teachings declare, "is the knowledge of the oneness of mankind and the fundamental oneness of religion."

Human beings today have been given the greatest mission ever laid upon mankind; the construction of a society of justice and peace. Before we can build, we must have the pattern of peace in our hearts and the practice of justice in our lives. Those who follow Bahá'u'lláh build upon the pattern of peace which God has ordained.

THE REVELATION OF BAHÁ'U'LLÁH

A Worldwide Spiritual Community

"The Tabernacle of Unity has been raised; regard ye not one another as strangers. . . . Of one tree are ye all the fruit and of one bough the leaves. . . . The world is but one country and mankind its citizens."

BAHÁ'U'LLÁH.

UPON the spiritual foundation established by Bahá'u'lláh during the forty-year period of His Mission (1853–1892), there stands today an independent religion represented by over three thousand local communities of believers.[1] These communities geographically are spread throughout all five continents. In point of race, class, nationality and religious origin, the followers of Bahá'u'lláh exemplify well-nigh the whole diversity of the modern world. They may be characterized as a true cross section of humanity, a microcosm which, for all its relative littleness, carries within it individual men and women typifying the macrocosm of mankind.

None of the historic causes of association served to create this world-wide spiritual community. Neither a common language, a common blood, a common civil government, a common tradition nor a mutual grievance acted upon Bahá'ís to supply a fixed centre of interest or a goal of material advantage. On the contrary, membership in the Bahá'í community in the land of its birth even to this day has been a severe disability, and outside of Persia the motive animating believers has been in direct opposition to the most inveterate prejudices of their environment. The Cause of Bahá'u'lláh has moved forward without the reinforcement of wealth, social prestige or other means of public influence.

Every local Bahá'í community exists by the voluntary association of individuals who consciously overcome the

[1] See Preface.

fundamental sanctions evolved throughout the centuries to justify the separations and antagonisms of human society. In America, this association means that white believers accept the spiritual equality of their Negro fellows. In Europe, it means the reconciliation of Protestant and Catholic upon the basis of a new and larger faith. In the Orient, Christian, Jewish and Muḥammadan believers must stand apart from the rigid exclusiveness into which each was born.

The central fact to be noted concerning the nature of the Bahá'í Faith is that it contains a power, fulfilled in the realm of conscience, which can reverse the principal momentum of modern civilization—the drive toward division and strife—and initiate its own momentum moving steadily in the direction of unity and accord. It is in this power, and not in any criterion upheld by the world, that the Faith of Bahá'u'lláh has special significance.

The forms of traditional opposition vested in nationality, race, class and creed are not the only social chasms which the Faith has bridged. There are even more implacable, if less visible differences between types and temperaments, such as flow inevitably from the contact of rational and emotional individuals, of active and passive dispositions, undermining capacity for co-operation in every organized society, which attain mutual understanding and harmony in the Bahá'í community. For personal congeniality, the selective principle elsewhere continually operative within the field of voluntary action, is an instinct which Bahá'ís must sacrifice to serve the principle of the oneness of mankind. A Bahá'í community, therefore, is a constant and active spiritual victory, an overcoming of tensions which elsewhere come to the point of strife. No mere passive creed nor philosophic gospel which need never be put to the test in daily life has produced this world fellowship devoted to the teachings of Bahá'u'lláh.

The basis of self-sacrifice on which the Bahá'í community stands has created a religious society in which all human relations are transformed from social to spiritual problems.

This fact is the door through which one must pass to arrive at insight of what the Faith of Bahá'u'lláh means to this age.

The social problems of the age are predominantly political and economic. They are problems because human society is divided into nations each of which claims to be an end and a law unto itself and into classes each of which has raised an economic theory to the level of a sovereign and exclusive principle. Nationality has become a condition which overrides the fundamental humanity of all the peoples concerned, asserting the superiority of political considerations over ethical and moral needs. Similarly, economic groups uphold and promote social systems without regard to the quality of human relationships experienced in terms of religion. Tensions and oppositions between the different groups are organized for dominance and not for reconciliation. Each step toward more complete partisan organization increases the original tension and augments the separation of human beings; as the separation widens, the element of sympathy and fellowship on the human level is eventually denied.

In the Bahá'í community the same tensions and instinctive antagonisms exist, but the human separation has been made impossible. The same capacity for exclusive doctrines is present, but no doctrine representing one personality or one group can secure a hearing. All believers alike are subject to one spiritually supreme sovereignty in the teachings of Bahá'u'lláh. Disaffected individuals may withdraw. The community remains. For the Bahá'í teachings are in themselves principles of life and they assert the supreme value of humanity without doctrines which correspond to any particular environment or condition. Thus members of the Bahá'í community realize their tensions and oppositions as ethical or spiritual problems, to be faced and overcome in mutual consultation. Their faith has convinced them that the "truth" or "right" of any possible situation is not derived from partisan victory but from the needs of the community as an organic whole.

A Bahá'í community endures without disruption because

only spiritual problems can be solved. When human relations are held to be political or social problems they are removed from the realm in which rational will has responsibility and influence. The ultimate result of this degradation of human relationships is the frenzy of desperate strife—the outbreak of inhuman war.

THE RENEWAL OF FAITH

"Therefore the Lord of Mankind has caused His holy, divine Manifestations to come into the world. He has revealed His heavenly books in order to establish spiritual brotherhood, and through the power of the Holy Spirit has made it possible for perfect fraternity to be realized among mankind." 'ABDU'L-BAHÁ.

In stating that the Cause of Bahá'u'lláh is an independent religion, two essential facts are implied.

The first fact is that the Bahá'í Cause historically was not an offshoot of any prior social principle or community. The teachings of Bahá'u'lláh are no artificial synthesis assembled from the modern library of international truth, which might be duplicated from the same sources. Bahá'u'lláh created a reality in the world of the soul which never before existed and could not exist apart from Him.

The second fact is that the Faith of Bahá'u'lláh is a religion, standing in the line of true religions: Christianity, Muḥammadanism, Judaism, and other prophetic Faiths. Its existence, like that of early Christianity, marks the return of faith as a direct and personal experience of the will of God. Because the divine will itself has been revealed in terms of human reality, the followers of Bahá'u'lláh are confident that their personal limitations can be transformed by an inflow of spiritual reinforcement from the higher world. It is for the privilege of access to the source of reality that they forgo reliance upon the darkened self within and the unbelieving society without.

The religious education of Bahá'ís revolutionizes their inherited attitude toward their own as well as other traditional religions.

To Bahá'ís, religion is the life and teachings of the prophet. By identifying religion with its founder, they exclude from its spiritual reality all those accretions of human definition, ceremony and ritualistic practice emanating from followers required from time to time to make compromise with an unbelieving world. Furthermore, in limiting religion to the prophet they are able to perceive the oneness of God in the spiritual oneness of all the prophets. The Bahá'í born into Christianity can wholeheartedly enter into fellowship with the Bahá'í born into Muhammadanism because both have come to understand that Christ and Muhammad reflected the light of the one God into the darkness of the world. If certain ·teachings of Christ differ from certain teachings of Moses or Muhammad, the Bahá'ís know that all prophetic teachings are divided into two parts: one, consisting of the essential and unalterable principles of love, peace, unity and co-operation, renewed as divine commands in every cycle; the other, consisting of external practices (such as diet, marriage and similar ordinances) conforming to the requirements of one time and place.

This Bahá'í teaching leads to a profounder analysis of the process of history. The followers of Bahá'u'lláh derive mental integrity from the realization made so clear and vivid by 'Abdu'l-Bahá that true insight into history discloses the uninterrupted and irresistible working of a Providence not denied nor made vain by any measure of human ignorance and unfaith.

According to this insight, a cycle begins with the appearance of a prophet or manifestation of God, through whom the spirits of men are revivified and reborn. The rise of faith in God produces a religious community, whose power of enthusiasm and devotion releases the creative elements of a new and higher civilization. This civilization comes to its fruitful autumn in culture and mental achievement, to give way eventually to a barren winter of atheism, when strife and discord bring the civilization to an end. Under the burden of immorality, dishonour and cruelty marking this phase of the cycle, humanity lies helpless until the spiritual leader, the prophet, once more returns in the power of the Holy Spirit.

Such is the Bahá'í reading of the book of the past. Its reading of the present interprets these world troubles, this general chaos and confusion, as the hour when the renewal of religion is no longer a racial experience, a rebirth of one limited area of human society, but the destined unification of humanity itself in one faith and one order. It is by the parable of the vineyard that Bahá'ís of the Christian West behold their tradition and their present spiritual reality at last inseparably joined, their faith and their social outlook identified, their reverence for the power of God merged with intelligible grasp of their material environment. A human society which has substituted creeds for religion and armies for truth, even as all ancient prophets foretold, must needs come to abandon its instruments of violence and undergo purification until conscious, humble faith can be reborn.

THE BASIS OF UNITY

"The best beloved of all things in My sight is Justice; turn not away therefrom if thou desirest Me, and neglect it not that I may confide in thee." BAHÁ'U'LLÁH.

Faith alone, no matter how whole-hearted and sincere, affords no basis on which the organic unity of a religious fellowship can endure. The faith of the early Christians was complete, but its degree of inner conviction when projected outward upon the field of action soon disclosed a fatal lack of social principle. Whether the outer expression of love implied a democratic or an aristocratic order, a communal or individualistic society, raised fundamental questions after the crucifixion of the prophet which none had authority to solve.

The Bahá'í teaching has this vital distinction, that it extends from the realm of conscience and faith to the realm of social action. It confirms the substance of faith not merely as a source of individual development but as a definitely ordered relationship to the community. Those who inspect the Bahá'í Cause superficially may deny its claim to be a religion for the reason that it lacks most of the visible marks by which religions are recognized. But in place of ritual or other formal worship it contains a social principle linking people to a community, the loyal observance of which makes spiritual faith coterminous with life itself. The Bahá'ís, having no professional clergy, forbidden ever to have a clergy, understand that religion, in this age, consists in an "attitude toward God reflected in life." They are therefore conscious of no division between religious and secular actions.

The inherent nature of the community created by Bahá'u'lláh has great significance at this time, when the relative values of democracy, of constitutional monarchy, of aristocracy and of communism are everywhere in dispute.

Of the Bahá'í community it may be declared definitely that its character does not reflect the communist theory. The rights of the individual are fully safeguarded and the fundamental distinctions of personal endowment natural among all people are fully preserved. Individual rights, however, are interpreted in the light of the supreme law of brotherhood and not made a sanction for selfishness, oppression and indifference.

On the other hand, the Bahá'í order is not a democracy in the sense that it proceeds from the complete sovereignty of the people, whose representatives are limited to carrying out the popular will. Sovereignty, in the Bahá'í community, is attributed to the Divine prophet, and the elected representatives of the believers in their administrative function look to the teachings of Bahá'u'lláh for their guidance, having faith that the application of His universal principles is the source of order throughout the community. Every Bahá'í administrative body feels itself a trustee, and in this capacity stands above the plane of dissension and is free of that pressure exerted by factional groups.

The local community on April 21 of each year elects by universal adult suffrage an administrative body of nine members called the Spiritual Assembly. This body, with reference to all Bahá'í matters, has sole power of decision. It represents the collective conscience of the community with respect to Bahá'í activities. Its capacity and power are supreme within certain definite limitations.

The various states and provinces unite, through delegates elected annually according to the principle of proportionate representation, in the formation of a National Spiritual Assembly for their country or natural geographical area. This National Spiritual Assembly, likewise composed of nine members, administers all national Bahá'í affairs and may assume jurisdiction of any local matter felt to be of more than local importance. Spiritual Assemblies, local and national, combine an executive, a legislative and a judicial function, all within the limits set by the Bahá'í teachings. They have no resemblance to religious bodies which can adopt articles of faith and regulate the processes of belief and worship. They are primarily responsible for the maintenance of unity within the Bahá'í community and for the release of its collective power in service to the Cause. Membership in the Bahá'í community is granted, on personal declaration of faith.[1]

Fifteen National Spiritual Assemblies have come into existence since the passing of 'Abdu'l-Bahá in 1921. Each National Spiritual Assembly will, in future, constitute an electoral body in the formation of an International Spiritual Assembly or House of Justice, a consummation which will perfect the administrative order of the Faith and create, for the first time in history, an international tribunal representing a world-wide community united in a single Faith.

Bahá'ís maintain their contact with the source of inspiration and knowledge in the sacred writings of the Faith by continuous prayer, study and discussion. No believer can ever have a finished, static faith any more than he can arrive at the end of his capacity for being. The community has but one meeting ordained in the teachings—the general meeting held every nineteen days given in the new calendar established by the Báb.

[1] See Preface.

This Nineteen Day Feast is conducted simply and informally under a programme divided into three parts. The first part consists in reading of passages from writings of Bahá'u'lláh, the Báb and 'Abdu'l-Bahá—a devotional meeting. Next follows general discussion of Bahá'í activities—the business meeting of the local community. After the consultation, the community breaks bread together and enjoys fellowship.

The experience which Bahá'ís receive through participation in their spiritual world order is unique and cannot be paralleled in any other society. Their status of perfect equality as voting members of a constitutional body called upon to deal with matters which reflect, even though in miniature, the whole gamut of human problems and activities; their intense realization of kinship with believers representing so wide a diversity of races, classes and creeds; their assurance that this unity is based upon the highest spiritual sanction and contributes a necessary ethical quality to the world in this age—all these opportunities for deeper and broader experience confer a privilege that is felt to be the fulfilment of life.

THE SPIRIT OF THE NEW DAY

"If man is left in his natural state, he will become lower than the animal and continue to grow more ignorant and imperfect. . . . God has purposed that the darkness of the world of nature shall be dispelled and the imperfect attributes of the natal self be effaced in the effulgent reflection of the Sun of Truth." 'ABDU'L-BAHÁ.

The complete text of the Bahá'í sacred writings has not yet been translated into English, but the present generation of believers has the supreme privilege of possessing the fundamental teachings of Bahá'u'lláh, together with the interpretation and lucid commentary of 'Abdu'l-Bahá, and more recently the exposition made by Shoghi Effendi of the teachings concerning the world order which Bahá'u'lláh came to establish. Of special significance to Bahá'ís of Europe and America is the fact that, unlike Christianity, the Cause of Bahá'u'lláh rests upon the Prophet's own words and not upon

58 RELIGION FOR MANKIND

a necessarily incomplete rendering of oral tradition. Furthermore, the commentary and explanation of the Bahá'í gospel
made by 'Abdu'l-Bahá preserves the spiritual integrity and
essential aim of the revealed text, without the inevitable alloy
of human personality which historically served to corrupt the
gospels of Jesus and Muḥammad. The Bahá'í, moreover, has
this distinctive advantage, that his approach to the teachings
is personal and direct, without the veils interposed by any
human intermediary.

The works which supply the Bahá'í teachings to English-
reading believers are *Kitáb-i-Íqán* (Book of Certitude) in which
Bahá'u'lláh revealed the oneness of the Prophets and the
identical foundation of all true religions, the law of cycles
according to which the Prophet returns at intervals of approximately one thousand years, and the nature of faith; *The Hidden
Words*, the essence of truths revealed by Prophets in the past;
prayers to quicken the soul's life and draw individuals and
groups nearer to God; *Tablets of Bahá'u'lláh* (Tarázát, Tablet of
the World, Kalimát, Tajallíyát, Bishárát, Ishráqát), which
establish social and spiritual principles for the new era; *Three
Tablets of Bahá'u'lláh* (Tablet of the Branch, Kitáb-i-'Ahd,
Lawḥ-i-Aqdas), the appointment of 'Abdu'l-Bahá as the
Interpreter of Bahá'u'lláh's teachings, the Testament of
Bahá'u'lláh, and His message to the Christians; *Epistle to the
Son of the Wolf* addressed to the son of a prominent Persian who
had been a most ruthless oppressor of the believers, a Tablet
which recapitulates many teachings Bahá'u'lláh had revealed
in earlier works; *Gleanings from the Writings of Bahá'u'lláh*. The
significant Tablets addressed to rulers of Europe and the
Orient, as well as to the heads of American Republics, about
the year 1870, summoning them to undertake measures for
the establishment of Universal Peace have been, in selected
excerpts, incorporated by Shoghi Effendi in his book *The
Promised Day Is Come*.

The largest and most authentic body of Bahá'u'lláh's
Writings in the English language consists of the excerpts chosen

and translated by Shoghi Effendi, and published under the title of *Gleanings from the Writings of Bahá'u'lláh*.

In *Prayers and Meditations by Bahá'u'lláh*, Shoghi Effendi has similarly given to the Bahá'í Community in recent years a wider selection and a superb rendering of devotional passages revealed by Bahá'u'lláh.

The published writings of 'Abdu'l-Bahá are: *Some Answered Questions*, dealing with the lives of the Prophets, the interpretation of Bible prophecies, the nature of man, the true principle of evolution and other philosophic subjects; *The Secret of Divine Civilization*, a work addressed to the people of Persia about sixty years ago to show them the way to sound progress and true civilization; *Tablets of 'Abdu'l-Bahá*, three volumes of excerpts from letters written to individual believers and Bahá'í communities, which illumine a vast range of subjects; *The Promulgation of Universal Peace*, from stenographic records of the public addresses delivered by the Master to audiences in Canada and the United States during the year 1912; *The Wisdom of 'Abdu'l-Bahá*, a similar record of His addresses in Paris; *'Abdu'l-Bahá in London*; and reprints of a number of individual Tablets, especially that sent to the Committee for a Durable Peace, The Hague, Holland, in 1919, and the Tablet addressed to the late Dr. Forel of Switzerland. The *Will and Testament* left by 'Abdu'l-Bahá has special significance, in that it provided for the future development of Bahá'í administrative institutions and the Guardianship.

The most comprehensive selection of the Writings of Bahá'u'lláh and 'Abdu'l-Bahá now available in the English language is *Bahá'í World Faith*.[1]

To these writings is now to be added the book entitled *Bahá'í Administration*, consisting of the general letters written by Shoghi Effendi as Guardian of the Faith since the Master's death in 1921, which explain the details of the administrative order of the Faith, and his letters on World Order, which

[1] A more recent compilation is *The Bahá'í Revelation* (Bahá'í Publishing Trust, London).

E

make clear the social principles embedded in Bahá'u'lláh's Revelation.

These latter letters were in 1938 published in a volume entitled *The World Order of Bahá'u'lláh*. Here the Guardian defines the relation of the Faith to the current social crisis, and sums up the fundamental tenets of the Bahá'í Faith. It is a work which gives to each believer access to a clear insight on the significance of the present era, and the outcome of its international perturbations, incomparably more revealing and at the same time more assuring than the works of students and statesmen in our times.

After laying the basis of the administrative order, and explaining the relations between the Faith of Bahá'u'lláh and the current movement and events which transform the world, the Guardian has written books of more general Bahá'í import. In *The Advent of Divine Justice*, Shoghi Effendi expounded the significance of 'Abdu'l-Bahá's teaching plan for North America against a background of ethical and social regeneration required for Bahá'í service today. *The Promised Day Is Come* examines the history of the Faith in its early days when the world repudiated the Báb and Bahá'u'lláh and inflicted supreme suffering upon them and their followers, and develops the thesis that war and revolution come as penalty for rejection of the Manifestation of God.[1]

In 1944, the centenary year of the Faith, the Guardian produced in *God Passes By* the authentic historical survey of the evolution of the Faith from its origin.

The literature has also been enriched by Shoghi Effendi's translation of *The Dawn-Breakers*, Nabíl's Narrative of the Early Days of the Bahá'í Revelation, a vivid eye-witness account of the episodes which resulted from the announcement of the Báb on May 23, 1844.

When it is borne in mind that the term "religious literature" has come to represent a wide diversity of subject matter,

[1] *Guidance for Today and Tomorrow* (Bahá'í Publishing Trust, London) is a comprehensive selection of the Guardian's writings.

ranging from cosmic philosophy to the psychology of personal experience, from efforts to understand the universe plumbed by telescope and microscope to efforts to discipline the passions and desires of disordered human hearts, it is clear that any attempt to summarize the Bahá'í teachings would indicate the limitations of the person making the summary rather than offer possession of a body of sacred literature touching the needs of man and society at every point. The study of Bahá'í writing does not lead to any simplified programme either for the solution of social problems or for the development of human personality. Rather should it be likened to a clear light which illumines whatever is brought under its rays, or to spiritual nourishment which gives life to the spirit. The believer at first chiefly notes the passages which seem to confirm his own personal beliefs or treat of subjects close to his own previous training. This natural but nevertheless unjustifiable over-simplification of the nature of the Faith must gradually subside and give way to a deeper realization that the teachings of Bahá'u'lláh are as an ocean, and all personal capacity is but the vessel that must be refilled again and again. The sum and substance of the Faith of Bahá'ís is not a doctrine, not an organization, but their acceptance of Bahá'u'lláh as Manifestation of God. In this acceptance lies the mystery of a unity that is general, not particular, inclusive, not exclusive, and limited in its gradual extension by no boundaries drawn in the social world nor arbitrary limitations accepted by habits formed during generations lacking a true spiritual culture.

What the believer learns reverently to be grateful for is a source of wisdom to which he may turn for continuous mental and moral development—a source of truth revealing a universe in which man's life has valid purpose and assured realization. Human history begins to reflect the working of a beneficent Providence; the sharp outlines of material sciences gradually fade out in the light of one fundamental science of life; a profounder sociology, connected with the inner life, little by little displaces the superficial economic and political beliefs which like waves dash high an instant only to subside into the moveless volume of the sea.

"The divine reality," 'Abdu'l-Bahá has said, "is unthinkable, limitless, eternal, immortal and invisible. The world of creation is bound by natural law, finite and mortal. The infinite reality cannot be said to ascend or descend. It is beyond the understanding of men, and cannot be described in terms which apply to the phenomenal sphere of the created world. Man, then, is in extreme need of the only power by which he is able to receive help from the divine reality, that power alone bringing him into contact with the source of all life.

"An intermediary is needed to bring two extremes into relation with each other. Riches and poverty, plenty and need: without an intermediary there could be no relation between these pairs of opposites. So we can say that there must be a Mediator between God and man, and this is none other than the Holy Spirit, which brings the created earth into relation with the 'Unthinkable One,' the Divine reality. The Divine reality may be likened to the sun and the Holy Spirit to the rays of the sun. As the rays of the sun bring the light and warmth of the sun to the earth, giving life to all created things, so do the Manifestations bring the power of the Holy Spirit from the Divine Sun of Reality to give light and life to the souls of men."

In expounding the teachings of Bahá'u'lláh to public audiences in the West, 'Abdu'l-Bahá frequently encountered the attitude that, while the liberal religionist might well welcome and endorse such tenets, the Bahá'í teachings after all bring nothing new, since the principles of Christianity contain all the essentials of spiritual truth. The believer whose heart has been touched by the Faith so perfectly exemplified by 'Abdu'l-Bahá feels no desire for controversy, but must needs point out the vital difference between a living faith and a passive formula or doctrine. What religion in its renewal brings is first of all an energy to translate belief into life. This impulse, received into the profoundest depths of consciousness, requires no startling "newness" of concept or theory to be appreciated as a gift from the divine world. It carries its own assurance as a renewal of life itself; it is a candle that has been lighted, and in comparison with the miracle of light the discussion of religion as a form of belief becomes secondary in importance. Were the Bahá'í Faith no more than a true revitalization of the revealed truths of former religions, it would by that quickening quality of inner life, that returning to God, still assert itself as the supreme fact of human experience in this age.

For religion returns to earth in order to re-establish a standard of spiritual reality. It restores the quality of human existence, its active powers, when that reality has become overlaid with sterile rites and dogmas which substitute empty shadow for substance. In the person of the Manifestation it destroys all those imitations of religion gradually developed through the centuries and summons humanity to the path of sacrifice and devotion.

Revelation, moreover, is progressive as well as periodic. Christianity in its original essence not only relighted the candle of faith which, in the years since Moses, had become extinguished—it amplified the teachings of Moses with a new dimension which history has seen exemplified in spread of faith from tribe to nations and peoples. Bahá'u'lláh has given religion its world dimension, fulfilling the fundamental purpose of every previous Revelation. His Faith stands as the reality within Christianity, within Muḥammadanism, within the religion of Moses, the spirit of each, but expressed in teachings which relate to all mankind.

The Bahá'í Faith, viewed from within, is religion extended from the individual to embrace humanity. It is religion universalized; its teaching for the individual, spiritually identical with the teaching of Christ, supplies the individual with an ethics, a sociology, an ideal of social order, for which humanity in its earlier stages of development was not prepared. Individual fulfilment has been given an objective social standard of reality, balancing the subjective ideal derived from religion in the past.

Bahá'u'lláh has removed the false distinctions between the "spiritual" and "material" aspects of life, due to which religion has become separate from science, and morality has been divorced from all social activities. The whole arena of human affairs has been brought within the realm of spiritual truth, in the light of the teaching that materialism is not a thing but a motive within the human heart.

The Bahá'í learns to perceive the universe as a divine creation in which man has his destiny to fulfil under a beneficent Providence whose aims for humanity are made known through Prophets who stand between man and the Creator. He learns his true relation to the degrees and orders of the visible universe; his true relation to God, to himself, to his fellow man, to mankind. The more he studies the Bahá'í teachings, the more he becomes imbued with the spirit of unity, the more vividly he perceives the law of unity working in the world today, indirectly manifest in the failure which has overtaken all efforts to organize the principle of separation and competition, directly manifest in the power which has brought together the followers of Bahá'u'lláh in East and West. He has the assurance that the world's turmoil conceals from wordly minds the blessings long foretold, now forgotten, in the sayings which prophesied the coming of the Kingdom of God.

The Sacred Literature of the Bahá'í Faith conveys enlightenment. It inspires life. It frees the mind. It disciplines the heart. For believers, the Word is not a philosophy to be learned, but the sustenance of being throughout the span of mortal existence.

"The Bahá'í Faith," Shoghi Effendi stated in a recent letter addressed to a public official, "recognizes the unity of God and of His Prophets, upholds the principle of an unfettered search after truth, condemns all forms of superstition and prejudice, teaches that the fundamental purpose of religion is to promote concord and harmony, that it must go hand-in-hand with science, and that it constitutes the sole and ultimate basis of a peaceful, an ordered and progressive society. It inculcates the principle of equal opportunity, rights and privileges for both sexes, advocates compulsory education, abolishes extremes of poverty and wealth, recommends the adoption of an auxiliary international language, and provides the necessary agencies for the establishment and safeguarding of a permanent and universal peace."

Those who, even courteously, would dismiss a Faith so firmly based, will have to admit that, whether or not by their test the teachings of Bahá'u'lláh are "new," the world's present plight is unprecedented, came without warning save in the utterances of Bahá'u'lláh and 'Abdu'l-Bahá, and day by day discloses dangers which strike terror to the responsible student of current affairs. Humanity itself now seems to share the prison and exile which an unbelieving generation inflicted upon the Glory of God eighty years ago.

The source and origin of this re-creative power lies in far-distant, unfamiliar, medieval Persia one hundred years ago. There, in Islám, as in Christian Europe and America, spiritual schools existed for cherishing the hope that in this age the promised One might appear. The longing for a Person endowed with the mission to connect humanity with God kindled fire in many souls who felt that the world had sunk to its lowest state, incapable of salvation save through its Creator's mercy.

THAT HOLY DAWN

To these humble servants of the altar of the heart the Báb revealed Himself in 1844. He was twenty-five years of age. The Báb, His title meaning "door" or "gate," exemplified a radiance, a beauty of being and of person, a power of spirit, a penetration of love which became the adoration of a mighty host. In that darkened, ignorant, tyrannical land the Báb arose as with the light of a dawning Sun. So powerful was He in quickening the human spirit, in establishing the standard of reality dividing the people into believers and non-believers, that within the span of six years His earthly destiny was fulfilled. Condemned for heresy, denounced as rebel, the Báb was imprisoned and executed in the city of Tabríz. It was a time of profound spiritual experience. Thousands of His followers advanced to martyrdom for His sake and in tribute to the pure religion He revealed for the world. The attitude of the true worshipper has been described by Bahá'u'lláh in these words of promise: "Great is his blessedness whosoever hath set himself towards Thee, and entered Thy presence, and caught the accents of Thy voice. . . . Whosoever hath recognized Thee will turn to none save Thee, and will seek from Thee naught else except Thyself."

Every testimony reveals the splendour of that holy Dawn, when men of sincerity and truth attained the purpose of their being in becoming filled with a new spirit and a new life. They had full assurance that this was no personal and no local experience, but a new enlightenment and impetus for the regeneration of the world. In the Báb they touched the mystery of the oneness of God, and in His spiritual being they felt the presence of all the Prophets through whom God has been manifested in the past. The Báb restored the power of providence to human affairs. Against Him sped the arrows of bitterest ecclesiastical and civil rancour. The Báb was the chosen Victim by whose sacrifice the human spirit could be given life, and a new direction established for the course of man's spiritual and social evolution. These words, addressed by the Báb to His nearest disciples, express the beauty of His teaching: "Such must be the purity of your character and the degree of your renunciation, that the people of the earth may through you recognize and be drawn closer to the Heavenly Father who is the Source of purity and grace."

Concerning His mission and the import of His teachings, the Báb declared that He prepared the way for the coming of Bahá'u'lláh, the Glory of God, the promised One in whom the prophetic hopes of the peoples would be fulfilled.

In such pure sacrifice was opened the door of divine guidance, and the mission of the Báb initiated the release of forces and powers which since, with increasing intensity, have acted upon mankind.

THE LAW IS REVEALED

Nineteen years after the declaration of the Báb, Bahá'u'-lláh's mission became known to the Báb's followers, and all save a few persons thereafter centred their faith in Him.

Through Bahá'u'lláh the ecstasy of spiritual renewal acquired substance in knowledge of spiritual truth and law. The Dawn of holiness became the risen Sun of a new Dispensation for mankind. Bahá'u'lláh suffered exile and imprisonment throughout forty years as the dominant powers of Islám tried in every way to extirpate this new Faith. What they accomplished was to establish Bahá'u'lláh in 'Akká, at the foot of Mount Carmel, where His spirit soared in majesty above the restless skirmishing of the sects who were exploiting the Holy Land in the name of their separate religions.

Bahá'u'lláh gave forth in writing a body of teachings for the new era. He provided for the needs of a united humanity and an ordered world civilization. He declared that all the Prophets had revealed one continuous, evolving and divine Faith, each as the Manifestation of God for one cycle and one stage in man's development. He stated that the law of the present cycle revolves around the principle of the oneness of mankind, which requires one social order and one universal Faith. Bahá'u'lláh interpreted the Holy Books of the past. He identified the Báb and Himself with the essence of reality in Abraham, Moses, Jesus and Muḥammad. He called upon the rulers to establish peace. He exalted the nature of man's soul and greatly amplified the body of spiritual knowledge concerning man and His destiny on earth and in the other worlds of God. Majesty and power, serene, glorious, heavenly, characterized this Person and this Message which is His blessed gift to mankind.

Bahá'u'lláh laid deep and strong the foundations of His Faith. His ordinances make it impossible for any clerical order to arise in this Dispensation and claim special authority, privilege or power. For the direction of affairs and the administration of activities He instituted elective bodies with defined duties and functions. He moreover appointed 'Abdu'l-Bahá to be the Interpreter of His Revelation and the Centre of His Covenant with mankind. In these provisions Bahá'u'lláh established a Faith which is no mere influence left for humanity to reflect to a lesser or greater degree according to its own volition. His Faith is a social organism imbued with a divine spirit, endowed with law and knowledge, provided with necessary institutions and agencies, and inspired by a sustaining power of guidance conveyed through His appointed representative, 'Abdu'l-Bahá.

"Darkness hath encompassed every land, O my God," Bahá'u'lláh cried in prayer, "and caused most of Thy servants to tremble. I beseech Thee, by Thy Most Great Name, to raise in every city a new creation that shall turn towards Thee."

Bahá'u'lláh's Covenant

Having revealed His truth and law, Bahá'u'lláh returned to His heavenly abode. In 'Abdu'l-Bahá the spirit of obedience to Bahá'u'lláh and passionate zeal for serving His Faith became a torrent of spiritual energy. Though 'Abdu'l-Bahá Himself was restrained physically under the terms of His imprisonment for sixteen years after Bahá'u'lláh ascended, nevertheless His irresistible will to serve found human instruments through which to some degree it might influence the whole world. In one single year a sequence of events had been set up which produced public reference to Bahá'u'lláh in the Parliament of Religions conducted by the Columbian Exhibition in Chicago in 1893, and the formation of the first Bahá'í group in the West in 1894.

His vision of the ultimate unfoldment of world civilization under the impetus of the Holy Spirit reflected through the Báb and Bahá'u'lláh concentrated 'Abdu'l-Bahá's effort on the most important task of this age: the development of capacity within souls to obey divine law and thereby rid the world of that degrading curse, that corrosive poison—acceptance of the struggle for existence as the underlying condition of man's social experience. That acceptance lay upon the nations like a doom. To transform this most grievous and perverted error into truth was 'Abdu'l-Bahá's destiny, His mission, His glory to the end of time.

One must realize this to grasp the essence of His teaching: His assurance that in no region of human action and no realm of human experience has the struggle for existence any sanction or validity from God. Neither in the nature of man, nor in the conflict of races, nor in the clash of nations, nor in the rancour of creeds did 'Abdu'l-Bahá admit the operation of any divine law reducing mankind to the level of the beast. Where He encountered inveterate prejudice and crystallized hate in which the struggle for existence had apparently become entrenched for ever, such a lamentable condition, He explained, was not part of the divine creative will for man, but man's self-inflicted punishment for repudiation of God—the darkness that supervenes when doors are closed against the Light, the terror that surrounds him when he leaves his home and lives in the jungle with the serpent and the tiger.

CHARTER OF WORLD ORDER

The exquisite passion which 'Abdu'l-Bahá poured forth upon the humblest believer lives on for us in His written word. "O ye friends of God! The world is like the body of man—it hath become sick, feeble and infirm. Its eye is devoid of sight, its ear hath become destitute of hearing and its faculties of sense are entirely dissolved. The friends of God must become as wise physicians, and care for and heal this sick person, in accord with the divine teachings. . . .

"The first remedy is to guide the people, so that they may turn unto God, hearken unto the divine commandments and go forth with a hearing ear and seeing eye. After this swift and certain remedy hath been applied, then according to the divine teachings they ought to be trained in the conduct, morals and deeds of the Kingdom of Abhá. The hearts should be purified and cleansed from every trace of hatred and rancour and enabled to engage in truthfulness, conciliation, uprightness and love toward the world of humanity, so that the East and the West may embrace each other like unto two lovers, enmity and animosity may vanish from the human world and the universal peace be established.

"O ye friends of God! Be kind to all peoples and nations, have love for all of them, exert yourselves to purify the hearts as much as you can, and bestow abundant effort in rejoicing the souls. . . . Consider love and union as a delectable paradise, and count annoyance and hostility as the torment of hell-fire. . . . Supplicate and beseech with your heart and search for divine assistance and favour, in order that you may make this world the paradise of Abhá and this terrestrial globe the arena of the supreme Kingdom."

'Abdu'l-Bahá perfected the art of intercourse between souls. He developed the faculty of kindness and consultation among the Bahá'ís as the foundation of existence in the new age. In the Will and Testament which He left as His final blessing and guidance for the Bahá'í community the believers of the world have been given the charter of their evolving Faith. By that momentous document 'Abdu'l-Bahá revealed the continuity of divine guidance for human affairs throughout this cycle in the succession of the station of Guardianship from generation to generation. To this station He attributed the sole power and authority to interpret the Bahá'í Sacred Writings, and this station He joined to the Universal House of Justice instituted by Bahá'u'lláh by making each successive Guardian its chairman for life. [See Preface.]

The Bahá'í Dispensation combines and co-ordinates what in the world has become hopelessly separate and divided: divine truth and social authority; spiritual law and legislation; devotion to God and justice to man; the rights of the individual and the paramount responsibility of the social body.

"In this sacred Dispensation," 'Abdu'l-Bahá left as His direction to His loved ones, "conflict and contention are in no wise permitted. Every aggressor deprives himself of God's grace. It is incumbent upon every one to show the utmost love, rectitude of conduct, straightforwardness and sincere kindliness unto all the peoples and kindreds of the world, be they friends or strangers. So intense must be the spirit of love and loving kindness, that the stranger may find himself a friend, the enemy a true brother, no difference whatsoever existing between them. For universality is of God and all limitations earthly."

LAWS, PRINCIPLES, TEACHINGS

Religion is the depository of spiritual truth. Its laws and principles revealed by the Manifestations of God constitute the reality of man's relations to God, to himself and to other men. What science is to the natural universe religion is to mankind in all that pertains to its spiritual, its supernatural endowment and aim. There is no chaos nor void where truth ceases to exist or laws to operate, but there is in man a realm of ignorance where he attempts to deny a divine law by substituting human desire and human opinion. The appearance of the new Manifestation brings all spiritual evasion and subterfuge to an end. He creates a condition in which only truth can survive.

In the Bahá'í Dispensation we find laws, principles and teachings, all reflecting the spirit of the new World Era. In this Dispensation religion brings fulfilment to feeling, will and reason in balance and harmony.

The western world first learned of the Faith through its principles. 'Abdu'l-Bahá expounded them in the form of general truths acceptable to the enlightened mind whatever its class, creed, race or nation. In one of His public addresses in America He presented the following summary:—

"The oneness of the world of humanity.

"The protection and guidance of the Holy Spirit.

"The foundation of all religion is one.

"Religion must be the cause of unity.

"Religion must accord with science and reason.

"Independent investigation of truth.

"Equality between men and women.

"The abandoning of all prejudices among mankind.

"Universal peace.

"Universal education.

"A universal language.

"Solution of the economic problem.

"An international tribunal.":

Of the source and meaning of these teachings He said: "His Holiness Bahá'u'lláh has dawned from the horizon of the Orient, flooding all regions with light and life which will never pass away. His teachings . . . embody the divine spirit of the age and are applicable to this period of maturity in the life of the human world. . . .

"Every one who truly seeks and justly reflects will admit that the teachings of the present day emanating from mere human sources and authority are the cause of difficulty and disagreement amongst mankind, the very destroyers of humanity, whereas the teachings of Bahá'u'lláh are the very healing of the sick world, the remedy for every need and condition. In them may be found the realization of every desire and aspiration, the cause of the happiness of the world of humanity, the stimulus and illumination of mentality, the impulse for advancement and uplift, the basis of unity for all nations, the fountain-source of love amongst mankind, the centre of agreement, the means of peace and harmony, the one bond which will unite the East and the West."

Those who sought no further than this preliminary discussion, conceived of the Faith as a leaven gradually penetrating the masses of mankind, urged and promoted by the enlightened and the idealistic in and through the reformation of the traditional movements and organizations. 'Abdu'l-Bahá, however, plainly set forth the sovereign quality of revealed religion, as, for example, in the following Tablet addressed to American Bahá'ís.

"In the contingent world there are many collective centres which are conducive to association and unity between the children of men. For example patriotism is a collective centre;

nationalism is a collective centre; identity of interests is a collective centre; political alliance is a collective centre; the union of ideals is a collective centre, and the prosperity of the world of humanity is dependent upon the organization and promotion of the collective centres. Nevertheless, all the above institutions are, in reality, the matter and not the substance, accidental and not eternal—temporary and not everlasting. With the appearance of great revolutions and upheavals, all these collective centres are swept away. But the collective centre of the Kingdom, embodying the Institutes and Divine Teachings, is the eternal collective centre. . . . The real Collective Centre is the body of the Divine Teachings, which include all the degrees and embrace all the universal relations and necessary laws of humanity."

Behind the principles of rational truth, therefore, we look for the deeper implications of law and ordinance.

In studying Bahá'u'lláh's laws and ordinances, we note that He revealed nothing in the form of a code or constitution. His teachings represent virtues and attitudes, or deal with matters which He did not intend to be altered during this cycle. The Bahá'í code will come into existence through the legislative institutions which Bahá'u'lláh created, and whose enactments are subject to revision from time to time as conditions change.

The laws of Bahá'u'lláh include: the obligation of daily prayer; an annual fasting period of nineteen days; prohibition of use of alcoholic liquor or drugs; monogamy; marriage contingent upon the consent of all four parents, or those living; obedience to civil government; obligation to engage in a useful trade, art or profession; prohibition of a clergy in the Bahá'í Faith.

Other ordinances and directions found in His writings can be summarized as follows:

Man's first duty is to know his own self and the conditions of progress and abasement. After maturity has been attained, wealth is needed for the attainment of social personality, and this is to be earned through the practice of a profession, art, trade or craft. Associate in a joyous spirit with the followers of all religions and the members of all races and nations. The supreme obligation is to attain a good character. Through trustworthiness mankind will obtain security and tranquillity. Respect possessors of talent. Meet all obligations due to others. Refrain from slander and backbiting. To acquire knowledge is incumbent on all, but knowledge must be of matters useful to mankind. Agriculture is of first importance. Human existence rests upon the two pillars of reward (for obedience to divine command) and punishment (for disobedience to it). Kings and rulers are to uphold religion as the means to world order and peace. Schools must train children in the principles of religion. Celibacy and seclusion from the world are not approved. Warfare for religious reasons is prohibited. Kings and rulers are exhorted to protect and assist the Bahá'í community. Governments must appoint or elect to office only such persons as have character and capacity. The repentant sinner must turn to God for forgiveness and not to any human being.

The realm of law and ordinance is defined and given a firm basis in the establishment of social institutions with definite functions for the Bahá'í community, and the conveyance of specific authority to be effective after Bahá'u'lláh's ascension. "The affairs of the people are placed in charge of the men of the House of Justice of God. They are the trustees of God among His servants and the daysprings of command in His countries.

"O people of God! The trainer of the world is justice, for it consists of two pillars: reward and retribution. These two pillars are two fountains for the life of the people of the world. Inasmuch as for each time and day a particular decree and order is expedient, affairs are therefore entrusted to the ministers of the House of Justice, so that they may execute that which they deem advisable at the time. Those souls who arise to please God will be inspired by the divine, invisible inspirations. It is incumbent upon all to obey."

The relation of this function to the spiritual realm of the Faith has been placed beyond the possibility of doubt and disagreement. "Administrative affairs," Bahá'u'lláh declared, "are all in charge of the House of Justice; but acts of worship must be observed according as they are revealed in the Book."

The aim of this term of social and spiritual evolution has been firmly fixed. "The ministers of the House of Justice must promote the Most Great Peace."

As 'Abdu'l-Bahá explained in His Will and Testament, this House of Justice is an international body whose members are to be elected by national representatives of the Bahá'ís.

In the Person of 'Abdu'l-Bahá, Bahá'u'lláh established authority as Interpreter of His Revelation and Exemplar of the Faith. The Dispensation of Bahá'u'lláh in reality is to be viewed as more than an initial spiritual impulse breathed into the human heart and left to humanity's own devices to direct and apply throughout an historical epoch. His Dispensation is an organism created to function in and through the entire epoch, for divine guidance has been promised to mankind henceforth, the day of God's Kingdom having dawned.

Shoghi Effendi, Guardian of the Faith, has disclosed this new dimension which religion in its fulfillment has attained. "For Bahá'u'lláh, we should readily recognize, has not only imbued mankind with a new and regenerating Spirit. He has not merely enunciated certain universal principles, or propounded a particular philosophy, however potent, sound and universal these may be. In addition to these He, as well as 'Abdu'l-Bahá after Him, has, unlike the Dispensations of the past, clearly and specifically laid down a set of laws, established definite institutions, and provided for the essentials of a Divine Economy. These are destined to be a pattern for future society, a supreme instrument for the establishment of the Most Great Peace, and the one agency for the unification of the world, and the proclamation of the reign of righteousness and justice upon the earth."

ADMINISTRATIVE ORDER

The Faith of Bahá'u'lláh expresses itself through a community and not through a church. Since this Dispensation began, the power of the Faith to assimilate and unify diverse peoples

F

has been demonstrated with ever-increasing might. Nowhere else in the world today does there exist any social body similar to the unique community which has arisen in response to His call. Spread in many parts of the world, separated by difference of language, custom, tradition and outlook as well as by the operation of conflicting political and economic policies in their environment, this community of believers could not be held together by personal agreement but by a power which surrounds them and combines them through a superhuman force.

The Bahá'í community feels itself immersed in a spiritual reality which encompasses it as by an invisible but potent atmosphere or sea. The influence of that surrounding spirit makes itself continuously felt like the virtue of health in a physical organism which adjusts it to continuous growth and development.

The believers think of the teachings of Bahá'u'lláh not as doctrines but as truths which come to life in their application to problems of conduct and human association. The concept of foreignness or the alien in mankind has been replaced by the ideal of fellowship. Bahá'u'lláh has given assurance that the process of destruction now operating is but the necessary preliminary to the process of construction which will eventually produce the harmonious co-ordination of the views and feelings, the interests and the institutions, the activities and the aims of all mankind.

On the foundations of spiritual equality before the law and the authority of their Faith, the Bahá'ís maintain their community worship and activity through local, national and international institutions which distribute power and authority in accordance with the natural duties and functions of an ordered society. All that pertains to daily action is assigned to the local Spiritual Assembly under the principle of decentralization of administrative control. The local communities are co-ordinated by a National Spiritual Assembly elected by delegates chosen on the basis of proportionate representation. These National Assemblies in turn will be the electoral bodies by whom the members of an International Assembly, or House of Justice, will be selected.[1] In the delegation of authority, the source or reservoir of power lies at the Centre of the world community, and duties and functions are assigned downward to the progressively smaller national and local units. This order follows inevitably from the fact that the whole body of authority was created in and through Bahá'u'lláh and by Him assigned to His ministers and institutions as servants of mankind. Historically, the Bahá'í World Order originated at the Centre, unlike those social bodies which develop from local units and whose central institutions reflect a secondary and imperfectly delegated power.

The Bahá'í thus realizes himself as part of a newly-created world, a world raised up by God above the tumults of the past, and endowed with a new destiny which the forces of disunity can assail but never destroy. The believer need no longer be partisan to the titanic struggles of competitive social values, whether capitalism, communism or state socialism, because such conflicts can never be resolved. What the world needs, He has learned, is a new mind and a new heart.

"This Administrative Order," Shoghi Effendi points out, "is fundamentally different from anything that any Prophet has previously established, inasmuch as Bahá'u'lláh has Himself revealed its principles, established its institutions, appointed the person to interpret His Word and conferred the necessary authority on the body designed to supplement and apply His legislative ordinances. Therein lies the secret of its strength, its fundamental distinction, and the guarantee against disintegration and schism. . . . Alone of all the Revelations gone before it, this Faith has, through the explicit directions, the repeated warnings, the authenticated safeguards incorporated and elaborated in its teachings, succeeded in raising a structure which the bewildered followers of bankrupt and broken creeds might well approach and critically examine, and seek, ere it is too late, the invulnerable security of its world-embracing shelter."

[1] See Preface.

THE FORMATION OF
AN ORGANIC RELIGIOUS COMMUNITY

IN ACCEPTING the message of Bahá'u'lláh, every Bahá'í has opened his mind and heart to the dominion of certain fundamental truths. These truths he recognizes as divine in origin, beyond human capacity to produce. In the realm of spirit he attests that these truths are revealed evidences of a higher reality than man. They are to the soul what natural law is to the physical body of animal or plant. Therefore the believer today, as in the Dispensation of Christ or Moses, enters into the condition of faith as a status of relationship to God and not of satisfaction to his own limited human and personal will or awareness. His faith exists as his participation in a heavenly world. It is the essence of his responsibility and not a temporary compromise effected between his conscience or reason and the meaning of truth, society, virtue or life.

The Bahá'í accepts a quality of existence, a level of being which has been created above the control of his own active power. Because on that plane the truth exists that mankind is one, part of his acceptance of the message of Bahá'u'lláh is capacity to see that truth as existing, as a heavenly reality to be confirmed on earth. Because likewise on that higher level the inmost being of Moses, Christ, Muḥammad, the Báb, and Bahá'u'lláh is one being, part of the believer's acceptance of the Bahá'í message is capacity to realize the eternal continuance of that oneness, so that thereafter never will he again think of those holy and majestic Prophets according to the separateness of their bodies, their countries and their times.

The Bahá'í, moreover, recognizes that the realm of truth is inexhaustible, the creator of truth God Himself. Hence the Bahá'í can identify truth as the eternal flow of life itself in a channel that deepens and broadens as man's capacity for truth enlarges from age to age. For him, that definition of truth which regards truth as tiny fragments of experience, to be taken up and laid down, as a shopper handling gems on a counter, to buy if one gem happens to please or seems becoming: such a definition measures man's own knowledge, or interest, or loyalty, but truth is a living unity which no man can condition. It is the sun in the heavens of spiritual reality, while self-will is the shadow of a cloud.

There are times for the revelation of a larger area of the indivisible truth to mankind. The Manifestation of God signalizes the times and He is the revelation. When He appears on earth He moves and speaks with the power of all truth, known and unknown, revealed in the past, revealed in Him, or to be revealed in the future. That realm of heavenly reality is brought again in its power and universality to knock at the closed door of human experience, a divine guest whose entrance will bless the household eternally, or a divine punishment when debarred and forbidden and condemned.

Bahá'u'lláh reveals that area of divine truth which underlies all human association. He enlarges man's capacity to receive truth in the realm of experience where all men have condemned themselves to social chaos by ignorance of truth and readiness to substitute the implacable will of races, classes, nations and creeds for the pure spiritual radiance beneficently shining for all. Spiritual reality today has become the principle of human unity, the law for the nations, the devotion to mankind on which the future civilization can alone repose. As long as men cling to truth as definition, past experience, aspects of self-will, so long must this dire period of chaos continue when the separate fragments of humanity employ life not to unite but to struggle and destroy.

In the world of time, Bahá'u'lláh has created capacity for union and world civilization. His Dispensation is historically new and unique. In the spiritual world it is nothing else than the ancient and timeless reality of Moses, Jesus and Muḥammad disclosed to the race in a stage of added growth and development so that men can take a larger measure of that which always existed.

Like the man of faith in former ages, the Bahá'í has been given sacred truths to cherish in his heart as lamps for darkness and medicines for healing, convictions of immortality and evidence of divine love. But in addition to these gifts, the Bahá'í has that bestowal which only the Promised One of all ages could bring: nearness to a process of creation which opens a door of entrance into a world of purified and regenerated human relations. The final element in his recognition of the message of Bahá'u'lláh is that Bahá'u'lláh came to found a civilization of unity, progress and peace.

"O Children of Men! Know ye not why We created you all from the same dust? That no one should exalt himself over the other. Ponder at all times how ye were created. Since we have created you all from the same substance it is incumbent on you to be even as one soul, to walk with the same feet, eat with the same mouth and dwell in the same land, that from your inmost being, by your deeds and actions, the signs of oneness and the essence of detachment may be made manifest. Such is My counsel to you, O concourse of light! Heed ye this counsel that ye may obtain the fruit of holiness from the sea of wondrous glory."

Thus He describes the law of survival revealed for the world today, mystical only in that He addressed these particular words to our deepest inner understanding. Their import is not confined to any subjective realm. The motive and the realization He invokes has become the whole truth of sociology in this era.

Or, as we find its expression in another passage: "All men have been created to carry forward an ever-advancing civilization." And the truth reappears in still another form: "How vast is the tabernacle of the Cause of God! It hath overshadowed all the peoples and kindreds of the earth, and will, ere long, gather together the whole of mankind beneath its shelter."

The encompassing reach of the Cause of God in each cycle means the particular aspect of experience for which men are held responsible. Not until our day could there be the creation of the principle of moral cause and effect in terms of mankind itself, in terms of the unifiable world.

The mission of 'Abdu'l-Bahá, following Bahá'u'lláh's ascension in 1892, was to raise up a community of believers through whom collectively He might demonstrate the operation of the law of unity. 'Abdu'l-Bahá's mission became fulfilled historically in the experience of the Bahá'ís of North America. In them He developed the administrative order, the organic society, which exemplifies the pattern of justice and order Bahá'u'lláh had creatively ordained. By His wisdom, His tenderness, His justice and His complete consecration to Bahá'u'lláh, 'Abdu'l-Bahá conveyed to this body of Bahá'ís a sense of partnership in the process of divine creation: that it is for men to re-create, as civilization, a human and earthly replica of the heavenly order existing in the divine will.

The Bahá'í administrative order has been described by the Guardian of the Faith as the pattern of the world order to be gradually attained as the Faith spreads throughout all countries. Its authority is Bahá'u'lláh, its sources the teachings He revealed in writing, with the interpretation and amplification made by 'Abdu'l-Bahá.

The first conveyance of authority by Bahá'u'lláh was to His eldest son. By this conveyance the integrity of the teachings was safeguarded, and the power of action implicit in all true faith directed into channels of unity for the development of the Cause in its universal aspects. No prior Dispensation has ever raised up an instrument like 'Abdu'l-Bahá through whom the spirit and purpose of the Founder could continue to flow out in its wholeness and purity until His purpose had been achieved. The faith of the Bahá'í thus remains untainted by those elements of self-will which in previous ages have translated revealed truth into creeds, rites and institutions of human origin and limited aim. Those who enter the Bahá'í community subdue themselves and their personal interests to its sovereign standard, for they are unable to alter the Cause of Bahá'u'lláh and exploit its teachings or its community for their own advantage.

'Abdu'l-Bahá's life exemplified the working of the one spirit and the one truth sustaining the body of believers throughout the world. He was the light connecting the Sun of Truth with the earth, the radiance enabling all Bahá'ís to realize that truth penetrates human affairs, illumines human problems, transcends conventional barriers, changes the climate of life from cold to warm. He infused Himself so completely into the hearts of the Bahá'ís that they associated the administrative institutions of the Faith with His trusted and cherished methods of service, so that the contact between their society and their religion has remained continuous and unimpaired.

The second conveyance of authority made by Bahá'u'lláh was to the institution He termed "House of Justice":—"The Lord hath ordained that in every city a House of Justice be established wherein shall gather counsellors to the number of Bahá (i.e. nine). . . . It behoveth them to be the trusted ones of the Merciful among men and to regard themselves as the guardians appointed of God for all that dwell on earth. It is incumbent upon them to take counsel together and to have regard for the interests of the servants of God, for His sake, even as they regard their own interests, and to choose that which is meet and seemly. . . . Those souls who arise to serve the Cause sincerely to please God will be inspired by the divine, invisible inspirations. It is incumbent upon all (i.e. all believers) to obey. . . . Administrative affairs are all in charge of the House of Justice; but acts of worship must be observed according as they are revealed in the Book."

The House of Justice is limited in its sphere of activity to matters not covered by the teachings of Bahá'u'lláh Himself: "It is incumbent upon the Trustees of the House of Justice to take counsel together regarding such laws as have not been expressly revealed in the Book." A high aim is defined for this central administrative organ of the Faith: "The men of the

House of Justice must, night and day, gaze toward that which hath been revealed from the horizon of the Supreme Pen for the training of the servants, for the upbuilding of countries, for the preservation of human honour."

In creating this institution for His community, Bahá'u'lláh made it clear that His Dispensation rests upon continuity of divine purpose, and associates human beings directly with the operation of His law. The House of Justice, an elective body, transforms society into an organism reflecting spiritual life. By the just direction of affairs this Faith replaces the institution of the professional clergy developed in all previous Dispensations.

By 1921, when 'Abdu'l-Bahá laid down His earthly mission, the American Bahá'í community had been extended to scores of cities and acquired power to undertake tasks of considerable magnitude, but the administrative order remained incomplete. His Will and Testament inaugurated a new era in the Faith, a further conveyance of authority and a clear exposition of the nature of the elective institutions which the Bahá'ís were called upon to form. In Shoghi Effendi, His grandson, 'Abdu'l-Bahá established the function of Guardianship with sole power to interpret the teachings and with authority to carry out the provisions of the Will. The Guardianship connects the spiritual and social realms of the Faith in that, in addition to the office of interpreter, he is constituted the presiding officer of the international House of Justice when elected; and the Guardianship is made to descend from generation to generation through the male line.

From the Will these excerpts are cited:

"After the passing of this wronged one, it is incumbent upon . . . the loved ones of the Abhá Beauty (i.e. Bahá'u'lláh) to turn unto Shoghi Effendi—the youthful branch branched from the two hallowed Lote-Trees (i.e. descended from both the Báb and Bahá'u'lláh) . . . as he is the sign of God, the chosen branch, the guardian of the Cause of God, . . . unto whom . . . His loved ones must turn. He is the expounder of the words of God, and after him will succeed the firstborn of his lineal descendants.

"The sacred and youthful branch, the guardian of the Cause of God, as well as the Universal House of Justice, to be universally elected and established, are both under the care and protection of the Abhá Beauty. . . . Whatsoever they decide is of God. . . . The mighty stronghold shall remain impregnable and safe through obedience to him who is the guardian of the Cause of God. . . . No doubt every vainglorious one that purposeth dissension and discord will not openly declare his evil purposes, nay rather, even as impure gold would he seize upon divers measures and various pretexts that he may separate the gathering of the people of Bahá."

"Wherefore, O my loving friends! Consort with all the peoples, kindreds and religions of the world with the utmost truthfulness, uprightness, faithfulness, kindliness, good-will and friendliness; that all the world of being may be filled with the holy ecstasy of the grace of Bahá. . . ."

"O ye beloved of the Lord! Strive with all your heart to shield the Cause of God from the onslaught of the insincere, for souls such as these cause the straight to become crooked and all benevolent efforts to produce contrary results. . . . All must seek guidance and turn unto the Centre of the Cause and the House of Justice."

In each country where Bahá'ís exist, they participate in the world unity of their Faith through the office of the Guardian at this time, and they maintain local and national Bahá'í institutions for conducting their own activities. [See Preface.]

In each local civil community, whether city, township or county, the Bahá'ís annually elect nine members to their local Spiritual Assembly. In America the Bahá'ís of each State, (a direction of the Guardian having effect for the first time in connection with the Convention of 1944, the one hundredth year of the Faith) join in the election of delegates by proportionate representation and these delegates, to the full number of one hundred and seventy-one, constitute the Annual Convention, which elects the members of the National Spiritual Assembly. These national bodies, in turn, will join in the election of an international Assembly, or House of Justice, when the world Bahá'í community is sufficiently developed.[1]

The inter-relationship of all these administrative bodies provides the world spirit of the Faith with the agencies required for the maintenance of a constitutional society which balances the rights of the individual with the paramount principle of unity preserving the whole structure of the Cause. The Bahá'í as an individual accepts guidance for his conduct and doctrinal beliefs, for not otherwise can he contribute his share to the general unity which is God's supreme blessing to the world today. This general unity is the believer's moral environment, his social universe, his psychic health and his goal of effort transcending any personal aim. In the Bahá'í order, the individual is the musical note, but the teachings revealed by Bahá'u'lláh are the symphony in which the note finds its real fulfilment; the person attains value by recognizing that truth transcends his capacity and includes him in a relationship which 'Abdu'l-Bahá said endowed the part with the quality of the whole. To receive, we give. In comparison to this divine creation, the traditional claims of individual conscience, of personal judgment, of private freedom, seem nothing more than empty assertions advanced in opposition to the divine will. It cannot be sufficiently emphasized that the Bahá'í relationship to this new spiritual society is an expression of faith, and faith alone raises personality out of the pit of self-will and moral isolation into which so much of the world has fallen.

There can be no organic society, in fact, without social truth and social law embracing the individual members and evoking a loyalty both voluntary and complete. The political and economic groups which the individual enters with reservations are not true societies but temporary combinations of restless personalities, met in a truce which cannot endure. Bahá'u'lláh has for ever solved the artificial dilemma which confuses and betrays the ardent upholder of individual freedom by His categorical statement that human freedom consists in obedience to God's law. The freedom revolving around self-will He

[1] See Preface.

declares "must, in the end, lead to sedition, whose flames none can quench. . . . Know ye that the embodiment of liberty and its symbol is the animal. . . . True liberty consists in man's submission unto My commandments, little as ye know it."

The Guardian, applying the terms of the Will and Testament to an evolving order, has given the present generation of Bahá'ís a thorough understanding of Bahá'í institutions and administrative principles. Rising to its vastly increased responsibility resulting from the loss of the beloved Master, 'Abdu'l-Bahá, the Bahá'í community itself has intensified its effort until in America alone the number of believers has been more than doubled since 1921.[1] It has been their destiny to perfect the local and national Bahá'í institutions as models for the believers in other lands. Within the scope of a single lifetime, the American Bahá'í community has developed from a small local group to a national unit of a world society, passing through the successive stages by which a civilization achieves its pristine pattern and severs itself from the anarchy and confusion of the past.

In Shoghi Effendi's letters addressed to this Bahá'í community, we have the statement of the form of the administrative order, its function and purpose, its scope and activity, as well as its significance which unites the thoughts and inspires the actions of all believers today.

From these letters[2] are selected a number of passages presenting fundamental aspects of the world order initiated by Bahá'u'lláh.

I. ON ITS NATURE AND SCOPE

"I cannot refrain from appealing to them who stand identified with the Faith to disregard the prevailing notions and the fleeting fashions of the day, and to realize as never before that the exploded theories and the tottering institutions of present-day civilization must needs appear in sharp contrast with those God-given institutions which are destined to arise upon their ruin. . . ."

[1] The number is now much larger and is constantly increasing.
[2] These letters are published in two volumes, *Bahá'í Administration* and *The World Order of Bahá'u'lláh*.

"For Bahá'u'lláh . . . has not only imbued mankind with a new and regenerating Spirit. He has not merely enunciated certain universal principles, or propounded a particular philosophy, however potent, sound and universal these may be. In addition to these He, as well as 'Abdu'l-Bahá after Him, has, unlike the Dispensations of the past, clearly and specifically laid down a set of Laws, established definite institutions, and provided for the essentials of a Divine Economy. These are destined to be a pattern for future society, a supreme instrument for the establishment of the Most Great Peace, and the one agency for the unification of the world, and the proclamation of the reign of righteousness and justice upon the earth. . . ."

"Unlike the Dispensation of Christ, unlike the Dispensation of Muḥammad, unlike all the Dispensations of the past, the apostles of Bahá'u'lláh in every land, wherever they labour and toil, have before them in clear, in unequivocal and emphatic language, all the laws, the regulations, the principles, the institutions, the guidance, they require for the prosecution of their task. . . . Therein lies the distinguishing feature of the Bahá'í Revelation. Therein lies the strength of the unity of the Faith, of the validity of a Revelation that claims not to destroy or belittle previous Revelations, but to connect, unify, and fulfil them. . . ."

"Feeble though our Faith may now appear in the eyes of men, who either denounce it as an offshoot of Islám, or contemptuously ignore it as one more of those obscure sects that abound in the West, this priceless gem of Divine Revelation, now still in its embryonic state, shall evolve within the shell of His law, and shall forge ahead, undivided and unimpaired, till it embraces the whole of mankind. Only those who have already recognized the supreme station of Bahá'u'lláh, only those whose hearts have been touched by His love, and have become familiar with the potency of His spirit, can adequately appreciate the value of this Divine Economy—His inestimable gift to mankind. . . ."

"This Administrative Order . . . will, as its component parts, its organic institutions, begin to function with efficiency and vigour, assert its claim and demonstrate its capacity to be regarded not only as the nucleus but the very pattern of the New World Order destined to embrace in the fulness of time the whole of mankind."

"Alone of all the Revelations gone before it this Faith has succeeded in raising a structure which the bewildered followers of bankrupt and broken creeds might well approach and critically examine, and seek, ere it is too late, the invulnerable security of its world-embracing shelter. . . ."

"To what else if not to the power and majesty which this Administrative Order—the rudiments of the future all-enfolding Bahá'í Commonwealth—is destined to manifest, can these utterances of Bahá'u'lláh allude: 'The world's equilibrium hath been upset through the vibrating influence of this most great, this new World Order. Mankind's ordered life hath been revolutionized through the agency of this unique, this wondrous System—the like of which mortal eyes have never witnessed. . . .' "

2. ON ITS LOCAL AND NATIONAL INSTITUTIONS

"A perusal of some of the words of Bahá'u'lláh and 'Abdu'l-Bahá on the duties and functions of the Spiritual Assemblies in every land (later to be designated as the local Houses of Justice), emphatically reveals the sacredness of their nature, the wide scope of their activity, and the grave responsibility which rests upon them.

"Addressing the members of the Spiritual Assembly in Chicago, the Master reveals the following: 'Whenever ye enter the council-chamber, recite this prayer with a heart throbbing with the love of God and a tongue purified from all but His remembrance, that the All-powerful may graciously aid you to achieve supreme victory: "O God, my God! We are servants of Thine that have turned with devotion to Thy Holy Face, that have detached ourselves from all beside

Thee in this glorious Day. We have gathered in this spiritual assembly, united in our views and thoughts, with our purposes harmonized to exalt Thy Word amidst mankind. O Lord, our God! Make us the signs of Thy Divine Guidance, the Standards of Thy exalted Faith amongst men, servants to Thy mighty Covenant. O Thou our Lord Most High! Manifestations of Thy Divine Unity in Thine Abhá Kingdom, and resplendent stars shining upon all regions. Lord! Aid us to become seas surging with the billows of Thy wondrous Grace, streams flowing from Thy all-glorious heights, goodly fruits upon the Tree of Thy heavenly Cause, trees waving through the breezes of Thy Bounty in Thy celestial Vineyard. O God! Make our souls dependent upon the Verses of Thy Divine Unity, our hearts cheered with the outpourings of Thy Grace, that we may unite even as the waves of one sea and become merged together as the rays of Thine effulgent Light; that our thoughts, our views, our feelings may become as one reality, manifesting the spirit of union throughout the world. Thou art the Gracious, the Bountiful, the Bestower, the Almighty, the Merciful, the Compassionate.'

"In the Most Holy Book is revealed:—'The Lord hath ordained that in every city a House of Justice be established wherein shall gather counsellors to the number of Bahá, and should it exceed this number it does not matter. It behoveth them to be the trusted ones of the Merciful among men and to regard themselves as the guardians appointed of God for all that dwell on earth. It is incumbent upon them to take counsel together and to have regard for the interests of the servants of God, for His sake, even as they regard their own interests, and to choose that which is meet and seemly. Thus hath the Lord your God commanded you. Beware lest ye put away that which is clearly revealed in His Tablet. Fear God, O ye that perceive.'

"Furthermore, 'Abdu'l-Bahá reveals the following:—'It is incumbent upon every one not to take any step without consulting the Spiritual Assembly, and they must assuredly obey with heart and soul its bidding and be submissive unto it, that things may be properly ordered and well arranged. Otherwise every person will act independently and after his own judgment, will follow his own desire, and do harm to the Cause.'

" 'The prime requisites for them that take counsel together are purity of motive, radiance of spirit, detachment from all else save God, attraction to His Divine Fragrances, humility and lowliness amongst His loved ones, patience and long-suffering in difficulties and servitude to His exalted Threshold. Should they be graciously aided to acquire these attributes, victory from the unseen Kingdom of Bahá shall be vouchsafed to them. In this day, assemblies of consultation are of the greatest importance and a vital necessity. Obedience unto them is essential and obligatory. The members thereof must take counsel together in such wise that no occasion for ill-feeling or discord may arise. This can be attained when every member expresseth with absolute freedom his own opinion and setteth forth his argument. Should any one oppose, he must on no account feel hurt for not until matters are fully discussed can the right way be revealed. The shining spark of truth cometh forth only after the clash of differing opinions. If, after discussion, a decision be carried unanimously, well and good; but if, the Lord forbid, differences of opinion should arise, a majority of voices must prevail.'

"Enumerating the obligations incumbent upon the members of consulting councils, the Beloved reveals the following: 'The first condition is absolute love and harmony amongst the members of the assembly. They must be wholly free from estrangement and must manifest in themselves the Unity of God, for they are the waves of one sea, the drops of one river, the stars of one heaven, the rays of one sun, the trees of one orchard, the flowers of one garden. Should harmony of thought and absolute unity be non-existent, that gathering shall be dispersed and that assembly brought to naught. The second condition: They must when coming together turn their faces to the Kingdom on high and ask aid from the Realm of Glory.

They must then proceed with the utmost devotion, courtesy, dignity, care and moderation to express their views. They must in every matter search out the truth and not insist upon their own opinion, for stubbornness and persistence in one's views will lead ultimately to discord and wrangling and the truth will remain hidden. The honoured members must with all freedom express their own thoughts, and it is in no wise permissible for one to belittle the thought of another, nay, he must with moderation set forth the truth, and should differences of opinion arise a majority of voices must prevail, and all must obey and submit to the majority. It is again not permitted that any one of the honoured members object to or censure, whether in or out of the meeting, any decision arrived at previously, though that decision be not right, for such criticism would prevent any decision from being enforced. In short, whatsoever thing is arranged in harmony and with love and purity of motive, its result is light, and should the least trace of estrangement prevail the result shall be darkness upon darkness. . . . If this be so regarded, that assembly shall be of God, but otherwise it shall lead to coolness and alienation that proceed from the Evil One. Discussions must all be confined to spiritual matters that pertain to the training of souls, the instruction of children, the relief of the poor, the help of the feeble throughout all classes in the world, kindness to all peoples, the diffusion of the fragrances of God and the exaltation of His Holy Word. Should they endeavour to fulfil these conditions the Grace of the Holy Spirit shall be vouchsafed unto them, and that assembly shall become the centre of the Divine blessings, the hosts of Divine confirmation shall come to their aid, and they shall day by day receive a new effusion of Spirit.'

"So great is the importance and so supreme is the authority of these assemblies that once 'Abdu'l-Bahá after having Himself and in His own handwriting corrected the translation made into Arabic of the Ishráqát (the Effulgences) by Shaykh Faraj, a Kurdish friend from Cairo, directed him in a Tablet to

G

submit the above-named translation to the Spiritual Assembly of Cairo, that he might seek from them, before publication, their approval and consent. These are His very words in that Tablet: 'His honour, Shaykh Faraj'u'lláh, has here rendered into Arabic with greatest care the Ishráqát and yet I have told him that he must submit his version to the Spiritual Assembly of Egypt, and I have conditioned its publication upon the approval of the above-named Assembly. This is so that things may be arranged in an orderly manner, for should it not be so any one may translate a certain Tablet and print and circulate it on his own account. Even a non-believer might undertake such work, and thus cause confusion and disorder. If it be conditioned, however, upon the approval of the Spiritual Assembly, a translation prepared, printed and circulated by a non-believer will have no recognition whatever.'

"This is indeed a clear indication of the Master's express desire that nothing whatever should be given to the public by any individual among the friends, unless fully considered and approved by the Spiritual Assembly in his locality; and if this (as is undoubtedly the case) is a matter that pertains to the general interest of the Cause in that land, then it is incumbent upon the Spiritual Assembly to submit it to the consideration and approval of the national body representing all the various local assemblies. Not only with regard to publication, but all matters without any exception whatsoever, regarding the interests of the Cause in that locality, individually or collectively, should be referred exclusively to the Spiritual Assembly in that locality, which shall decide upon it, unless it be a matter of national interest, in which case it shall be referred to the national body. With this national body also will rest the decision whether a given question is of local or national interest. (By national affairs is not meant matters that are political in their character, for the friends of God the world over are strictly forbidden to meddle with political affairs in any way whatever, but rather things that affect the spiritual activities of the body of the friends in that land.)

"Full harmony, however, as well as co-operation among the various local assemblies and the members themselves, and particularly between each assembly and the national body, is of the utmost importance, for upon it depends the unity of the Cause of God, the solidarity of the friends, the full, speedy and efficient working of the spiritual activities of His loved ones."

"Regarding the establishment of 'National Assemblies,' it is of vital importance that in every country, where the conditions are favourable and the number of friends has grown and reached a considerable size, such as America, Great Britain and Germany, that a 'National Spiritual Assembly' be established, representative of the friends throughout that country.

"Its immediate purpose is to stimulate, unify and co-ordinate by frequent personal consultations, the manifold activities of the friends as well as the local Assemblies; and by keeping in close and constant touch with the Holy Land, initiate measures, and direct in general the affairs of the Cause in that country.

"It serves also another purpose, no less essential than the first, as in the course of time it shall evolve into the National House of Justice (referred to in 'Abdu'l-Bahá's Will as the 'secondary House of Justice'), which according to the explicit text of the Testament will have, in conjunction with the other National Assemblies throughout the Bahá'í world, to elect directly the members of the International House of Justice, that Supreme Council that will guide, organize and unify the affairs of the Movement throughout the world. [Elected 1963.]

"It is expressly recorded in 'Abdu'l-Bahá's Writings that these National Assemblies must be indirectly elected by the friends; that is, the friends in every country must elect a certain number of delegates, who in their turn will elect from among all the friends in that country the members of the National Spiritual Assembly. In such countries, therefore, as America, Great Britain and Germany, a fixed number of secondary electors must first be decided upon. . . . The friends then in every locality where the number of adult declared believers exceeds nine must directly elect its quota of secondary electors assigned to it in direct proportion to its numerical strength. These secondary electors will then, either through correspondence, or preferably by gathering together, and first deliberating upon the affairs of the Cause throughout their country (as the delegates to the Convention), elect from among all the friends in that country nine who will be the members of the National Spiritual Assembly.

" This National Spiritual Assembly, which, pending the establishment of the Universal House of Justice, will have to be re-elected once a year, obviously assumes grave responsibilities, for it has to exercise full authority over all the local Assemblies in its province, and will have to direct the activities of the friends, guard vigilantly the Cause of God, and control and supervise the affairs of the Movement in general.

"Vital issues, affecting the interests of the Cause in that country such as the matter of translation and publication, the Mashriqu'l-Adhkár, the Teaching Work, and other similar matters that stand distinct from strictly local affairs, must be under the jurisdiction of the National Assembly.

"It will have to refer each of these questions, even as the local Assemblies, to a special Committee, to be elected by the members of the National Spiritual Assembly, from among all the friends in that country, which will bear to it the same relation as the local committees bear to their respective local Assemblies.

"With it, too, rests the decision whether a certain point at issue is strictly local in its nature, and should be reserved for the consideration and decision of the local Assembly, or whether it should fall under its own province and be regarded as a matter which ought to receive its special attention. The National Spiritual Assembly will also decide upon such matters which in its opinion should be referred to the Holy Land for consultation and decision.

"With these Assemblies, local as well as national, harmoniously, vigorously, and efficiently functioning throughout the

Bahá'í world, the only means for the establishment of the Supreme House of Justice will have been secured. And when this Supreme Body will have been properly established, it will have to consider afresh the whole situation, and lay down the principle which shall direct, so long as it deems advisable, the affairs of the Cause. . . .

"The need for the centralization of authority in the National Spiritual Assembly, and the concentration of power in the various local Assemblies, is made manifest when we reflect that the Cause of Bahá'u'lláh is still in its age of tender growth and in a stage of transition; when we remember that the full implications and the exact significance of the Master's world-wide instructions, as laid down in His Will, are as yet not fully grasped, and the whole Movement has not sufficiently crystallized in the eyes of the world.

"It is our primary task to keep the most vigilant eye on the manner and character of its growth, to combat effectively the forces of separation and of sectarian tendencies, lest the Spirit of the Cause be obscured, its unity be threatened, its Teachings suffer corruption; lest extreme orthodoxy on one hand, and irresponsible freedom on the other, cause it to deviate from that Straight Path which alone can lead it to success. . . ."

"Hitherto the National Convention has been primarily called together for the consideration of the various circumstances attending the election of the National Spiritual Assembly. I feel however, that in view of the expansion and the growing importance of the administrative sphere of the Cause, the general sentiments and tendencies prevailing among the friends, and the signs of increasing interdependence among the National Spiritual Assemblies throughout the world, the assembled accredited representatives of the American believers should exercise not only the vital and responsible right of electing the National Assembly, but should also fulfil the functions of an enlightened, consultative and co-operative body that will enrich the experience, enhance the prestige, support the authority, and assist the deliberations of the National Spiritual Assembly. It is my firm conviction that it is the bounden duty, in the interest of the Cause we all love and serve, of the members of the incoming National Assembly, once elected by the delegates at Convention time, to seek and have the utmost regard, individually as well as collectively, for the advice, the considered opinion and the true sentiments of the assembled delegates. Banishing every vestige of secrecy, of undue reticence, of dictatorial aloofness, from their midst, they should radiantly and abundantly unfold to the eyes of the delegates, by whom they are elected, their plans, their hopes, and their cares. They should familiarize the delegates with the various matters that will have to be considered in the current year, and calmly and conscientiously study and weigh the opinions and judgments of the delegates. The newly elected National Assembly, during the few days when the Convention is in session and after the dispersal of the delegates, should seek ways and means to cultivate understanding, facilitate and maintain the exchange of views, deepen confidence, and vindicate by every tangible evidence their one desire to serve and advance the common weal. Not infrequently, nay oftentimes, the most lowly, untutored and inexperienced among the friends will, by the sheer inspiring force of selfless and ardent devotion, contribute a distinct and memorable share to a highly involved discussion in any given Assembly. Great must be the regard paid by those whom the delegates call upon to serve in high position to this all-important though inconspicuous manifestation of the revealing power of sincere and earnest devotion.

"The National Spiritual Assembly, however, in view of the unavoidable limitations imposed upon the convening of frequent and long-standing sessions of the Convention, will have to retain in its hands the final decision on all matters that affect the interests of the Cause in America, such as the right to decide whether any local Assembly is functioning in accordance with the principles laid down for the conduct and advancement of the Cause. It is my earnest prayer that they will utilize their highly responsible position, not only for the wise and efficient conduct of the affairs of the Cause, but also for the extension and deepening of the spirit of cordiality and whole-hearted and mutual support in their co-operation with the body of their co-workers throughout the land. The seating of delegates to the Convention, i.e. the right to decide upon the validity of the credentials of the delegates at a given Convention, is vested in the outgoing National Assembly, and the right to decide who has the voting privilege is also ultimately placed in the hands of the National Spiritual Assembly, either when a local Spiritual Assembly is being for the first time formed in a given locality, or when differences arise between a new applicant and an already established local Assembly. While the Convention is in session and the accredited delegates have already elected from among the believers throughout the country the members of the National Spiritual Assembly for the current year, it is of infinite value and a supreme necessity that as far as possible all matters requiring immediate decision should be fully and publicly considered, and an endeavour be made to obtain after mature deliberation, unanimity in vital decisions. Indeed, it has ever been the cherished desire of our Master, 'Abdu'l-Bahá, that the friends in their councils, local as well as national, should by their candour, their honesty of purpose, their singleness of mind, and the thoroughness of their discussions, achieve unanimity in all things. Should this in certain cases prove impracticable the verdict of the majority should prevail, to which decision the minority must under all circumstances, gladly, spontaneously and continually, submit.

"Nothing short of the all-encompassing, all-pervading power of His Guidance and Love can enable this newly-enfolded order to gather strength and flourish amid the storm and stress of a turbulent age, and in the fulness of time vindicate its high claim to be universally recognized as the one Haven of abiding felicity and peace."

3. ON ITS INTERNATIONAL INSTITUTIONS

"It should be stated, at the very outset, in clear and un-ambiguous language, that these twin institutions of the Administrative Order of Bahá'u'lláh should be regarded as divine in origin, essential in their functions and complementary in their aim and purpose. Their common, their fundamental object is to ensure the continuity of that divinely-appointed authority which flows from the Source of our Faith, to safeguard the unity of its followers and to maintain the integrity and flexibility of its teachings. Acting in conjunction with each other these two inseparable institutions administer its affairs, co-ordinate its activities, promote its interests, execute its laws and defend its subsidiary institutions. Severally, each operates within a clearly defined sphere of jurisdiction; each is equipped with its own attendant institutions—instruments designed for the effective discharge of its particular responsibilities and duties. Each exercises, within the limitations imposed upon it, its powers, its authority, its rights and prerogatives. These are neither contradictory, nor detract in the slightest degree from the position which each of these institutions occupies. Far from being incompatible or mutually destructive, they supplement each other's authority and functions, and are permanently and fundamentally united in their aims.

"Divorced from the institution of the Guardianship the World Order of Bahá'u'lláh would be mutilated and permanently deprived of that hereditary principle which, as 'Abdu'l-Bahá has written, has been invariably upheld by the Law of God. 'In all the Divine Dispensations,' He states, in a Tablet addressed to a follower of the Faith in Persia, 'the eldest son hath been given extraordinary distinctions. Even the station of prophethood hath been his birthright.' Without such an institution the integrity of the Faith would be imperilled, and the stability of the entire fabric would be gravely endangered. Its prestige would suffer, the means required to enable it to take a long, an uninterrupted view over a series of generations would be completely lacking, and the necessary guidance to define the sphere of the legislative action of its elected representatives would be totally withdrawn.

"Severed from the no less essential institution of the Universal House of Justice this same System of the Will of 'Abdu'l-Bahá would be paralysed in its action and would be powerless to fill in those gaps which the Author of the *Kitáb-i-Aqdas* has deliberately left in the body of His legislative and administrative ordinances.

" 'He is the Interpreter of the Word of God,' 'Abdu'l-Bahá referring to the functions of the Guardian of the Faith, asserts, using in His Will the very term which He Himself had chosen when refuting the argument of the Covenant-breakers who had challenged His right to interpret the utterances of Bahá'u'lláh. 'After him,' He adds, 'will succeed the first-born of his lineal descendants.' 'The mighty stronghold,' He further explains, 'shall remain impregnable and safe through obedience to him who is the Guardian of the Cause of God.' 'It is incumbent upon the members of the House of Justice, upon all the Aghsán, the Afnán, the Hands of the Cause of God, to show their obedience, submissiveness and subordination unto the Guardian of the Cause of God.'

" 'It is incumbent upon the members of the House of Justice,' Bahá'u'lláh, on the other hand, declares in the Eighth Leaf of *The Exalted Paradise*, 'to take counsel together regarding those things which have not outwardly been revealed in the Book, and to enforce that which is agreeable to them. God will verily inspire them with whatsoever He willeth, and He verily is the Provider, the Omniscient.' 'Unto the Most Holy Book' (the *Kitáb-i-Aqdas*), 'Abdu'l-Bahá states in His Will, 'every one must turn, and all that is not expressly recorded therein must be referred to the Universal House of Justice. That which this body, whether unanimously or by a majority doth carry, that is verily the truth and the purpose of God Himself. Whoso doth deviate therefrom is verily of them that love discord, hath shown forth malice, and turned away from the Lord of the Covenant.'

"Not only does 'Abdu'l-Bahá confirm in His Will Bahá'u'-lláh's above-quoted statement, but invests this body with the additional right and power to abrogate, according to the exigencies of time, its own enactments, as well as those of a preceding House of Justice. 'Inasmuch as the House of Justice,' is His explicit statement in His Will, 'hath power to enact laws that are not expressly recorded in the Book and bear upon daily transactions, so also it hath power to repeal the same. . . . This it can do because these laws form no part of the divine explicit text.'

"Referring to both the Guardian and the Universal House of Justice we read these emphatic words: 'The sacred and youthful Branch, the Guardian of the Cause of God, as well as the Universal House of Justice to be universally elected and established, are both under the care and protection of the Abhá Beauty, under the shelter and unerring guidance of the Exalted One (the Báb) (may my life be offered up for them both). Whatsoever they decide is of God.'

"From these statements it is made indubitably clear and evident that the Guardian of the Faith has been made the Interpreter of the Word and that the Universal House of Justice has been invested with the function of legislating on matters not expressly revealed in the teachings. The interpretation of the Guardian, functioning within his own sphere, is as authoritative and binding as the enactments of the International House of Justice, whose exclusive right and prerogative is to pronounce upon and deliver the final judgment on such laws and ordinances as Bahá'u'lláh has not expressly revealed. Neither can, nor ever will, infringe upon the sacred and prescribed domain of the other. Neither will seek to curtail the specific and undoubted authority with which both have been divinely invested. . . ." [See Preface.]

"Let no one, while this System is still in its infancy, misconceive its character, belittle its significance or misrepresent its purpose. The bedrock on which this Administrative Order is founded is God's immutable Purpose for mankind in this day.

The source from which it derives its inspiration is no less than Bahá'u'lláh Himself. Its shield and defender are the embattled hosts of the Abhá Kingdom. Its seed is the blood of no less than twenty thousand martyrs who have offered up their lives that it may be born and flourish. The axis round which its institutions revolve are the authentic provisions of the Will and Testament of 'Abdu'l-Bahá. Its guiding principles are the truths which He Who is the unerring Interpreter of the teachings of our Faith has so clearly enunciated in His public addresses throughout the West. The laws that govern its operation and limit its functions are those which have been expressly ordained in the *Kitáb-i-Aqdas*. The seat round which its spiritual, its humanitarian and administrative activities will cluster are the Mashriqu'l-Adhkár and its Dependencies. The pillars that sustain its authority and buttress its structure are the twin institutions of the Guardianship and of the Universal House of Justice. The central, the underlying aim which animates it is the establishment of the New World Order, as adumbrated by Bahá'u'lláh. The methods it employs, the standard it inculcates, incline it to neither East nor West, neither Jew nor Gentile, neither rich nor poor, neither white nor coloured. Its watchword is the unification of the human race; its standard the 'Most Great Peace'; its consummation the advent of that golden millenium —the Day when the kingdoms of this world shall have become the Kingdom of God Himself, the Kingdom of Bahá'u'lláh."

Fifty years have passed since the Cause of Bahá'u'lláh was first brought to North America.[1] Three generations of believers have worked and sacrificed and prayed in order to produce a body of Bahá'ís large enough to demonstrate the principles here summarized in a few pages for the present-day student of these teachings. 'Abdu'l-Bahá employed as unifying element for the American community, during that period when only rudimentary local administrative bodies could be established, the construction of the House of Worship, the Mashriqu'l-Adhkár, in Wilmette. He in fact referred to the House of Worship as the "inception of the Kingdom." Around its construc-

[1] In 1893.

tion devotedly gathered the American friends. 'Abdu'l-Bahá approved their action in setting up a religious corporation to hold title to the property and provide a basis for collective action. In surveying those days from 1904 to 1921, one realizes how, in every stage of progress, the believers rushed forward in devotion before they could perceive the full results of action or comprehend the full unfoldment of their beloved Master's intention. In their hearts they knew that unity is the keynote of their Faith, and they were assured that the new power of unity would augment until it encompassed the whole of mankind. But as to the nature of world order, the foundation of universal peace, the principles of the future economy, while the clear picture eluded them, they went forward with enthusiasm to the Light.

In a continent consecrated to the pioneer, the early American Bahá'ís pioneered in the world of spirit, striving to participate in a work of supreme importance whose final result was the laying of a foundation on which human society might raise a house of justice and a mansion of peace.

THE NEW CALENDAR

HISTORY has no record of any society which has ever, for any considerable period, followed a calendar established by civil authority. The French Revolution produced an abortive scheme which soon fell into oblivion, and we need not anticipate any greater success for the chronology of more recent revolutions. The testimony of human experience has without exception proved that human beings measure time and record dates according to a calendar based upon the coming of the Manifestation of God. Just as our space world is a higher creation, so is the time world in which our lives unfold and our cultures evolve. The Jew lives by his calendar, the Christian's time world is according to the "year of our Lord," and the Muslim dates all affairs from the journey of Muḥammad. In cosmopolitan cities like Constantinople, where men of different faiths established permanent communities, inter-community contacts involved at times the translation of dates from one calendar into five or six different chronologies. The survival of these community calendars into the modern world is one of the great and majestic signs of the creative power of Revelation. Man's world is in essence nothing else than a projection of the Divine will and a remembrance of the fire of His Love.

The persistence of these different chronologies is likewise a sign and indication that Revelation was never fulfilled for any people in the past. A world of humanity divided into creeds and cultures and traditions is a world which has never realized its true identity. These races, these clans, these nations and self-assertive artificial sovereignties are still to become men, since only they are men who know the reality of Man.

Now an era has dawned whose Revelation is not merely one more step of progress along an historical path marked out ages ago. In the Báb, in Bahá'u'lláh, Revelation closed the chapters of the Book of Prophecy and opened a new and greater Book for the maturity of humanity and the union of men in Man. The standard now is oneness and the scale worldwide. One of the significant signs is the folding up of all the ancient calendars. Their time has run out and their span is ended. "The world is a new world." "A new creation hath been called into being." The people of the new day know that the year One of a World Calendar dawned at that holy time which the West miscalled 1844, and the East by relative names in chronologies dating from Prophets whose cycles are no more. What an overwhelming victory the Divine power won for man in that renewal of time, symbol of the renewal of the spirit of life itself. All who can attest that today, *now*, is of the year 99[1] of the coming of the Lord to earth, and not of a twelfth or nineteenth or fiftieth century, share in that victory because they themselves have also, like time and the spirit, been renewed. All debts of former times are annulled and cancelled by the Supreme. No race need be hated and no people need fall into hate because of deeds of their ancestors or because of sufferings recorded in the ancient books, provided they drink the healing waters of the new Well-Spring of Eternity. Within a time world which has been created by the Divine will, the souls of men are safe and secure. Therein are rewards, bounties and spiritual prizes, while in the times of illusion there is but penalty and pain for those who worship their ancestors but deny God.

THE BAHÁ'Í YEAR

In this renewal of time when "the world's great age is born anew" the cycle of the year coincides with the cycle of the sun. The Bahá'í year begins at the vernal equinox, when the physical earth enters its season of renewal and spring. One sees here a sign of the fundamental oneness of truth, when a spiritual reality and an astronomical fact can be harmonized. Moreover, the Bahá'í day begins at sunset and not at midnight,

[1] 1942 A.D.

ending with the going down of the sun twenty-four hours later. Here again is the rhythm of spirit and organism identified. How can the unit of human experience begin at midnight, when nothing of the cosmic or spiritual world has its beginning?

Nineteen months of nineteen days each, plus four intercalary days, complete the full cycle of the earth's revolution around the sun in the Bahá'í chronology. This division of the days into months inaugurates a new social rhythm whose full implications cannot yet be realized. The gods of Greece and Rome that lingered on in our Januaries and our Junes no longer have even twilight existence. They have become one with the dark that can never return. In their place we have the radiance of the attributes of God: Splendour, Glory, Beauty, Grandeur, Light, Mercy, Words, Perfection, Names, Might, Will, Knowledge, Power, Speech, Questions, Honour, Sovereignty, Dominion, Loftiness. The truth whose Revelation sustains this plan of months will, as the cycle unfolds, reorder not merely the names and designations of days, months and years, but also the rhythm of our lives and of our society. The Bahá'í recalls the blessed teaching that "work performed in the spirit of service is worship". The new calendar connotes a new economics, a new and better way of life.

Embedded in the Bahá'í year as a revealed truth and not dogma or convention of human origin is the month consecrated to fasting. This is the last month of the year, 'Alá, month of Loftiness, its nineteen days culminating in the great and glorious Feast of Naw-Rúz, the New Year of the Bahá'í and of the physical earth. During those days, from sunrise to sunset, the Bahá'í abstains from both food and drink. Thus by an act of specific self-denial the believer is prepared to realize the deeper implications of death and renewal. Like the earth itself he has had his winter of dearth, that he may have the spring of ecstasy.

The Bahá'í month is signalized throughout the year by the special observance of its first day. At that time the believers in their local communities gather together for their Nineteen Day Feast. They receive in humility the supreme Feast, the holy and creative Word, the message revealed by the Manifestation for His cycle and age. They consult and discuss on matters pertaining to the Bahá'í community and service to their Faith. They break bread together, Bahá'ís of different races and peoples, all those who have found the way of union and agreement in the Cause of Bahá'u'lláh. The fulfilment of all holy communion is here, as the fulfilment of the Word in the coming of the Glory of God.

BAHÁ'Í ANNIVERSARIES

The Bahá'í year, moreover, re-enacts the scenes of the greatest spiritual drama of the ages. The Bahá'í year contains Anniversaries of events of soul-shaking import. Attending them, the Bahá'í draws near to the very essence of that Love and Sacrifice on which human existence is established.

The Feast of Riḍván, the Anniversary of the Declaration of Bahá'u'lláh, falls through the period April 21–May 2. The first, ninth and twelfth days of this Festival are observed as holy days. In 1863, in the garden if Riḍván outside Baghdád, Bahá'u'lláh, a prisoner and an exile, revealed His Station to the followers of the Báb, and became the Promised One of all the Revelations.

May 23, 1844, the Declaration of the Báb, is observed by the Bahá'ís of the world in profound reverence. Then was the Dawn of the true Day. 'Abdu'l-Bahá was born on that very date, May 23, 1844, but that event, great as it is in the annals of the Faith, is submerged within the significance of the Báb's Declaration.

May 29, 1892, marks the Ascension of Bahá'u'lláh, and its Anniversary, observed as it is by believers at the same hour, moves as a beam of prayer around the whole world, just as time itself is not simultaneous for this sphere but continuous from East to West.

The Martyrdom of the Báb on July 9, 1850, in the public square of the medieval city of Tabríz, gives the Bahá'ís an

Anniversary characterized by a most poignant realization of how Revelation returns to a darkened world through the Crucified Ones and the Anointed Ones of the Supreme Will. The Báb's Words reverberate out again in their eternal majesty. Devoted hearts lift themselves up to be filled like cups with the wine of sacrifice.

October 20, 1819, signalized the birth of the Báb; and November 12, 1817, signalized the birth of Bahá'u'lláh. These Anniversaries prepare the Bahá'ís to understand more reverently the unfoldment of the higher Will through a human temple.

On November 26 the Bahá'ís celebrate the Day of the Covenant held in honour of the unique Station bestowed by Bahá'u'lláh upon His eldest son, 'Abdu'l-Bahá. At this time a spirit of joyous intimacy characterizes the gathering of the friends. For there still live and serve faithfully many blessed believers who were seen by the Master, who were addressed by Him in converse and in written Tablet. They were gathered more closely in the arms of spiritual affection. Such Bahá'ís have ecstacy and priceless experience to share with the newer believers. Two days later, on November 28, the Bahá'ís observe 'Abdu'l-Bahá's Ascension, their moving sorrow mitigated only by His Will and Testament wherein He gave to the Bahá'ís the world-surpassing treasure of the Guardianship and the comfort and inspiration of the Plan of Bahá'u'lláh's new world order.

Nine days in the Bahá'í year are holy days when if possible work is to be suspended and the individual believer is to withdraw into meditation and prayer. These are: the first, ninth and twelfth days of Riḍván; the Anniversary of the Declaration of the Báb; the Anniversary of the Birth of Bahá'u'lláh; the Anniversary of the Birth of the Báb; the Anniversary of the Ascension of Bahá'u'lláh; the Anniversary of the Martyrdom of the Báb; the Feast of Naw-Rúz.

Shoghi Effendi, through his secretary, has given some definite information about the Bahá'í calendar: "The Bahá'í day starts

H

and ends at sunset. . . . The Guardian would advise that, if
feasible, the friends should commemorate certain of the feasts
and anniversaries at the following time: The Anniversary of the
Declaration of the Báb on May 22, at about two hours after
sunset. The first day of Ridván, at about 3.00 p.m. on the
twenty-first of April. The Anniversary of the Martyrdom of
the Báb on July 9 at about noon. The Anniversary of the
Ascension of Bahá'u'lláh, on May 29 at 3.00 a.m. The Ascension of 'Abdu'l-Bahá on November 28, at 1.00 a.m."

Through this new Calendar, the procession of the days, the
months and the years has been hallowed and sanctified for the
believer. The great Anniversaries, like acts in a new type of
social drama, purge and purify his soul, socialize his feelings
and prepare him for life in a unified world. The Bahá'í is
surrounded by influences from the supernatural realm; and
these influences, with their extreme purity, surround him with
an atmosphere through which the darts of psychic suggestion
and spiritism cannot penetrate. Whatever his local conditions
and circumstances, whether he be a member of a large and
active Bahá'í community or be an isolated believer, he knows
that on the occasion of the Anniversaries and Festivals of his
religion, he is not spiritually solitary, unaided, alone. To him
in the clear light of imagination, there comes the thought of
how the Anniversary is observed by the Guardian on Mount
Carmel. He feels the descent of guidance and acceptance from
on high in that sacred spot. A mighty wave of consecration
rolls out across the earth. Each Bahá'í has the blessedness of
access to that world experience, that unifying element operating
in the spirit of mankind. "The Word of God hath set the heart
of the world afire; how regrettable if ye fail to be enkindled
with its flame ! Please God, ye will regard this blessed night as
the night of unity, will knit your souls together, and resolve
to adorn yourselves with the ornament of a goodly and praiseworthy character. . . ."

THE FIRST WORLD HOLY DAY

WHEN 'Alí-Muḥammad declared His Mission in the city of Shíráz, Persia, on May 23, 1844, He created the first occasion in all known history which can be observed by the peoples of the entire world with equal right, for one purpose, and in the same spirit. For He whom we know as the Báb came as one of the Prophets of God, but His mission was not a preliminary but a culmination of the great cycle of the past. Through Him shone forth the Dawn-Light of the day of the creation of mankind. When he revealed the divine Word, the separation of the peoples was annulled, their division transcended, their hostility overcome. Man as the highest kingdom of reality under the Prophets received the inspiration to arise as one organic and mysterious being and enter into his true heritage as the sign of God and the expression of His will. The Báb summoned the races and peoples to respond to their glorious destiny by uniting in obedience to the divine decree.

There is no distinction between the Manifestations of God. Human beings cannot say that their Prophet is superior to others, revealed a more sublime Word, or endowed them with special authority over the people of other Faiths. What is distinctive is the stage of development in men at the time the Prophet comes to them to re-illumine the one true path. The Báb is the first World Prophet, and the day of His Declaration the first World Holy Day, because in our own time the process of spiritual and social evolution had completed the preliminary stages in the unfoldment of human attributes and attained to the condition of universal civilization.

Not all humanity has yet become conscious of what happened on May 23, 1844. Those who have this realization demonstrate their conviction of the oneness of God by meeting

certain tests which infallibly determine both their knowledge
and their sincerity.

The first condition of universality is recognition of the
unique station of the Manifestation of God, the Prophet, as the
sole connection between mankind and the Creator. One may
have all rational knowledge, but lacking this recognition he
lingers outside the precincts of spiritual truth.

The second condition is the acceptance of the equality of all
the Manifestations, the founders of revealed religion. To reject
one, whether He be Christ, Moses or Muḥammad, is to reject
all the Messengers by substituting one's own limited conception
for the reality itself. For if we reject one portion of the Path,
we are not on the Path. The identifying landmarks are lost;
we must try and recover the way.

The third condition is understanding of the principle or
method by which the guiding truth is brought to this world,
by recurrence of revelation, and in accordance with a progressive enlargement of the scope of truth. Thus it is not enough to
say one believes in all the Prophets because they all brought the
same message. Such a view is one's own limitation arbitrarily
imposed upon the successive statements of truth as revealed and
accessible in the Sacred Scriptures of all Faiths. Were religion
only that scheme of recurrent repetition which some philosophers teach, the very essence of progress and development
would be removed from human life.

The fourth condition is acceptance of mankind itself; the
willingness to discard the old formulas of separation which
sought to justify pride of race, creed or class, and reduced true
ethical principles to the realm of convention and convenience.
These myriad barriers which divide humanity are nothing
more than expressions of prejudice. True faith impels one to
help banish these shadows from the world.

The fifth condition is confident realization that the day of
spiritual victory has dawned; that the promise of ancient faiths
is being swiftly fulfilled; that the world is being inspired to conquer superstition, overcome ignorance and surmount inertia;

that the nations *will* attain peace; that world civilization has already been created as the pattern of reality for the new age.

To observe with reverence and gratitude the date of May 23, 1844, far from belittling or ignoring the Holy Days of the past, in reality exalts each of them by connecting it with its essential aim and fulfilment. For in the Báb have returned Jesus, Muḥammad, Moses and all the Prophets. There is no other way in which the peoples of today can honour their ancestral traditions than by honouring Him in whom faith is life and not memory nor imagination.

PART III

A SPIRITUAL SOCIETY

RELIGIOUS EDUCATION FOR

A PEACEFUL SOCIETY

THE UNIVERSE OF PALOMAR

THE LARGEST telescope yet designed has been raised by scientists on a mountain under the clear California sky. Its lens, measuring sixteen feet eight inches in diameter, gathers light with so much more intensity than the human eye that its reflected image discloses an endless heaven hung with brilliant orbs. Its power is so encompassing that it extends human vision to bodies whose distance from the earth, measured by the time required for the journey of a ray of light, is not less than one billion years.

Since the speed of light is 186,000 miles a second, no terrestrial system of measurement can contain this utter remoteness or translate it into ordinary human meaning.

The universe of Palomar engulfs the small and familiar worlds sustained by the imagination of the poet, the shepherd and the mariner of ancient times. Its infinity of space and time can never be subjugated by hope or fear. It is a motion we cannot stay, a direction we cannot divert, a peace we cannot impair, a power we cannot control. Here existence realizes the fulness of its purpose. The design and the material, the means and the end, the law and the subject, seem wholly one.

At Palomar the mind of man, standing on tiptoe, can behold the cosmic spectacle and grow by the eternal majesty it feeds on, but searching east or west or north or south one finds here no candle lighted to welcome the errant human heart.

"This nature," the Bahá'í teachings observe, "is subjected to an absolute organization, to determined laws, to a complete order and a finished design, from which it will never depart; to such a degree, indeed, that if you look carefully and with keen sight, from the smallest invisible atom up to such large bodies of the world of existence as the globe of the sun or the other great stars and luminous spheres, whether you regard their arrangement, their composition, their form or their movement you will find that all are in the highest degree of organization, and are under one law from which they will never depart.

"But when you look at nature itself, you see that it has no intelligence, no will . . . . Thus it is clear that the natural movements of all things are compelled; there are no voluntary movements except those of animals, and above all, those of man. Man is able to deviate from and to oppose nature, because he discovers the constitution of things, and through this he commands the forces of nature; all the inventions he has made are due to his discovery of the constitution of things. . . .

"Now, when you behold in existence such organizations, arrangements, and laws, can you say that all these are the effects of nature, though nature has neither intelligence nor perception? If not, it becomes evident that this nature, which has neither perception nor intelligence, is in the grasp of Almighty God Who is the Ruler of the world of nature; whatever He wishes He causes nature to manifest."[1]

Another passage states: "Know that every created thing is a sign of the revelation of God. Each, according to its capacity, is, and will ever remain, a token of the Almighty. . . . So pervasive and general is this revelation that nothing whatsoever in the whole universe can be discovered that does not reflect His splendour. . . . Were the Hand of Divine Power to divest of this high endowment all created things, the entire universe would become desolate and void."[2]

The Bahá'í teachings also declare: "Earth and heaven cannot contain Me; what can alone contain Me is the heart of him that believes in Me, and is faithful to My Cause."[3]

[1] 'Abdu'l-Bahá, Some Answered Questions, Ch. I.
[2] Bahá'u'lláh, Bahá'í World Faith, p. 97.
[3] ibid. p. 98.

MAN'S INNER WORLD

From man's inner world of hope and fear the cry for help has never been raised so desperately nor so generally across the whole earth. Civilization is in conflict with the man of nature. Civilization betrays the man of understanding and feeling. The individual has become engulfed in struggles of competitive groups employing different weapons to attain irreconcilable ends. The beginning and the end of his actions lie concealed in the fiery smoke of furious, interminable debate. His personal world has been transformed into an invaded area he knows not how to defend.

Sickness of soul, like physical ailment, manifests itself in many forms. It need not be a localized pain nor an acute sense of shock and disability. An ailment can produce numbness as well as torment, or it can spare the victim's general health but deprive him of sight, hearing or the use of a limb.

Soul sickness that goes deep into the psychic organism seldom finds relief in hysteria or other visible adjustments to ill-being. It expresses itself in successive re-orientations to self and to society, each of which results in a conviction representing a definite choice or selection between several possibilities. When the conviction hardens, all possibilities but one are denied and dismissed. If individuals come to realise that effort to express certain qualities through their daily lives is continuously unsuccessful, they will, in the majority of cases, abandon the exercise of that quality and concentrate on others. If individuals find that their civilization makes demands on them for the exercise of qualities they personally condemn, in most cases the necessary adjustment is made.

The modern individual is in the same position as the mountain climber bound to other climbers by a rope. At all times he is compelled to choose between freedom and protection—to balance his rights and his loyalties, and compromise between his duty to protect others and his duty to develop something unique and important in himself. As long as the route and the goal are equally vital to all the climbers, the necessary adjustments can be made without undue strain. But modern life binds together in economic, political and other arrangements groups of people who never entered into a pact of mutual agreement, who inwardly desire and need diverse things. The rope that binds them is a tradition, a convention, an inherited obligation no longer having power to fulfil.

Here, in essence, is the tragic sickness of modern man. What he sows he cannot reap. What he reaps he cannot store until a new harvest ripens. He feeds on another's desire, he wills to accomplish an alien task, he works to destroy the substance of his dearest hope. Moral standards stop at the frontier of the organized group. Partisan pressures darken the heavens of understanding.

Humanity is undergoing a complete transformation of values. The individual is being transplanted from his customary, sheltered, traditional way of life to the vast and disruptive confusions of a world in torment. The institutions which have afforded him social or psychic well-being are themselves subject to the same universal dislocation. The label no longer identifies the quality or purpose of the organization. One cannot retreat into the isolation of primitive simplicity; one cannot advance without becoming part of a movement of destiny which no one can control or define.

Where can a new and creative way of life be found? How can men attain knowledge of the means to justify their legitimate hope, fulfil their normal emotions, satisfy their intelligence, unify their aims and civilize their activities? The astronomer has his polished lens of Palomar to reveal the mysteries of the physical universe. Where can mankind turn to behold the will and purpose of God?

CONSCIENCE: THE MIRROR HUNG IN A DARKENED ROOM

Many persons feel that in man there is a power of conscience that will unfailingly, like the compass needle, point to the right goal. If in any individual case, this conception believes, the power of conscience fails to operate, it is because the human being himself has betrayed his own divine endowment. He has heard the voice but refused to heed. He has seen the right course of action but preferred to take the evil path.

If we examine this contention as applied to ourselves and others familiar to us over a considerable period of time, we find that conscience, as a faculty, cannot be understood by reference to any such naïve and conventional view.

The individual has no private wire to God. The dictates or impulses we call conscience indicate different courses of action at different times. The truth, the law, the appropriate principle or the perfect expression of love is not when wanted conveyed to our minds like a photograph printed from a negative developed in the subconscious self. No individual can afford to rely for guidance in all vital affairs on the testimony offered from within.

Individual conscience appears to be compounded of many ingredients at this stage of mass development: childhood training, personal aptitude, social convention, religious tradition, economic pressure, public opinion and group policy.

It is when we examine individual conscience in the area of social action and public responsibility that its limitations become clear. Public policy is the graveyard in which the claim to perfect personal guidance lies interred. In every competitive situation involving social groups, conscientious persons are found on both sides of the struggle. The conscience of one leads to a definition of value or a course of action which stultifies the other. Conscientious persons in the same group seldom agree on matters affecting the whole group. Individual conscience retreats to the realm of the private person when it cannot share or alter the conscience and conviction of others.

The result is that while theoretical exaltation of conscience is seldom abandoned, the operation of conscience, outside the small area controlled by personal will, is continuously suppressed. Policy is the conscience of the group, and dominant groups sanction collective actions frequently abhorrent to the individual. Our dominant groups are the successors to the primitive tribes in which the individual was once completely submerged. Like the primitive tribe, their basic policy is to survive.

Conscience is not a form of wisdom or knowledge. It cannot be disassociated from the development of the individual or from the condition of his society. But one may say that conscience is a mirror hung in a room. If the room is darkened the mirror reflects but dimly. Light is needed—the light of truth and love. Then will the mirror of spiritual awareness disclose to the individual the essential nature of his own problem of choice, and open for him the door that leads from the private person to mankind. The helplessness of the individual today is due to the absence of light.

"When man allows the spirit, through his soul, to enlighten his understanding, then does he contain all creation; because man, being the culmination of all that went before and thus superior to all previous evolutions, contains all the lower world within himself. Illuminated by the spirit through the instrumentality of the soul, man's radiant intelligence makes him the crowning-point of creation.

"But on the other hand when man does not open his mind and heart to the blessing of the spirit, but turns his soul towards the material side, towards the bodily part of his nature, then is he fallen from his high place and he becomes inferior to the inhabitants of the lower animal kingdom. In this case the man is in a sorry plight! For if the spiritual qualities of the soul, open to the breath of the Divine Spirit, are never used, they become atrophied, enfeebled, and at last incapacitated; while the soul's material qualities alone being exercised, they become terribly powerful, and the unhappy, misguided man becomes more savage, more unjust, more vile, more cruel, more malevolent than the lower animals themselves.

"If, on the contrary, the spiritual nature of the soul has been so strengthened that it holds the material side in subjection, then does the man approach the divine; his humanity becomes so glorified that the virtues of the celestial assembly are manifest in him; he radiates the mercy of God, he stimulates the spiritual progress of mankind, for he becomes a lamp to show light on their path."[1]

In such words the Bahá'í teachings describe the two paths which open before each human being, choice of which he himself is free to make.

SECTARIANISM—FROM CREATION TO CHAOS

If individual conscience cannot illumine from man's inner world the nature of basic social problems, what of religion? Have the traditional faiths such command of spiritual truth that they can serve as the guide and conscience of mankind? Do these sects and denominations constitute the moral Palomar bestowing vision upon a divided, a desperate humanity? Has God spoken to our age from these minarets, these temples, mosques, chapels and churches which represent the meaning and purpose of religion to the masses in East and West?

The world of sectarian religion is not a universe, ordered by one central creative will, but the fragments of a world which no human authority has power to restore. There are the main bodies of ancient, revealed religion: Hinduism, Buddhism, Zoroastrianism, Judaism, Muḥammadanism and Christianity, standing apart like continents separated by the salt, unplumbed sea. There are in each of these bodies a large number of independent, mutually exclusive subdivisions. Their diverse claims to organic sovereignty maintain in the realm of faith the same condition which exists among nations, principalities, kingdoms and empires. They deal with one another by treaty and truce; there are conquests and seizures, colonies and alliances, plans and strategies, wars and revolutions, all without control of the greater and vital movements of society or even foreknowledge of what was and is to come.

This is why mankind has suffered two world wars, social dislocation and a plague of immorality, faithlessness, materialism and discontent. No universal religious body has existed to

[1] 'Abdu'l-Bahá, The Reality of Man, p. 6

stay the swift descent of our age into the gloom of savage strife. Events do not wait upon doctrinal readjustments. When peace does not exist in the world of the soul it cannot exist in any other realm of human intercourse and experience. The masses have been given no moral unity, no common purpose which, stamped with divine authority, could raise them above the fatal disunities and conflicts distilled by their economic and political institutions.

Yet each of these faiths was divinely revealed, imbued with a universal spirit, charged with a high creative mission, and established itself through the sacrifice and heroism of those early believers who beheld the Word of God. Each faith has reconsecrated human life and by its lifeblood nourished great progress in civilization. What has happened to the first, true vision? What has extinguished the flame upon the altar of worship?

The superhuman character of revelation has gradually undergone dilution and admixture. The human explanation of a truth has been substituted for the truth itself. The performance of ceremonial rites has come to occupy the place held by the mystery of spiritual rebirth. Obligation to a professionalized institution has weakened the duty laid upon individuals to serve society and mankind. The aim of a regenerated, righteous, peaceful civilization inspired by the founders of religion has become diverted into hope for the victory of the church. Sectarianism in essence is not freedom of religion. It is an opportunity to abandon the way of life revealed from on high and substitute belief for sacrifice, ritual for virtue, creed for understanding, and a group interest for the basic rights of mankind.

All things exist in a process of life and death, growth and development, extinction and renewal. The fact that what men devise as a counterfeit for truth is eventually destroyed, does not confirm the rejection of religion by the cynic or the materialist. On the contrary, the succession of faiths throughout the period of known history points to a complete vindication of faith in God, since He divides truth from error, the spirit from the letter. He punishes and He rewards. For every death he sends a new life.

"O army of life !" the Bahá'í teachings warn, "East and West have joined to worship stars of faded splendour and have turned in prayer unto darkened horizons. Both have utterly neglected the broad foundation of God's sacred laws, and have grown unmindful of the merits and virtues of His religion. They have regarded certain customs and conventions as the immutable basis of the Divine Faith, and have firmly established themselves therein. They have imagined themselves as having attained the glorious pinnacle of achievement and prosperity when, in reality, they have touched the innermost depths of heedlessness and deprived themselves wholly of God's bountiful gifts.

"The cornerstone of the Religion of God is the acquisition of the Divine perfections and the sharing in His manifold bestowals. The essential purpose of faith and belief is to ennoble the inner being of man with the outpourings of grace from on high. If this be not attained, it is indeed deprivation itself. It is the torment of infernal fire."[1]

And even more definitely: "Superstitions have obscured the fundamental reality, the world is darkened and the light of religion is not apparent. This darkness is conducive to differences and dissensions; rites and dogmas are many and various; therefore discord has arisen among the religious systems whereas religion is for the unification of mankind. True religion is the source of love and agreement amongst men, the cause of the development of praiseworthy qualities; but the people are holding to the counterfeit and imitation, negligent of the reality which unifies, so they are bereft and deprived of the radiance of religion."[2]

"When the lights of religion become darkened the materialists appear. They are the bats of night. The decline of religion is their time of activity; they seek the shadows when the world is darkened and the clouds have spread over it."[3]

1 'Abdu'l-Bahá, Selected Writings. p. 43.
2 'Abdu'l-Bahá, Bahá'í World Faith, p. 137.
3 ibid., p. 238.

"If the edifice of religion shakes and totters, commotion and chaos will ensue and the order of things will be utterly upset."[1]

"Religious fanaticism and hatred," the Bahá'í teachings affirm, "are a world-devouring fire,whose violence none can quench. The Hand of Divine Power can alone deliver mankind from this desolating affliction."[2]

INTERNATIONALISM: THE END OF AN ERA

When changes take place in the spiritual life of a people, they produce effects not only upon the realm of personal conscience or upon the definitions of denominational faith—their results flow forth throughout the civilization. Society, indeed, is the outer surface of human action, as religion is the inner surface. The persons who are impressed with certain values from the religious teaching of their childhood, strive to fulfil them as adults in their civilization. The nations of the world are not composed of separate races of human beings called citizens or subjects; all this mass of humanity who serve as citizens or subjects are at the same time members of different racial groups and members of different religious bodies.

Since religious training has for the most part been based upon pre-rational states of childhood, the vital assumptions of faith or theology continue from generation to generation without analysis or investigation. The child assumes that his religion sets him off in some mysterious but inevitable and justifiable manner from those people who belong to a different religion. This pre-rational experience becomes an imperative directing his activities in other fields, all the more effective because it works behind his conscious and rational thought. Religion has thus prepared the way for the spirit of exclusive nationalism, class competition and other self-centred types of social institution. The pre-rational experience of justifiable division matures in the irrational attitudes of partisan loyalty which set

---

[1] ibid., p. 239.
[2] Bahá'u'lláh, *Gleanings from Writings*, CXXXII.

I

people off from one another in political and economic matters, eventuating in strife and ruin.

The modern nation represents the most powerful and effective social unity ever achieved. It has co-ordinated the human qualities and possibilities to an unprecedented degree, liberating people from servitude to nature and laying the foundations of orderly progress by reconciling the political claims of the state with the social and cultural needs of the individual. But like every human institution, the nation cannot become an end unto itself. It cannot draw arbitrary lines and decree that human evolution must stop short at this line or that. The nation cannot reduce all questions of human relations to political principle, and solve them by a formal relationship to the state.

The movement of life is irresistible. When the modern nation had organized its area and completed the creation of the necessary institutions, it became mature and incurred obligation to establish useful relationships with other nations. The nation became more and more involved in activities and affairs outside its boundaries and beyond its jurisdiction. Internationalism has been the principle of civilization for more than a hundred years, but the nations could not realize themselves as means to an end, as instruments called upon, for the sake of humanity, to create a sovereignty of and for the entire world. This moral resolution has been lacking.

Denied fulfilment in world order, modern internationalism has organized the nations for their own destruction. The social organism made an end unto itself becomes self-consuming. First there has been an interval of spiritual blindness, a miscalculation of the essential nature of human life; then a denial of the obligation to join with other nations for the sake of peace, then a denunciation of some threatening foe, and, finally, a plunge into the maelstrom where every trend toward world unity is accelerated faster than the public intelligence can comprehend.

Power to make permanent and workable decisions has been temporarily lost. Our international relations rest upon formal agreements which have not yet become translated into world relationships and hence remain subject to abrupt dissolution if the strains of social dislocation go to the breaking point. In this condition of crisis humanity stands, unable to return to the simpler societies of the past and unable to generate sufficient power for true unity in a world civilization. The races and peoples meet in a fateful encounter, each cherishing its separateness as a duty and a right. One may say that humanity does not yet exist, for men are not directed by a world consciousness or impelled by a mutual faith.

"Today the world of humanity," the Bahá'í teachings stated a generation ago, "is in need of international unity and conciliation. To establish these great fundamental principles a propelling power is needed. It is self-evident that unity of the human world and the Most Great Peace cannot be accomplished through material means. They cannot be established through political power, for the political interests of nations are various and the policies of peoples are divergent and conflicting. They cannot be founded through racial or patriotic power, for these are human powers, selfish and weak. The very nature of racial differences and patriotic prejudices prevents the realization of this unity and agreement. Therefore it is evidenced that the promotion of the oneness of the kingdom of humanity, which is the essence of the teachings of all the Manifestations of God, is impossible except through the divine power and the breaths of the Holy Spirit. Other powers are too weak and are incapable of accomplishing this."[1]

"Among the teachings . . . is man's freedom, that through the ideal Power he should be free and emancipated from the captivity of the world of nature; for as long as man is captive to nature he is a ferocious animal, as the struggle for existence is one of the exigencies of the world of nature. This matter of the struggle for existence is the fountainhead of all calamities and is the supreme affliction."[2]

[1] 'Abdu'l-Bahá, *Selected Writings*, p. 5.
[2] 'Abdu'l-Bahá, *Bahá'í World Faith*, p. 288, written in 1919.

"Universal peace is a matter of great importance, but unity of conscience is essential, so that the foundation of this matter may become secure, its establishment firm and its edifice strong."[1]

In the Bahá'í writings, peace is revered because in essence it is a spiritual mystery in which humanity has been invited in our day, for the first time, to partake. Peace is a divine creation; a reconciliation of human and divine purpose. Peace appears first as a universal religion; as its influence gathers force and its principles spread then peace can permeate the body of society, redeeming its institutions and its activities and consecrating its aims.

"Universal peace," these writings promise, "is assured . . . as a fundamental accomplishment of the religion of God; that peace shall prevail among nations, governments and peoples, among religions, races and all conditions of mankind. This is one of the special characteristics of the Word of God revealed in this Manifestation."[2]

SPIRITUAL EDUCATION: THE INSTRUMENT OF PEACE

The issues of human existence turn upon the axis of education. Education alone can overcome the inertia of our separateness, transmute our creative energies for the realization of world unity, free the mind from its servitude to the past and reshape civilization to be the guardian of our spiritual and physical resources.

The true purposes of education are not fulfilled by the knowledge conferred through civil education, since this knowledge ends with the purposes of the individual or the needs of the state. They are not fulfilled by sectarian education, since sectarian knowledge excludes the basic principle of the continuity and progressiveness of revelation.

The true purposes of education are not achieved by independent pursuit of knowledge undertaken through study of

[1] ibid., p. 285.
[2] ibid., p. 247.

the classics, the great philosophies or even the religious systems of the past. Such education enhances the individual capacity and deepens the insight of a group. It opens the door to a world of superior minds and heroic accomplishment. But that world is the reflection of the light of truth upon past conditions and events. It is not the rising of the sun to illumine our own time, inspire a unified world movement, and regenerate withered souls.

Nor may we hope that psychology can develop the necessary transforming power for a dislocated society, a scientific substitute for the primitive offices of religion. The explorer in the world of the psyche sees the projection of his own shadow, finds the answer determined by his own question. He can prove mechanistic determinism or demonstrate the freedom and responsibility of the soul. The area within which he works is suitable for the development of personal healing. He can learn the habitual reactions of persons in a group or of groups in a society, but this knowledge is statistical until applied by a comprehensive organ of intelligence on a world scale.

"The human spirit which distinguishes man from the animal," the Bahá'í teachings state, "is the rational soul; and these two names—the human spirit and the rational soul—designate one thing. This spirit, which in the terminology of the philosophers is the rational soul, embraces all beings, and as far as human ability permits discovers the realities of things and becomes cognizant of their peculiarities and effects, and of the qualities and properties of beings. But the human spirit, unless assisted by the spirit of faith, does not become acquainted with the divine secrets and the heavenly realities. It is like a mirror which, although clear, polished and brilliant, is still in need of light. Until a ray of the sun reflects upon it, it cannot discover the heavenly secrets."[1]

This significant comment is also found: "With the love of God all sciences are accepted and beloved, but without it, are fruitless; nay, rather, the cause of insanity. Every science is like

[1] 'Abdu'l-Bahá, Bahá'í World Faith, p. 317.

unto a tree; if the fruit of it is the love of God, that is a blessed tree. Otherwise it is dried wood and finally a food for fire."[1]

A new and universal concept of education is found in the literature of the Bahá'í Faith.

"When we consider existence, we see that the mineral, vegetable, animal and human worlds are all in need of an educator.

"If the earth is not cultivated it becomes a jungle where useless weeds grow; but if a cultivator comes and tills the ground, it produces crops which nourish living creatures. It is evident, therefore, that the soil needs the cultivation of the farmer. . . .

"The same is true with respect to animals: notice that when the animal is trained it becomes domestic, and also that man, if he is left without training becomes bestial, and, moreover, if left under the rule of nature, becomes lower than an animal, whereas if he is educated he becomes an angel. . . .

"Now reflect that it is education that brings the East and the West under the authority of man; it is education that produces wonderful industries; it is education that spreads glorious sciences and arts; it is education that makes manifest new discoveries and laws. If there were no educator there would be no such things as comforts, civilization, facilities, or humanity. . . .

"But education is of three kinds: material, human and spiritual. Material education is concerned with the progress and development of the body, through gaining its sustenance, its material comfort and ease. This education is common to animals and man.

"Human education signifies civilization and progress: that is to say, government, administration, charitable works, trades, arts and handicrafts, sciences, great inventions and discoveries of physical laws, which are the activities essential to man as distinguished from the animal.

"Divine education is that of the Kingdom of God: it consists

[1] ibid., p. 366.

in acquiring divine perfections, and this is true education; for in this estate man becomes the centre of divine appearance, the manifestation of the words, 'Let us make man in our image and after our likeness.' This is the supreme goal of the world of humanity.

"Now we need an educator who will be at the same time a material, human and spiritual educator, and whose authority will be effective in all conditions. . . .

"It is clear that human power is not able to fill such a great office, and that the reason alone could not undertake the responsibility of so great a mission. How can one solitary person without help and without support lay the foundations of such a noble construction? He must depend on the help of the spiritual and divine power to be able to undertake this mission. One Holy Soul gives life to the world of humanity, changes the aspect of the terrestrial globe, causes intelligence to progress, vivifies souls, lays the foundation of a new existence, establishes the basis of a marvellous creation, organizes the world, brings nations and religions under the shadow of one standard, delivers man from the world of imperfections and vices, and inspires him with the desire and need of natural and acquired perfections. Certainly nothing short of a divine power could accomplish so great a work." [1]

Who is this educator? "The holy Manifestations of God, the divine prophets, are the first teachers of the human race. They are universal educators and the fundamental principles they have laid down are the causes and factors of the advancement of nations. Forms and imitations which creep in afterward are not conducive to that progress. On the contrary these are destroyers of the human foundations laid by the heavenly educators." [2]

"Religion is the outer expression of the divine reality. Therefore it must be living, vitalized, moving and progressive. If it be without motion and non-progressive it is without the

[1] 'Abdu'l-Bahá, *Some Answered Questions*, Ch. III.
[2] 'Abdu'l-Bahá, *Bahá'í World Faith*, p. 250.

divine life; it is dead. The divine institutes are continuously active and evolutionary; therefore, the revelation of them must be progressive and continuous."[1]

THE MANIFESTATION OF GOD

The focal point of the Bahá'í teachings is clarification of man's relationship to God. As long as peoples differ, or are unaware, or accept a substitute for this relationship, we cannot distinguish between truth and error, or discriminate between principle and superstition. Until we apprehend human beings in the light of the creative purpose, it is impossible to know ourselves or others. Social truth is merely experiment and hypothesis unless it forms part of a spiritual reality.

The founders of revealed religions, who have been termed prophets, messengers, messiahs and saviours, in the Bahá'í teachings are designated Manifestations of God. These beings, walking on earth as men, stand in a higher order of creation and are endowed with powers and attributes human beings do not possess. In the world of truth they shine like the sun, and the rays emanating from that sun are the light and the life of the souls of men.

The Manifestation is not God. The Infinite cannot be incarnated. God reveals His will through the Manifestation, and apart from what is thus manifested His will and reality remain for ever unknown. The physical universe does not reveal the divine purpose for man.

"Every one of them," the Bahá'í teachings state, "is the Way of God that connects this world with the realms above, and the standard of His truth unto every one in the kingdoms of earth and heaven. They are the Manifestations of God amidst men, the evidences of His truth, and the signs of His glory."[2]

What almighty power is exercised by a will manifested through a person who has been flouted, denied, imprisoned, tortured and crucified? No human authority could survive

[1] ibid., p. 224.
[2] Bahá'u'lláh, Kitáb-i-Íqán

such savage onslaughts as have greeted each messenger who has come from the heavenly realm to this lowest of worlds. The divine power expresses itself by compulsion in the kingdoms of nature. In the kingdom of man the divine power operates in such a manner that men are free to accept and adore, or repudiate and condemn. The divine power compels that from age to age men must come to a decision, but the decision itself is free. By that decision, when the prophet has revealed the will of God, men separate into two organic companies: those who believe and those who deny.

The whole pattern and process of history rests upon the succession of dispensations by which man's innate capacities are developed and by which the course of social evolution is sustained. The rise and fall of civilizations proceeds as the effect of prior spiritual causation. An ancient civilization undergoes moral decadence; by division of its own people and attack from without its power and authority are destroyed; and with that destruction collapses the culture and the religious system which had become parasites upon its material wealth. Concurrently, a new creative spirit reveals itself in the rise of a greater and better type of society from the ruins of the old.

The critical point in this process is the heroic sacrifice offered the prophet by those who see in Him the way to God, and His official condemnation by the heads of the prevailing religious system. That condemnation, because men cannot judge God, recoils back upon the religion and the civilization itself. They have condemned themselves. In the same manner, the small and weak minority who have seen the Face of God in His Manifestation grow from strength to strength. The future is with them. In their spiritual fellowship the seeds of the new civilization are watered and its first, tender growth safeguarded by their heart's blood.

Through the Manifestation of God the power of the Holy Spirit accomplishes the will of God. Nothing can withstand that power. Because its work is not instantaneous, a darkened age cannot perceive the awful process of cause and effect—the divine will as cause, and human history as effect—guiding human destiny from age to age.

But the Bahá'í teachings penetrate farther into the mystery when they affirm that in spirit and in aim the successive prophets are one being, one authority, one will. This teaching on the oneness of the Manifestations of God is the essential characteristic of a revelation which represents religion for the cycle of man's maturity and the creation of world peace.

"There can be no doubt whatever that the peoples of the world, of whatever race or religion, derive their inspiration from one heavenly Source and are the subjects of one God. The difference between the ordinances under which they abide should be attributed to the varying requirements of the age in which they were revealed." [1]

Those who deny and condemn the prophet, therefore, are not defending the divine purpose from sinister betrayal by one who introduces new laws and principles; on the contrary, since the Manifestation in Himself is one, they condemn their own prophet when He returns to regenerate the world and advance the true Faith of God. Thus is the moral nature of human life, and man's responsibility to God, sustained throughout the devious course of history. Faith is no mere belief, but a connection with the only power that confers immortality on the soul and saves humanity as a whole from complete self-destruction.

"A man who has not had a spiritual education," the Bahá'í writings attest, "is a brute." [2] "We have decreed, O people, that the highest and last end of all learning be the recognition of Him who is the Object of all knowledge; and yet behold how ye have allowed your learning to shut you out, as by a veil, from Him who is the Day-spring of this Light, through whom every hidden thing has been revealed." [3]

The oneness of the Manifestations has been thus established in the Bahá'í writings: "In the Word of God there is . . . unity,

[1] Bahá'u'lláh, *Gleanings from Writings*, CXI.
[2] 'Abdu'l-Bahá, *Some Answered Questions*, Ch. XXIX.
[3] Bahá'u'lláh, *Epistle to the Son of the Wolf*, p. 129.

the oneness of the Manifestations of God, His Holiness Abraham, Moses, Jesus Christ, Muḥammad, the Báb and Bahá'u'lláh. This is a unity divine, heavenly, radiant, merciful; the one reality appearing in successive manifestations. For instance, the sun is one and the same but its points of dawning are various. During the summer season it rises from the northern point of the ecliptic; in winter it appears from the southern point of rising. Although these dawning-points are different, the sun is the same sun which has appeared from them all. The significance is the reality of prophethood which is symbolized by the sun, and the holy Manifestations are the dawning-places or zodiacal points."[1]

The coming of the Manifestation in this age signalizes the termination of a long epoch in human history, the prophetic era in which mankind was gradually prepared for the promised day of universal peace. In Bahá'u'lláh the spirit of faith is renewed and given expression in teachings which affirm the organic unity of the whole human race. Nothing sacred and valid revealed in former dispensations is denied, but the spirit of faith has been endowed with a worldwide and universal meaning.

The Bahá'í teachings overcome prejudices of race, nation and sect by inspiring sentiment of brotherhood. They create not only a pure well of feeling but constitute also a unified body of knowledge in which the power of reason can be fulfilled. They connect social truth with the truth of worship, and broaden the field of ethics to include right relationships of races as well as individual persons. They formulate law and principle which will bring order into international affairs.

"In this present age the world of humanity," the teachings declared before the first World War (anticipating the conditions of today) "is afflicted with severe sicknesses and grave disorders which threaten death. Therefore His Holiness Bahá'u'lláh has appeared. He is the real physician bringing divine remedy and healing to the world of man."[2]

1 'Abdu'l-Bahá, *Bahá'í World Faith*, p. 259.
2 'Abdu'l-Bahá, *Selected Writings*, p. 12.

"The first teaching of Bahá'u'lláh is the investigation of reality. Man must seek the reality himself, forsaking imitations and adherence to mere hereditary forms. As the nations of the world are following imitations in lieu of truth and as imitations are many and various, differences of belief have been productive of strife and warfare. So long as these imitations remain the oneness of the world of humanity is impossible. Therefore we must investigate the reality in order that by its light the clouds and darkness may be dispelled. If the nations of the world investigate reality they will agree and become united."[1]

"The source of all learning is the knowledge of God, exalted be His glory, and this cannot be attained save through the knowledge of His divine Manifestation."[2] This knowledge offers to men the substance of the education needed for the establishment of a society worthy of the blessings of justice and peace.

[1] 'Abdu'l-Bahá, *Bahá'í World Faith*, p. 238.
[2] Bahá'u'lláh, *Words of Wisdom*.

THE WORLD ECONOMY OF BAHÁ'U'LLÁH

To an unprecedented degree, the power of constructive thought has been released from the realm of private affairs for study of the basic social structure, as responsible men in all countries have come to realize their new obligation to give concern to the general problem of depression and unrest.

The time is therefore favourable for more widespread knowledge of the fact that a plan of world order was advanced in the last century, which not only anticipates many proposals now receiving serious consideration, but rests upon the substantial foundation of a true analysis of the malady afflicting modern life.

It is, in fact, a matter of importance for the serious student of current conditions, whether his interest is primarily economic, political or sociological, to learn that a body of literature has existed for over two generations in which are to be found explicit principles and teachings meeting the very difficulties now so profoundly felt throughout the world.

The world economy of Bahá'u'lláh transcends in scope and purpose the belated response to the risk of calamity made by economists and statesmen under the pressure of events in recent years. His principles are established upon organic laws of human evolution. They interpret the modern problem not as a temporary maladjustment of industry and trade—the effects of an "industrial revolution"—but as a movement in humanity itself. They make the necessary connection between the spiritual and practical affairs of men which alone can breathe the breath of life into any social mechanism.

Careful study of this body of literature makes it apparent that Bahá'u'lláh stood at that major turning-point of social evolution where the long historic trend toward diversity—in language, custom, civil and religious codes and economic practices—came to an end, and the movement was reversed in the direction of unity. The human motive in the former era was necessarily competitive. The human motive in the new era is necessarily co-operative.

From this point of view it becomes clear that the European Wars and the uninterrupted sequence of international disturbances since 1918 are, essentially, vital indications that by sheer spiritual inertia humanity has continued to function under the old competitive motive when conditions have arisen which make co-operation and unity imperative to the very existence of mankind. Instead of temporary "maladjustment" we have the urgent necessity to transform the whole structure of civilization. Institutions and social organisms created in the age of diversity and competition have become unfit to serve human needs in the age of co-operation and peace. Our present "crisis" discloses more and more clearly the tragic fact that people turn for the divine gifts of peace and sustenance to agencies adapted for the opposite ends of war and destruction.

The new conditions affecting every branch of human activity today are the result of the physical unity of the world achieved during the last century through technological equipment. As the arena of human affairs has become one unit, and is no longer a series of unrelated territories, the law of cause and effect, for the first time in history, operates for society as positively as it operates for the material universe. The consequence is that every public action has its immediate reaction. National and racial or class movements are no longer isolated and irresponsible; they no longer can be made to secure definite and limited objectives, like a small, compact and medieval army turned loose among unarmed peasants, but every social movement and influence today affects the general structure of society and brings about results of a general character.

Just as this new law of cause and effect connects in one common destiny hitherto isolated geographical areas, so likewise, within the single political or economic area of each nation, consequences of political or economic action now cannot be confined to their own special field, but flow throughout the whole nation and produce effects in all fields.

That is, not only has humanity become an organic unit by reason of geographical relationship, but in addition its structure of civilization has become interdependent by reason of the new relationships affecting such apparently unrelated activities as business and religion, or government and philosophy. The real significance of this vital fact is that politics is no longer politics alone, and economics is no longer economics alone, but both are nothing else than facets of the one, indivisible substance of human life.

We have arrived, in other words, at a stage in human evolution when moral value—that which serves the good of humanity and not merely the interest of any one group—determines not alone the desirability but also the feasibility of every public policy and every social programme.

That is why the present world crisis escapes every effort to bring it under the control of normal social agencies. When another international war seems imminent, we call the crisis "political" and effort is made to control it by political bodies. When the economic depression seems most acute, we call the crisis "economic" and seek to control it by economic bodies. It would be just as logical to call the crisis "religious" and base our hopes of recovery upon the influence of the churches. In reality, the crisis is at once political, economic and religious, but humanity possesses no responsible, authoritative agency capable of co-ordinating all the factors and arriving at a world plan which takes all factors into account.

These considerations reveal the vital importance of a new principle of action, a new attitude and a new quality of understanding such as the student of society encounters in the teachings of Bahá'u'lláh. Here one makes contact with a world view raised above local and partisan interests, and a spirit of faith in divine Providence so profound that it sustains the certitude that mankind will be guided through the most terrible storm of confusion and strife the world has ever faced.

In contradistinction to those social plans which attempt to rationalize an abstract system of political economy and apply it, with or without the element of compulsion, to the body of humanity in naïve disregard of the complexity of human nature, the principles of Bahá'u'lláh operate from the heart outward to the social structure. His principles interpret the realities of man's spiritual nature, upholding an ideal civilization which will come into being gradually, by voluntary action of those who understand it, accept it as truth and strive for its attainment as the fulfilment of their own highest aspiration.

His aim was the unity of mankind in the world of the mind and spirit, that the external unity in process of realization might become man's blessing, the means of peace and co-operation, rather than a bitter curse, the means of chaos and strife. Through the leaven of spiritual knowledge those prejudices which now divide the hearts and confuse the minds, setting nation against nation, class against class and creed against creed, will be transmuted into a common loyalty and positive fellowship identifying social order with true ethics and true mystical experience.

If we desire material abundance, leisure, security, opportunity for broader knowledge, a larger conquest of nature and a social environment enabling men to enjoy creative relationships—if we seek to give actuality to those visions and desires which society now resists and makes impossible—the door of attainment is unity and co-operation. As unity of personality brings power to individuals, so human fellowship will release yet-dormant capacities in the race.

Bahá'u'lláh exemplified the possibility of this human fellowship and its capacity to transform society from the clash of hostile communities to an organic structure embracing the world. The literature expressing his insight into human reality, when responsive to the transforming spirit of the one God, links together those necessary steps in evolution which lead from the new outlook required by the individual to a world order co-ordinating the different aspects of social activity now functioning separately and aimlessly: education, religious devotion, industry, finance, trade, government.

Before adding certain important details to these fundamental tenets, it is desirable to meet the attitude which represents the chief danger to human welfare at this time, namely the opinion that a few superficial alterations in the political and economic organization are sufficient to overcome the difficulties we now confront.

THE NATURE OF WORLD UNREST

Warfare and strife have ever been present in human society, but since the outbreak of military operations in this century, the principle of war has been enormously reinforced. The cessation of hostilities by no means meant the termination of war. The military period served to exhaust and destroy all the human and social resources at the command of governments, but the consuming flame was communicated from the field of battle to the broader field of business, where its destructiveness assumed new forms.

In passing from the military to the economic domain, the principle of war escaped the control vested by society in government, which throughout history has served to confine the area and duration of violent combat within the attainment of definite objectives. The principle of war today—that is, the condition of organized conflict—spreads throughout the body of society, engaging all civil activities and setting not only nation against nation but class against class and interest against interest. In this domain no government nor any other social institution is powerful enough to stamp out the flames. Civilization has become one continuous crisis, a state of unending civil war. Meanwhile, under the steady pressure of fear arising as much from the possibility of domestic revolution as of foreign aggression, the military establishments directed by all leading governments have accumulated means of violence sufficient virtually to destroy the human race.

K

As long as war can be regarded as abnormal, a temporary emergency within the control of responsible governments, ended at will by victory or surrender, its operation does not interrupt fixed social habits nor affect fundamental ideas. A people during war temporarily abandons its civil routine and its inherited moral and religious tenets, as a family abandons a house injured by storm, to re-enter it when the storm has subsided and repair whatever damage has been done. But when the principle of war has carried over from the limited field of government operation to the unlimited field of general social activity, we have a condition in which the inherited capital of social loyalty and constructive idealism is readily impaired. The steady, relentless pressure exercised by a society divided against itself and reduced to the elemental struggle for existence affects the form and nature both of government and other responsible institutions. It affects also the aims and habits of the mass of the people. The failure of social philosophies emanating from ancient religious teachings opens the door to philosophies and doctrines essentially materialistic in aim and outlook. These compete for the control of the state and its complex agencies of legislation, finance and public education, altering radically the traditional relations of political parties. Industry has the alternative of entering this political struggle at the risk of separating the interests of labour, capital and consumer, or of concentrating upon its business task at the risk of finding its international markets crippled by nationalistic policies abroad and its domestic market interfered with by socialistic programmes at home. As materialistic philosophies spread among a confused, a burdened and disillusioned people, religious bodies follow industry in its effort to control legislation and education in order to safeguard their special interests and values, with the result that the power of the state to adopt broad and fundamental public policies is sacrificed to the clash of determined interests. Only occasionally, and timidly, can the state rise above this interminable wrangle to consider its true relations to the world situation as a whole.

The individual, meanwhile, finds himself more and more conditioned by this general, ever-changing and menacing competition. He finds himself becoming a lone being in a social jungle threatening his welfare at many points. Isolated goodwill and personal integrity tend to lose their meaning as he finds that they no longer produce their habitual result in terms of his life and work. He feels that there is no longer any connection between ultimate faith and today's shelter and food. He finds materialism in his church and idealism in his economic party. Above all, he witnesses the confounding of leadership in high places and recognizes that the balance of competing forces is so complete that no social group can through political influence successfully enforce its will upon the whole population. Under these conditions the final impact of world unrest upon the mass of people is anti-social, manifested in indifference, in uneasy fear or in determination to seek the short cut through direct action.

The combined and successive shocks to human nature of the butchery during the wars, the depreciation of currencies, the post-war revolutions, unemployment, public dishonesty, and the rise of materialistic philosophies to the stature of fully developed institutions, not to mention other vital factors such as the inadequacy of the education afforded by public school and sectarian church, and the social blindness exhibited by responsible leaders in all fields of human activity since 1914, has been underestimated in the promotion of plans promising general improvement. The ultimate triumph of the principle of war has been to reduce the richly varied capacities of people to the sheer instinct to survive. Society is no longer under control— it is a rudderless ship, an unpiloted plane. No one can predict events, and no authority can deal properly with the emergencies that continually arise.

An adequate social diagnosis, one on which a permanent plan of betterment may be founded, can at this time scarcely afford to overlook these three essential facts: first, that through their inability to establish real peace and their endorsement of universally destructive instruments of warfare, governments no longer protect life and property, but, on the contrary, have become the chief sources of peril to mankind; second, that as the result of the concentration of the means of production and distribution, without corresponding social policy, industry and commerce no longer feed, clothe and shelter the people, but, on the contrary, have increased the area and intensity of poverty and destitution[1]; and, third, that through the diversity and strife of creeds, and their materialistic dependence upon civil authority to enforce moral principles, established religion no longer intensifies the inner life of man, relating people one to another in the spirit of co-operation and sincere consultation for mutual protection and general betterment, but, on the contrary, poisons the very sources of loyalty and understanding and fans the flame of competition and dissension which, passing out from the church into life, sanctions nationalism in the state and self-aggrandisement in business affairs.

By gradual, imperceptible stages, the constructive instruments of civilization have acquired destructive aims. The condition called "peace" is one in which antagonisms and strifes grow to the breaking point within each nation; the condition called "war" is the only one in which people in each nation attain solidarity and exercise collective will. The logical end of either condition is the same.

Regarded from the institutional point of view, this age marks the end of a civilization which no longer serves mankind. From the point of view of human experience, it marks the complete and final frustration of the instinct of physical self-preservation, which man shares with the beast, as the dominating social motive. Both statements reflect the same truth, for it is the instinct of physical self-preservation which throughout history has impelled humanity to organize the competitive institutions of state, industry and church which are miscalled "civilization."

---

[1] This passage refers to the general depression of the 1930's, and was written before the second war and its subsequent boom.

Disillusion would only be justified if human society could be successfully established on the war principle. An age which has fully proved that war no longer leads to the fruits of victory, and that a competitive economy no longer produces wealth, is an age permeated and sustained by providential forces. The complexity of the problem, and the greatness of the crisis, is in itself the true measure of human capacity.

To realize that antagonism and hatred, no matter how magnified by the leverage of social institutions, no matter how gilded and refined by cultural and doctrinal philosophies, threaten the very existence of humanity, is to perceive that human life functions under other and higher laws than those which condition the life of the brute. It is likewise to perceive that, all along, the external man-made world of civilization has had no true inner correspondence with the spiritual nature and infinitely varied talents, desires and thoughts of the race. Only by continuous suppression of one entire aspect of his being—his latent and passive reality—has man, acting from emergency to emergency, made competition the dominant motive in comparison to co-operation. Both motives are always present; if competition has created governments and industrial systems, the vision of unfulfilled love has supplied the power and inspiration for true music, art and poetry in every age.

The rise of science in the modern age has enormously reinforced the latent powers of men in comparison to those faculties developed during the era of external struggle against the physical environment. Important as its technological achievement has been, the ultimate value of science lies not in its inventions but in its assertion of yet-undeveloped resources within the mind and soul. The faculties that make for discovery in the realm of the material universe can, and will, be employed in the more important realm of spiritual reality. Science restores the balance between man as being and man as desiring and doing. It reveals a new measure of human capacity, and confirms the integrity of the race as the vehicle for further evolution. While the effects of science so far have been negative no less than positive, a spiritual science concerned with the central problem of human welfare can provide the agencies necessary for the functioning of the spirit of co-operation throughout society.

The providential character of the crisis actually consists in the fact that it is a crisis—a challenge to human understanding not to be diverted or put off to a more convenient season. Because it is worldwide, it lays its burden as heavily upon America as Europe, upon the East no less than upon the West, upon government as upon industry, and upon religion as upon government. Humanity shares one universal experience of suffering and grief, bears one unavoidable responsibility, reacts to one supreme stimulus serving to quicken the slumbering, passive "inner" powers—hence humanity grows in understanding of its fundamental reality and is trained to function through collective resources and instruments.

The present unrest has no real meaning or ultimate value until it is recognized as a movement in humanity and only secondarily a disturbance in the institutional elements of civilization. Political exigencies and economic crises have become so acute that the symptoms are mistaken for the actual disease. The first principle, and the foundation upon which the new order stands, is the oneness of humanity—the interdependence of the race in a common origin and destiny. The social organization that now fails to function is one constructed upon the assumption of diversity and separateness, which has produced a society motivated by competition.

THE ANALOGY OF ROME

Fortunately, the history of our own civilization offers, on a smaller scale, an era closely paralleling the present condition.

The Roman Empire, at a certain point, also established a civilization opposed to the best interests of humanity. Its institutional society likewise entered a time of "transition" when the competitive instinct began to fail, faced with political, economic and religious problems too complex for solution by traditional means. But through the power of the Christian faith, those problems were transmuted into a higher human process. The claims of that faith no doubt remained consistently ignored or condemned by those indoctrinated with the social science of the period, but the fact remains that the stream of human evolution abandoned the institutions of civilization and flowed onward through the channels of a movement reflecting the needs and capacities of humanity. The restoration of society came about through the loyalty of regenerated individuals welded in a co-operative group, not through the reorganization of tariffs, wages, public statutes and trade. Up to the limit of human capacity, the people of faith constituted a society in which a bond and relationship, like that animating the members of a family, replaced the formal procedures and unfeeling contacts sanctioned by the political and economic science of the ruined state.

The essence of that experience was the triumph of humanity over civilization. The early Christians dipped themselves in the eternal stream of human reality, recovered the vision of God, and armed only with devotion and faith, stood fast against the shocks of a collapsing society and eventually laid the foundation for a "new age." Their faith in Christ released the mysterious forces of the spirit within; by sacrifice they were able to re-create society on a higher moral basis, nearer the ultimate aim of a co-operative world.

The early Christian world was, however, a definitely limited area, hemmed in by barbaric hordes and prevented from expanding the Christian experience to include humanity. The movement outward came to an end; Christianity organized itself for defence, admitting within itself the fatal influences of dissension and force; the new social body after it had repudiated the law of universal love revealed the presence of spiritual disease by dividing on issues of scientific truth; this fissure gradually widened until Protestantism made it permanent, and modern civilization, with its inner conflict between "secular" and "religious" values was the inevitable result. Nothing in this gradual decay can be made to serve as argument against the true significance of religion. Christianity restored the power of the heart.

The "truth" of Christianity, and of all religions founded by a prophetic spirit, is, however, not a constant but a variable; a rise toward the vision of God, followed by a darkening and degeneration. It is a spring-time of spiritual fertility, followed by summer and the harvest of autumn, and terminating in the cold of winter. Civilization may be likened to a clock that must be periodically wound. The historic process that reduced Christianity from a source of inner-renewal to a mere institutionalism operated also in the case of Judaism, Muḥammadanism, Buddhism and the other religions. Each regenerated an area of humanity, revived civilization, created new and better conditions for mankind and slowly died, to yield place to another prophet and a renewal of faith.

A NEW CYCLE OF HUMAN POWER

Bahá'u'lláh, whose mission was promulgated by 'Abdu'l-Bahá in Europe and America, completed the circle of religion as the expression of man's real nature and possibility in relation to God, to society and to the physical universe. He joined the arcs described by Jesus and the prophets of other races. In His teaching are made those necessary connections between ethics, science and sociology which carry into society and civilization the full integrity of the principle of love. Bahá'u'lláh is the first interpreter of humanity as a unified organism capable of co-ordinating its resources of mind and heart. "Let not a man glory in this, that he loves his country," Bahá'u'lláh declared more than sixty years ago, "rather let him glory in this, that he loves his kind." Standing in the same relation of sacrifice toward the unmoral institutions of modern society that Jesus held toward the civilization of Palestine and Rome, Bahá'u'lláh manifested a spiritual power which likewise created a movement of faith and devotion among the people paralleled by extreme hatred and antagonism on the part of the official leaders in his environment. Today his teaching has the dimension of history—a story written indelibly in the blood of Persian martyrs.

The movement entered the West in the person of 'Abdu'l-Bahá, who travelled throughout Europe and America during 1911 and 1912 to expound Bahá'u'lláh's doctrine in relation to the political, economic and social problems of the age.

Speaking in the City Temple, London, in September, 1911 —on the eve of the great war which he foresaw and warned people against—he used these significant words: "This is a new cycle of human power. All the horizons of the world are luminous, and the world will become indeed as a garden and a paradise. It is the hour of the unity of the sons of men and of the drawing together of all races and all classes. You are loosed from ancient superstitions which have kept men ignorant, destroying the foundations of true humanity.

"The gift of God to this enlightened age is the knowledge of the oneness of mankind and of the fundamental oneness of religion. War shall cease between nations, and by the will of God the 'Most Great Peace' shall come; the world will be seen as a new world, and all men will live as brothers.

"In the days of old an instinct for warfare was developed in the struggle with wild animals; this is no longer necessary; nay, rather co-operation and mutual understanding are seen to produce the greatest welfare of mankind. Enmity is now the result of prejudice only. . . . There is one God; mankind is one; the foundations of religion are one. Let us worship Him, and give praise for all His great prophets and messengers who have manifested His brightness and glory."

This conception of world unrest as the gathering of the latent resources of mankind for release in a "new cycle of human power" emanates from the depths of truth. It focuses in one point the complex issues which specialists in many fields are separately unable to meet; it recovers for human imagination, human understanding and human will the control of events apparently dominated by an uncontrollable social "machine."

But with this statement should be paralleled another statement, made by 'Abdu'l-Bahá at Baptist Temple, Philadelphia, June 9, 1912: "True religion is the source of love and agreement among men, the cause of the development of praiseworthy qualities; but the people are holding to the counterfeit and imitation, negligent of the reality which unifies, so they are bereft and deprived of the radiance of religion. They follow superstitions inherited from their fathers and ancestors. . . . That which was meant to be conducive to life has become the cause of death; that which should have been an evidence of knowledge is now a proof of ignorance; that which was a factor in the sublimity of human nature has proved to be its degradation. Therefore the realm of the religionist has gradually narrowed and darkened and the sphere of the materialist has widened and advanced; for the religionist has held to imitation and counterfeit, neglecting and discarding holiness and the sacred reality of religion. When the sun sets it is time for bats to fly. They come forth because they are creatures of night."

Here we have the obverse of the picture—the negative condition opposed to the positive, the blind submission to external "institutional" truth in contradistinction to faith in human values; in other words, civilization in active opposition to the real interests of humanity. Between these polar extremes, currents of immeasurable power flow through modern society, destroying all forms of organized selfishness and at the same time quickening human minds and hearts with the capacity to realize that only through unity and co-operation can the race survive.

The concentration of moral force and intelligence upon one objective creates a tool for the accomplishment of the greatest task. The objective laid upon conscience and reason alike in this stage of evolution is world order and peace. In this aim the ideals of religion become identical with the requirements of economics and social science.

Up to the economic depression, world peace was held to be merely a political problem, a matter of treaty between the sovereign states. The depression served to reveal the fact that world peace in reality is a question of social justice and not merely the cessation of military strife. It revealed also that from the point of view of social justice the states are no longer sovereign, but have become areas of economic and psychological revolution. This fact makes the United Nations[1], as now constituted, an inadequate instrument for international control. It is as though the Federal Government at Washington consisted merely of delegates from nearly fifty sovereign states, whose deliberations to become effective had to be ratified separately by each state legislature and who possessed no Federal army or navy, while each state maintained a complete military establishment in competition with every other state, and refused to yield to Washington any essential elements of its local sovereignty. Such a condition in one country could not be termed a national government, nor can the United Nations be regarded as an international government. The Security Council seems to represent the limit of attainment possible to the old civilization; it is not yet an organization of humanity.

OBJECTIVES OF SOCIAL PROGRESS

Chaos and revolution will continue, with increased momentum, until social justice creates an instrument of world government, a government possessing the sovereignty of mankind, to which the national states are subordinated as provinces having only local jurisdiction. This is the central issue of the world today, the inescapable obligation written in financial, political, social and moral terms that all may eventually read.

For world government differs from the present national governments not merely through an extension of the physical area of jurisdiction, but in the dimension of social responsibility as well. It alone can effect disarmament, create a safe currency, reconcile the discord of classes, establish an education conforming to basic human needs, and overcome the sinister peril resident in the divergent theories of capitalism and communism.

[1] In the original article, the League of Nations.

Not until world government exists can the divorce between "religious" and "secular" values be ended, the greatest curse in human experience. World government implies social administration by the elect of mankind—men whose executive talents are imbued with moral principles. It is the partisan politician who maintains social disunity that he may have the privilege of fishing in troubled waters.

World government is the only possible source of stability for local communities everywhere.

As world government is the first, so a regenerated local community is the second objective of social progress. The essential human relations are all maintained locally. It is our community environment which finally determines the quality of human life. Here our inner attitudes begin that cycle of social influence culminating either in peace or war. Here takes place the impact of education upon the unprejudiced child soul which produces the motives and reactions of adult life.

The transformation needed to make the local community over from the condition of a diseased cell in a disordered social body, into the condition of a healthy cell in a sound organism, is the extension of the social relationship from the political to the economic realm. In a vital social organism, the individual would have not merely the inalienable right to vote and receive the protection of the courts, but also the inalienable right of economic livelihood—not insulting charity but fundamental human right. The political structure today is a sieve through which runs away in loss the noblest aspirations and the most effective motives and qualities of mankind. Nothing can redeem the fact that modern government originated as an agency for the conduct of war rather than for the maintenance of peace.

This new and higher human status, moreover, does not depend upon the success of socialism and far less upon the success of communism. Both these social theories fail to correspond to the standard of human reality. They are, at bottom, an effort to organize materials and processes and not an effort to unify human beings. The emphasis is entirely upon the mechanism instead of upon the nature of man. Their complete application might produce the semblance of external order, but this would be at the expense of the human spirit. Only after we have uncovered the spiritual principles of human association can we evolve a social order corresponding to the divine reality.

Both world government and regenerated local community are possibilities in a human evolution the realization of which depends upon the existence of a new scale of personal motives and a new range of social understanding. The ultimate goal of a world economy therefore has a third objective, correlated to the two objectives already outlined. The third objective is the need of spiritual education—the reinforcement of man's passive idealism to the point where people consciously strive together for mutual ends, and are no longer socially indifferent, waiting for "good times" to come *per se* or to be received as a gift from a few bankers, manufacturers and statesmen.

The profit motive alone will not sustain a balanced, enduring civilization. Far stronger, far truer—in fact, far more humanly natural—is the motive of self-expression and fulfilment found in children and surviving in the few artists, artisans and spiritually conscious men and women who refuse to be moulded by the external forces prevailing in their environment. The inadequacy of the profit motive appears when we imagine the result if it were extended to family life. Every family is a co-operative economy attempting to maintain itself in a competitive community. The dissolution of the family marks the end of an age.

At present, education is limited to the aim of assuring personal survival in a competitive society, and the effect of this mental and moral strangulation is to leave the essential core of personality—its understanding of fundamental purpose and its motives—to the overwhelming influence of an already perverted society. As the expression of a collective social mentality, education can and must deal with the basic human values.

Spiritual education has little connection with the systems of education developed by churches for partisan ends. It is education of the whole being for useful life in a united society which derives its laws and principles from the universal law of love. It is education conscious of the modes of social evolution and hence subduing the means of life to its true purpose and outcome. One single generation raised by spiritual education above the false guides who rationalize class, race, national and religious prejudices can give humanity a definite foothold in the new age of co-operation and unity.

These three objectives—world government, a regenerated community and spiritual education—are interdependent. Neither can exist without the other two. All three are latent in human society at the present time. They are emerging to the degree that the highest type of people in all countries recognize one or more of them as the most worthy values for idealism and effort. The sheer inertia of past evolution, however, still carries the race in other directions. By comparing the numbers and resources devoted to the promotion of these three ideals, with the numbers and resources available for the promotion of all vested interests dependent on a competitive order, we appreciate anew the depth of the crisis in which we are plunged.

What is needed above all at this time is a valid source of conviction that, whatever the immediate future may be, bright or dark, the reinforcement of universal truth stands behind the movement toward world order and peace, and that the opposition is in essence negative and will ultimately be overthrown. Conscious faith alone can turn the scale between evolution and revolution, between order and chaos.

PRINCIPLES OF BAHÁ'U'LLÁH

Bahá'u'lláh is the source of this conscious faith. His teachings transform political and economic problems into occasions for human virtue and love. A summary of the teachings will emphasize the following essential truths.

1. There is an organic cycle in human evolution, marked by the duration of the life of a religion, approximately one

thousand years. A social cycle begins with the appearance of a prophetic founder of religion, whose influence and teaching renews the inner life of man and releases a new wave of progress. Each cycle destroys the outworn beliefs and institutions of the former cycle and creates a civilization based on beliefs in closer conformity with actual human needs. This civilization in turn decays, with the passing of time, as human doctrines are substituted for the reality taught by the prophet, and must give way to a fresh conception of God.

2. In the past the influence of each founder of religion has been limited to one race or region by reason of the physical separation of the races and nations. The present cycle has worldwide influence and meaning. It upholds faith in the spiritual oneness of humanity and will accomplish the creation of an organic world order. As Bahá'u'lláh is the spiritual proof of the coming of a universal cycle, so the rise of science is its intellectual proof and evidence. The rise of science has made the definite cleavage between the age of competition and the age of co-operation. Science has drawn man up from his physical helplessness in nature, multiplied his powers and at the same time given him an entirely new degree of moral responsibility. If the old tribal morality persists, science will be a destroyer. Its forces can only be controlled by a united humanity striving for the general welfare and well-being.

3. Sectarian churches will be abandoned and replaced by a spiritual centre in each community devoted to meditation and prayer, without a professional clergy. Religious ideas and practices not in conformity with science are superstitions and will not survive. Not ritual and creed but the inspiration of the prophet's life and message is the foundation of religion. As science progresses, men will not fail to recognize that humanity has ever depended on the vision of love and brotherhood revealed by the prophets from age to age, and that they have the unique office of inspiring a higher capacity for life through conscious knowledge of the will of God. The prophet is the focal point of human evolution.

4. As the local community is dependent upon the national community, so the nation is dependent upon the community of nations. The theory of national sovereignty has been overthrown by the fact of economic interdependence; it should be discarded in political practice. Statesmen are responsible to the Creator for the protection of the people. They must take steps to create a world body on which alone complete sovereignty can be conferred. More essential than the fact that metals and products are distributed throughout the world, beyond the control of any one nation, is the fact that humanity is one organism and must have one law and one executive control. All morality is fulfilled in loyalty to mankind through the orderly processes of world government.

5. The law of the struggle for existence does not exist for man when he becomes conscious of his mental and spiritual powers. It is replaced by the higher law of co-operation.

Under this higher law the individual will enjoy a far larger status than that of passive political citizenship. His organic rights will include universal education and the means of livelihood. Local communities will be organized so as to give this status effect. Public administration will pass from partisan politics, which betray the people, to those who can regard office as a sacred trusteeship in which they can serve divine principles of justice and brotherhood. Income taxes are to be paid to the local community rather than the national state, which will give the community a secure material basis and enable it to provide the necessary agencies for the welfare and protection of the people. The national treasury is to receive its income from local communities rather than from individuals. The emphasis is thrown back upon the local community, where the issues of life are first raised and are first to be met.

The present national state, during the era of war, developed many agencies and instruments which will be unnecessary when an international state is established. The international state will enact statutes making for world order and progress.

6. Economic stability depends upon moral solidarity and the realization that wealth is the means and not the end of life, rather than upon the working out of any elaborate socialistic or communistic plan. The essential point is the rise of a new mind, a new spirit of co-operation and mutual help, not universal subservience to a formal system, the effect of which would be to remove all individual moral responsibility. Under conditions of co-operation and peace, the tragedy of unemployment could be transformed into the opportunity for leisure for cultural progress and personal development. Employees are to receive not only wages but also a fixed share of the profit of industry, as partners in a firm. The foundation of industry is agriculture, and first concern must be given those who live and work upon the land. Industry will become simpler as men attain a balance between being and doing.

Bahá'u'lláh also reveals a method or system of inheritances by which the handing down of great fortunes can be made to serve the community as a whole, without depriving the individual of a just measure of liberty. By this method, an inheritance is divided into proportionate parts for the surviving relatives, and significantly enough, teachers who have contributed to the deceased's character and development are given a share of the estate.

Another principle emphatically laid down is that loyalty to representative and just government is a requisite of the religious attitude toward society. No justification is given the view that ecclesiastical doctrines and policies can claim a higher loyalty than that rendered the civil state. Faith in God may not be controlled by the state; the state may not require the individual to betray his spiritual conviction; but apart from this, matters of public policy are wholly under government control.

7. Neither democracy nor aristocracy alone supplies the correct basis for society. Democracy is helpless against internal dissension; aristocracy survives by foreign aggression. A combination of both principles is necessary—the administration of affairs by the *élite* of mankind, elected by universal suffrage and

L

controlled by a world constitution embodying principles
having moral reality.

8. The spiritual basis of humanity consists in universal education—combining in every individual both economic and
cultural values, co-ordinating mind and emotion, and quickening the powers of the soul through knowledge of the tenets of
true religion. "The source of all knowledge,"as Bahá'u'lláh has
said, "is knowledge of God."

The basic social principle confirmed by Bahá'u'lláh is the law
of consultation. He has declared that the solution of all problems depends on the sincere meeting for discussion of all parties
to the question, and their willingness to abide by the decisions
so made. The spark of clashing opinion, as 'Abdu'l-Bahá has
said, reveals the truth. At present the "truth" of practically any
situation is obscured by prejudices and vested interests. From
the human point of view, truth must include all parties. The
new social organism cannot be anticipated in detail. It must
evolve.

9. At this time of transition between the old age of competition and the new age of co-operation, the very life of humanity
is in peril. It is a major stage in human history, a turning-point
in the evolution of mankind. Between spiritual ignorance,
nationalistic ambition, class strife, economic fear and greed,
tremendous forces are arrayed for another and fatal international war. Only a divinely-sent, providential power, an
influence like that of Christ, can avert the supreme catastrophe.
The world is in dire need of the conviction of kinship and
solidarity, of mutual co-operation and interdependence, of
common principles and a definite programme combining the
validity of religion with the aim and purpose of social science.

The bitter experiences of this century throw a revealing light
upon the statements made by 'Abdu'l-Bahá to public audiences
in Europe and America during 1911 and 1912. The following
quotations will serve to illustrate the character and scope of His
outlook, and indicate the manner in which He appealed to
humanity rather than to institutional values.

THE RELIGION OF GOD

"The body politic today is in need of a physician. It is similar
to a human body afflicted with severe ailments. A doctor diag-
noses the case and prescribes treatment. He does not prescribe,
however, until he has made the diagnosis. The disease which
afflicts the body politic is lack of love and absence of altruism.
In the hearts of men no real love is found and the condition is
such that unless their susceptibilities are quickened by some
power so that unity, love and accord may develop within
them, there can be no healing, no agreement among mankind.
Love and unity are the needs of the body politic today. Without
these there can be no progress or prosperity attained. Therefore
the friends of God must adhere to the power which will create
this love and unity in the hearts of the sons of men. Science
cannot cure the illness of the body politic. Science cannot
create amity and fellowship in human hearts. Neither can
patriotism nor racial allegiance effect a remedy. It must be
accomplished solely through the divine bounties and spiritual
bestowals which have descended from God in this day for that
purpose. This is an exigency of the times and the divine
remedy has been provided. The spiritual teachings of the religion of God alone can create this love, unity and accord in
human hearts." (June 8, 1912, at 309 West 78th Street, New
York City.)

THE BODY POLITIC

"Although the body politic is one family, yet because of
lack of harmonious relations some members are comfortable
and some in direct misery, some members are satisfied and
some members are hungry, some members are clothed in most
costly garments and some families are in need of food and
shelter. Why? Because this family (of mankind) lacks the
necessary reciprocity and symmetry. This household is not well
arranged. This household is not living under a perfect law. All
the laws which are legislated do not ensure happiness. They do
not provide comfort. Therefore a law must be given to this

family by means of which all the members will enjoy well-being and happiness." (September, 1912, at a meeting of Socialists, Montreal.)

SOCIALISM AND COMMUNISM

"The question of socialization is very important. It will not be solved by strikes for wages. All the governments of the world must be united and organize an assembly the members of which should be elected from the parliaments and the nobles of the nations. These must plan with utmost wisdom and power so that neither the capitalist may suffer from economic losses nor the labourers become needy. In the utmost moderation they should make the law, then announce to the public that the rights of the working people are to be strongly protected; also the rights of the capitalists are to be protected. When such a general plan is adopted by the will of both sides, should a strike occur, all the governments of the world collectively should resist it. Otherwise, the labour problem will lead to much destruction, especially in Europe. Terrible things will take place.

"The owners of properties, mines and factories should share their incomes with their employees and give a certain fair percentage of their products to their working men in order that the employees may receive, beside their wages, some of the general income of the factory, so that the employee may strive with his heart in the work." (Spoken in 1912 at the home of a government official, reported in *Star of the West*, vol. 13, page 231.)

"Lycurgus, king of Sparta, who lived long before the day of Christ, conceived the idea of absolute equality in government. He proclaimed laws by which all the people of Sparta were classified into certain divisions. . . . Lycurgus, in order to establish this for ever as a law, brought nine thousand grandees together, told them he was going upon a long journey and wished this form of government to remain effective until his return. They swore an oath to protect and preserve his law. He then left his kingdom, went into voluntary exile, and never returned. No man ever made such a sacrifice to ensure equality among his fellowmen. A few years passed and the whole system of government he had founded collapsed, although established upon such a wise and just basis.

"Difference of capacity in human individuals is fundamental. It is impossible for all to be alike, all to be equal, all to be wise. Bahá'u'lláh has revealed principles and laws which will accomplish the adjustment of varying human capacities." (July 1, 1912, at 309 West 78th Street, New York City.)

MATERIAL AND SPIRITUAL CIVILIZATION

"In the western world material civilization has attained the highest point of development but divine civilization was founded in the land of the East. The East must acquire material civilization from the West and the West must receive spiritual civilization from the East. This will establish a mutual bond. When these two come together, the world of humanity will present a glorious aspect and extraordinary progress will be achieved." (June 2, 1912, at Church of the Ascension, New York City.)

"While thousands are considering these questions, we have more essential purposes. The fundamentals of the whole economic condition are divine in nature and are associated with the world of the heart and spirit. This is fully explained in the Bahá'í teaching, and without knowledge of its principles no improvement in the economic state can be realized. . . . Economic questions are most interesting, but the power which moves, controls and attracts the hearts of men is the love of God." (July 23, 1912, at Hotel Victoria, Boston.)

THE SUPREME TRIBUNAL

"At present Universal Peace is a matter of great importance, but unity of conscience is essential, so that the foundation of this matter may become secure, its establishment firm and its edifice strong. . . . Although the League of Nations has been

brought into existence, yet it is incapable of establishing
Universal Peace. But the Supreme Tribunal which His Holiness
Bahá'u'lláh has described will fulfil this sacred task with the
utmost might and power. And His plan is this: that the national
assemblies of each country and nation—that is to say parliaments—should elect two or three persons who are the choicest
men of that nation, and are well informed concerning international laws and the relations between governments, and
aware of the essential needs of the world of humanity in this
day. The number of these representatives should be in proportion to the number of inhabitants of that country. The election
of these souls who are chosen by the national assembly, that is,
the parliament, must be confirmed by the upper house, the
congress and the cabinet and also by the president or monarch
so that these persons may be the elected ones of all the nation
and the government. From among these people the members
of the Supreme Tribunal will be elected, and all mankind will
thus have a share therein, for every one of these delegates is
fully representative of his nation. When the Supreme Tribunal
gives a ruling on any international question, either unanimously
or by majority rule, there will no longer be any pretext for the
plaintiff or ground of objection for the defendant. In case any
of the governments or nations, in the execution of the irrefutable
decision of the Supreme Tribunal, be negligent or dilatory, the
rest of the nations will rise up against it, because all the governments and nations of the world are supporters of this Supreme
Tribunal. Consider what a firm foundation this is! But by a
limited and restricted League the purpose will not be realized
as it ought and should." (December 17, 1919, in a letter written
to the Central Organization for a Durable Peace, The Hague.)

The Oneness of Reality

"The source of perfect unity and love in the world of human
existence is the bond and oneness of reality. When the divine
and fundamental reality enters human hearts and lives, it
conserves and protects all states and conditions of mankind,

establishing that intrinsic oneness of the world of humanity which can only come into being through the efficacy of the Holy Spirit. For the Holy Spirit is like unto the life in the human body, which blends all differences of parts and members in unity and agreement.

"Consider how numerous are these parts and members, but the oneness of the animating spirit of life unites them all in perfect combination. It establishes such a unity in the bodily organism that if any part is subjected to injury or becomes diseased all the other parts and functions sympathetically respond and suffer owing to the perfect oneness existing. Just as the human spirit of life is the cause of co-ordination among the various parts of the human organism, the Holy Spirit is the controlling cause of the unity and co-ordination of mankind. That is to say, the bond or oneness of humanity cannot be effectively established save through the power of the Holy Spirit, for the world of humanity is a composite body and the Holy Spirit is the animating principle of its life. . . .

"Today the greatest need of the world is the animating, unifying presence of the Holy Spirit. Until it becomes effective, penetrating and interpenetrating hearts and spirits, and until perfect reasoning faith shall be implanted in the minds of men, it will be impossible for the social body to be inspired with security and confidence. Nay, on the contrary, enmity and strife will increase day by day and the differences and divergences of nations will be woefully augmented. Continual additions to the armies and navies of the world will be made, and the fear and certainty of the great pandemic war—the war unparalleled in history—will be intensified." (September 16, 1912, at 5338 Kenmore Avenue, Chicago.)

"The most important principle of divine philosophy is the oneness of the world of humanity, the unity of mankind, the bond conjoining East and West, the tie of love which blends human hearts. . . . For thousands of years we have had bloodshed and strife. It is enough; it is sufficient. Now is the time to associate together in love and harmony.

"All the divine Manifestations have proclaimed the oneness of God and the unity of mankind. They have taught that men should love and mutually help each other in order that they might progress. Now if this conception of religion be true, its essential principle is the oneness of humanity. The fundamental truth of the Manifestations is peace. This underlies all religion, all justice. The divine purpose is that men should live in unity, concord and agreement and should love one another. Consider the virtues of the human world and realize that the oneness of humanity is the primary foundation of them all." (April 19, 1912, at Columbia University, New York City.)

THE DIVINE PROPHETS

"The holy Manifestations of God, the divine prophets, are the first teachers of the human race. They are universal educators and the fundamental principles they laid down are the causes and factors of the advancement of nations. Forms and imitations which creep in afterward are not conducive to that progress. On the contrary these are destroyers of human foundations established by the heavenly educators.

"Therefore there is need of turning back to the original foundation. The fundamental principles of the prophets are true and correct. The imitations and superstitions which have crept in are at wide variance with the original precepts and commands. His Holiness Bahá'u'lláh has revoiced and re-established the quintessence of the teachings of all the prophets setting aside the accessories and purifying religion from human interpretation." (May 3, 1912, at Hotel Plaza, Chicago.)

"Religion is the outer expression of the divine reality. Therefore it must be living, vitalized, moving and progressive. If it be without motion and non-progressive it is without the divine life; it is dead. The divine institutes are continuously active and evolutionary; therefore the revelation of them must be progressive and continuous." (May 24, 1912, at Unitarian Conference, Boston.)

"The divine Manifestations since the day of Adam have

striven to unite humanity so that all may be accounted as one soul. The function and purpose of a shepherd is to gather and not disperse his flock. The prophets of God have been divine shepherds of humanity. They have established a bond of love and unity among mankind, made scattered peoples one nation and wandering tribes a mighty kingdom. They have laid the foundation of the oneness of God and summoned all to Universal Peace. All these holy, divine Manifestations are one. They have served one God, promulgated the same truth, founded the same institutions and reflected the same light. Their appearances have been successive and correlated; each one has announced and extolled the one who was to follow and all laid the foundation of reality. They summoned and invited the people to love and made the human world a mirror of the World of God. Therefore the divine religions they established have one foundation; their teachings, proofs and evidences are one; in name and form they differ but in reality they agree and are the same." (May 28, 1912, at Metropolitan Temple, New York City.)

THE DIVINE SPIRIT OF THE AGE

"That which was applicable to human needs during the early history of the race could neither meet nor satisfy the demands of this day and period of newness and consummation. . . . From every standpoint the world of humanity is undergoing a reformation. The laws of former governments and civilizations are in process of revision, scientific ideas and theories are developing and advancing to meet a new range of phenomena. . . . This is the cycle of maturity and reformation in religion as well. Dogmatic imitations of ancestral beliefs are passing. They have been the axis around which religion revolved but now are no longer useful; on the contrary, in this day they have become the cause of human degradation and hindrance.

"Heavenly teachings applicable to the advancement in human conditions have been revealed in this merciful age. This reformation and renewal of the fundamental reality of religion constitute the true and outworking spirit of modernism, the unmistakable light of the world, the manifest effulgence of the Word of God, the divine remedy for all human ailments and the bounty of eternal life to all mankind.

"His Holiness Bahá'u'lláh, the Sun of Truth, has dawned from the horizon of the Orient, flooding all regions with the light and life which will never pass away. His teachings which embody the divine spirit of the age and are applicable to this period of maturity in the life of the human world are: The oneness of the world of humanity; The protection and guidance of the Holy Spirit; The foundation of all religion is one; Religion must be the cause of unity; Religion must accord with science and reason; Independent investigation of truth; Equality between men and women; The abandonment of prejudice; Universal Peace; Universal education; A universal language; Solution of the economic problem; An International Tribunal.

"Everyone who truly seeks and justly reflects will admit that the teachings of the present day emanating from mere human sources and authority are the cause of difficulty and disagreement amongst mankind, the very destroyers of humanity, whereas the teachings of Bahá'u'lláh are the very healing of the sick world, the remedy for every need and condition. In them may be found the realization of every desire and aspiration, the cause of the happiness of the world of humanity, the stimulus and illumination of mentality, the impulse for advancement and uplift, the basis of unity for all nations, the fountain source of love amongst mankind, the centre of agreement, the means of love and harmony, the one bond which will unite the East and the West." (November 17, 1912, at Genealogical Hall, New York City.)

IMMEASURABLE UPWARD PROGRESS

"In this present cycle there will be an evolution in civilization unparalleled in the history of the world. The world of humanity has heretofore been in the stage of infancy; now it is approaching maturity. Just as the individual human organism, having attained the period of maturity, reaches its fullest degree of physical strength and ripened intellectual faculties, so that in one year of this ripened period there is witnessed an unprecedented measure of development, likewise the world of humanity in this cycle of its completeness and consummation will realize an immeasurable upward progress." (April 21, 1912, 1219 Connecticut Avenue, Washington, D.C.)

"According to an intrinsic law, all phenomena of being attain to a summit and degree of consummation, after which a new order and condition is established. As the instruments and science of war have reached the degree of thoroughness and proficiency, it is hoped that the transformation of the human world is at hand and that in the coming centuries all the energies and inventions of man will be utilized in promoting the interests of peace and brotherhood. . . .

"The powers of earth cannot withstand the privileges and bestowals which God has ordained for this great and glorious century. Peace is a need and exigency of the time. Man can withstand anything except that which is divinely intended and indicated for the time and its requirements. Now, praise be to God, in all countries of the world peace lovers are to be found and these principles are being spread among mankind, especially in this country. Praise be to God, this thought is prevailing and souls are continually arising as defenders of the oneness of humanity, endeavouring to assist and establish international peace. There is no doubt that this wonderful democracy will be able to realize it and the banner of international agreement will be unfurled here to spread onward and outward among all the nations of the world." (May 13, 1912, at meeting of New York Peace Society, Hotel Astor.)

Though these quotations are but a few fragments of the complete text, nevertheless they reveal the outline of a religious philosophy which penetrates to the soul of history and explains the strange disorders tormenting the present age. In Bahá'u'lláh a spiritual sun has arisen above the darkness of the world, a touchstone dividing the false and the true, compelling a final struggle between the forces of materialism and those of reality. He evokes a new and universal loyalty which alone can sustain the burden of world administration and develop in men their latent higher powers. He reinforces the hope of peace and the desire for social justice, by the assurance that they emanate from the very order of human evolution. Enshrined in the teaching of Bahá'u'lláh is the principle of a worldwide social structure, an organism fitted to the present needs of humanity. His teachings universalize the teachings given by prophets in the past.

THE BAHÁ'Í FAITH AND LABOUR

THE TURBULENCE agitating human affairs today was foreseen in the Bahá'í writings and depicted as that state of anarchy which disrupts the old order when it resists the spirit of progress and change. The immeasurable new possibilities of human life today call for world solidarity, a world mind and world institutions. A renewal of faith, vitalizing the new and greater social concept, alone can transform such chaos into a peaceful society. "Unification of the whole of mankind is the hallmark of the state which human society is now approaching. Unity of family, of tribe, of city-state, and nation, have been successively attempted and fully established. World Unity is the goal toward which a harassed humanity is striving. Nation-building has come to an end. A world growing to maturity, must abandon this fetish, recognize the oneness and wholeness of human relationships, and establish once and for all the machinery that can best incarnate this fundamental principle of its life."[1]

This new social idea involves the development of a world economy as the essential condition for the achievement of security, justice and moral liberty by the individual or the group. No one nation or empire or class, the Bahá'í teachings insist, can today operate a sound, self-centred economy, for no political entity is today self-sufficient. Whatever social policy is adopted in denial of the truth of interdependence, it remains an expedient subject to pressure beyond control. It became apparent a generation ago that people must choose between commonwealth and war.

A sound economy begins with the individual. The Bahá'í concept of labour is endowed with a spiritual meaning not

[1] Shoghi Effendi, *The Unfoldment of World Civilization.*

subject to exploitation by any special interest. It binds the individual by conscience to his own unique and God-given destiny and provides the basis for his right relationship to the whole community.

Labour is made a sacred obligation for all. "It is incumbent on every one ... to engage in some occupation, such as arts, trades and the like. ... Occupy yourselves with what will profit yourselves and others. ... The most despised of men before God, is he who sits and begs."[1] "If a man engages with all his power in the acquisition of a science or in the perfection of an art, it is as though he has been worshipping God in the churches and temples."[2]

The importance of the creative element in the individual is strongly emphasized. Appeal is made to the elemental instinct for perfection. What one does is the record of his spiritual life on earth—the real "business" of living. Any system which denies the individual his right to the fruit of existence intervenes between him and the world of spirit and can claim no moral sanction for its eventual outcome in an impoverished society. The individual himself cannot disclaim all responsibility for abandoning that right. The source of all security and justice lies in obedience to the laws of being. Awareness of truth confers vision, and acceptance of moral obligation produces integrity. Through vision and integrity every social problem can be brought to solution. "The fundamentals of the whole economic condition are divine in nature and are associated with the world of the heart and spirit."[3]

Materialism, accepting the theory that human life is inevitably and for ever a struggle for existence, and recognizing only force as the means to suppress the struggle, emerges as the real and ultimate enemy to be overcome wherever its influence is manifested. "Man ... should be free and emancipated from the captivity of the world of nature; for as long as man is

[1] Bahá'u'lláh, *Tablet of Glad Tidings.*
[2] 'Abdu'l-Bahá, *Bahá'í World Faith*, pp. 377-8
[3] 'Abdu'l-Bahá, Talk in Boston, Mass., 1912.

captive to the law of nature he is a ferocious animal, as the struggle for existence is one of the exigencies of the world of nature."[1]

As long as social sovereignty remains partly national and partly international in character and influence, the problem of the existing inequitable distribution of wealth will continue to provoke conflicting theories and methods of solution. Materialism in an individual is a personal evil and a private misfortune. Materialism in the state or powerful group represents public disaster. It is a force generated to dominate its own people. Communism and other theories of equality attainable through violence are repudiated by the Bahá'í teachings because they are in opposition to the very nature of order in society. From moral failure their compulsions deceive the mind to acquiesce in the employment of vital human powers and instincts for non-human ends. A momentum of revolution has been set up which can survive only as long as it can continue to pervert and destroy. The principle defined in the Bahá'í teachings is voluntary sharing of wealth—a moral standard of human relations. "This voluntary sharing is greater than equality, and consists in this, that man should not prefer himself to others, but rather should sacrifice his life and property for others. But this should not be introduced by coercion so that it becomes a law and man is compelled to follow it."[2] "Equality is attained through force, but benevolence is a good deed performed voluntarily. . . . For compulsion breeds discord, and disrupts the order in human affairs."[3]

If this principle seems weak and ineffective, it is because the sense of common community has failed for lack of a vital religious motive. Men have been subordinated to an industrial process conceived to be a system governed by its own laws and rules. "The principal cause of these difficulties," the Bahá'í teachings remarked more than forty years ago, "lies in the laws

---

[1] 'Abdu'l-Bahá. Letter to Central Organization for a Durable Peace, The Hague, 1919.
[2] ibid.
[3] 'Abdu'l-Bahá, Letter to Andrew Carnegie, 1913.

of the present civilization; for they lead to a small number of individuals accumulating incomparable fortunes, beyond their needs, while the greater number remains destitute, stripped and in the greatest misery. This is contrary to justice, to humanity, to equity. . . .

"Then rules and laws should be established to regulate the excessive fortunes of certain private individuals, and limit the misery of millions of the poor masses; thus a certain moderation would be obtained. However, absolute equality is just as impossible, for absolute equality in fortunes, honours, commerce, agriculture, industry would end in a want of comfort, in discouragement, in disorganization of the means of existence, and in universal disappointment; the order of the community would be quite destroyed. Thus there is a great wisdom in the fact that equality is not imposed by law; it is, therefore, preferable for moderation to do its work. The main point is, by means of laws and regulations to hinder the constitution of the excessive fortunes of certain individuals, and to protect the essential needs of the masses."

The partnership of capital and labour was upheld in the same statement. "Laws and regulations should be established which would permit the workmen to receive from the factory owner their wages and a share in the fourth or fifth part of the profits, according to the wants of the factory; or in some other way the body of workmen and the manufacturers should share equitably the profits and advantages. . . .

"It would be well, with regard to the social rights of the manufacturers, workmen and artisans, that laws be established giving moderate profits to manufacturers, and to workmen the necessary means of existence and security for the future. . . . In the same way, the workmen should no longer rebel and revolt, nor demand beyond their rights. . . . The mutual rights of both associated parties will be fixed and established according to custom by just and impartial laws. . . . The intervention of courts of justice and of the government in difficulties pending between manufacturers and workmen is legal, for the reason that current affairs between workmen and manufacturers cannot be compared with ordinary affairs between private persons, which do not concern the public, and with which the government should not occupy itself."[1]

Through science this age has acquired unlimited capacity to produce wealth in terms of shelter, food and all necessities, and also of means for the mental and cultural progress of individuals and peoples. But science, like industry, cannot define its own social code nor exercise control over the results of its own activity. These resources, which are new and providential, have come to humanity as a sacred trust. Misused, they have multiplied insecurity and mortgaged the nations. They are like trees whose fruit is bitter and poisonous until fully ripened and mature. A technical economy matures and ripens not through its science but through its spiritual enlightenment and its common loyalty to a common standard of human rights. The more efficient the tool, the greater must be the skill of the user.

"A world community in which all economic barriers will have been permanently demolished and the interdependence of Capital and Labour definitely recognized; in which the clamour of religious fanaticism and strife will have been for ever stilled; in which the flame of racial animosity will have been finally extinguished; in which a single code of international law—the product of the considered judgment of the world's federated representatives—shall have as its sanction the instant and coercive intervention of the combined forces of the federated units; and finally a world community in which the fury of a capricious and militant nationalism will have been transmuted into an abiding consciousness of world citizenship —such indeed, appears, in its broadest outline, the Order anticipated by Bahá'u'lláh, an Order that shall come to be regarded as the fairest fruit of a slowly-maturing age."[2]

---

[1] 'Abdu'l-Bahá, *Some Answered Questions*, Ch. LXXVIII.
[2] Shoghi Effendi, *The Goal of a New World Order*.

M

THE BAHÁ'Í TEMPLE

THE COMPLETION of the Bahá'í House of Worship discloses a physical edifice impressive in size, striking in architecture, and superb in its clear white surface carved to the pattern of symbolic design.

In appearance the structure suggests to the western mind an oriental influence. To the easterner it conveys the effect of occidental tradition. The Bahá'í Temple blends and harmonizes, without artificial effort, many of the creative elements which characterize the historical cultures of mankind. What is familiar acquires new significance by association with what has been remote and strange. The essential spirit of this edifice is too universal to be confined within the form and mould of any race or creed.

Here the utilitarian function of structure has become aesthetically fulfilled in the achievement of a means suitable for unified worship of the one true God. A sense of the living cosmos attaches to the building, as if the architect had striven, with physical material, to encompass a holy place, and had learned measure and proportion, height and depth, stillness and motion, by observation of the flight of suns and stars through the heavenly world. Outwardly the House of Worship reflects a passionate, yet reverent spiritual reality, embodying a fullness of welcome, a certitude of truth, and an integrity of peace which the soul of religion contains before faith is darkened by doctrine and narrowed by creed.

FEATURES OF ITS DESIGN

Certain important elements of design in harmonious relationship compose the dynamic nature of the unity which this kingly jewel of temples exemplifies.

The edifice rests upon a great platform, circular in shape, surrounded by eighteen ascending steps. From this foundation rises a nine-sided architectural unit, the main storey, each side constituting an entrance arch buttressed by pylons or towers. The nine symmetrical sides form a series of concave arcs intersecting the line of the circle marked by the towers. This main storey becomes, in its turn, a platform supporting the gallery, the clerestory and the dome. The gallery unit, likewise nine-sided, sets back from the circumference of the main storey. It repeats the effect of the entrance arches below in its series of nine window arches, but the nine smaller towers of this level do not coincide vertically with the nine pylons below. They rise at points midway between the lower pylons, and their coincidence is with the perpendicular lines formed by the nine ribs which spring from the base of the clerestory to meet above the top of the dome. Clerestory and dome, set back from the outer line of the gallery, form circles and not nonagons, their circumference being divided into nine convex arcs by the ribs. The dome itself is a hemisphere, but the great ribs meeting above it transform the effect of finality and resignation emanating from domed structures into the upward thrust of aspiration fulfilled in answered prayer.

In the solution of the unique problem set for him in designing this house of worship of a world faith, the architect has been less the conventional draughtsman than the sculptor. One feels that his material has not been arranged by thought but subdued by will. He has wrestled with titans of atheism and anarchy; he has struggled through jungles of materialism. It is in the essence of spiritual victory that he achieved this structure of massive weight, immovable power, patterned motion and soaring altitude, to provide a shrine for the mention of God.

Having designed the structure, the architect then proceeded to treat each wall as if it were a facet for the transmission of radiant light from the sun to the interior, and from illumination inside the temple to the world at night. The outer surface is, in reality, a series of patterned windows, for the physical function of wall has been transferred to pylon, tower, rib and column. These elements carry the weight. The surface between these elements can therefore become a medium for light and not its interference. This intention has been realized through the development of architectural concrete, a process by which in plastic condition a mixture of white quartz and cement has been poured into moulds made from hand-carved models, emerging as units of a surface hard and enduring as granite, clear in texture, and bearing a design delicate as lace.

SYMBOL OF A NEW ERA

The Bahá'í Temple at Wilmette, Illinois, has not arisen as the meeting place of a local congregation. It is the central shrine and house of worship of the followers of Bahá'u'lláh in North America. In the western world, this edifice is the first public expression made by the believers of the creative energy and spiritual aims of the Faith of Bahá'u'lláh. Its construction, however, has been made possible by the contributions given by Bahá'ís of Europe, Asia and Africa, Australia and New Zealand, as well as of the United States, Canada, and South America. The undertaking has been a world project when one realizes that the Bahá'í community of East and West is representative, in the racial and religious background of its members, of the diverse families of mankind. The period of time covered by the undertaking, from the original intention to the completion of the structure and its exterior decoration, has been about forty years.

During this period of time the nature of man's collective life has been transformed. The authority and control of ancient religion over human destiny has failed. Royal and imperial thrones have toppled to the dust. Aggressive social philosophies, nurtured in class conflict intensified by the industrial revolution, have become the creed and hope of millions of men. National sovereignty, the particular spiritual achievement of the old era, the most potent instrument for internal order yet created, has

encountered the world spirit of the new cycle, refusing so far
to subdue itself to the higher sovereignty of truth. Under the
impact of two international wars, a major depression and many
domestic upheavals, the claim to self-sufficient power and
independent policy has jeopardized the very life of mankind.
The Bahá'í House of Worship, built by those who knew the
destiny of these years as clearly foretold in the Bahá'í sacred
writings, has reflected the spirit of the new era arising amidst
the agony of the old.

For the Healing of All the World

The nine selected utterances of Bahá'u'lláh carved above the
entrances of the Temple reveal its fundamental meaning in the
life of our age:—

"The earth is but one country; and mankind its citizens."

"The best beloved of all things in My sight is Justice; turn
not away therefrom if thou desirest Me."

"My love is My stronghold; he that entereth therein is safe
and secure."

"Breathe not the sins of others so long as thou art thyself a
sinner."

"Thy heart is My home; sanctify it for My descent."

"I have made death a messenger of joy to thee; wherefore
dost thou grieve?"

"Make mention of Me on My earth that in My heaven I may
remember thee."

"O rich ones on earth! The poor in your midst are My trust;
guard ye My trust."

"The source of all learning is the knowledge of God, exalted
be His glory."

The Bahá'í Temple expresses the renewal of religion. It
realizes a faith which relates the soul to a universal, a revealed
and a divine truth wherein all human beings, of whatever race,
class or creed, can meet and share the true equality emanating
from their common dependence upon God. It serves a teaching
which goes beyond all the social philosophies to make possible

a world order capable not only of co-ordinating and guiding economic effort but also of safeguarding and fostering the highest qualities of man. Bahá'u'lláh declared the oneness of mankind, a spiritual creation inaugurating the universal era of knowledge, justice and peace which ancient Prophets foretold and promised the people would come.

"There can be no doubt whatever that the peoples of the world," He has written, "of whatever race or religion, derive their inspiration from one heavenly Source and are the subjects of one God." The theme unfolds in these clear, majestic truths —"The utterance of God is a lamp, whose light is these words: Ye are the fruits of one tree, and the leaves of one branch. Deal ye one with another in the utmost love and harmony. . . . So powerful is the light of unity that it can illuminate the whole earth !" "The well-being of mankind, its peace and security, are unattainable unless and until its unity is firmly established. This unity can never be achieved so long as the counsels which the Pen of the Most High hath revealed are suffered to pass unheeded." It sweeps to its fulfilment in this passage taken from Bahá'u'lláh's message written to Queen Victoria of England from His prison in 'Akká, Palestine, more than eighty years ago: "That which the Lord hath ordained as the sovereign remedy and mightiest instrument for the healing of all the world is the union of all its peoples in one universal Cause, one common Faith." [Written about 1870.]

THE REAL TEMPLE IS THE WORD

'Abdu'l-Bahá, eldest son of Bahá'u'lláh, and Centre of His Covenant, travelled in America during 1912, proclaiming the Bahá'í teachings and promulgating the principles of universal peace. On one occasion He addressed a national gathering of Bahá'ís held at Chicago in the interests of this Temple. "Among the institutes of the Holy Books," 'Abdu'l-Bahá said, "is that of the foundation of places of worship. That is to say, an edifice or temple is to be built in order that humanity might find a place of meeting, and this is to be conducive to unity and fellowship among them. The real temple is the very Word of God; for to it all humanity must turn and it is the centre of unity for all mankind. It is the collective centre, the cause of accord and communion of hearts, the sign of the solidarity of the human race, the source of life eternal. Temples are the symbols of the divine uniting force, so that when people gather there in the House of God they may recall the fact that the law has been revealed for them and that the law is to unite them. They will realize that just as this temple was founded for the unification of mankind, the law preceding and creating it came forth in the manifest Word. . . . That is why His Holiness Bahá'u'lláh has commanded that a place of worship be built for all the religionists of the world; that all religions, races and sects may come together within its universal shelter; that the proclamation of the oneness of mankind shall go forth from its open courts of holiness; the announcement that humanity is the servant of God and that all are submerged in the ocean of His mercy. It is the Mashriqu'l-Adhkár.[1]

"The world of existence may be likened to this Temple and place of worship; for just as the external world is a place where the people of all races and colours, varying faiths, denominations and conditions come together, just as they are submerged in the same sea of divine favours, so likewise all may meet under the dome of the Mashriqu'l-Adhkár and adore the one God in the same spirit of truth; for the ages of darkness have passed away and the century of light has come."

For many persons universality in religion has been difficult to grasp. Its essential simplicity has proved elusive. They consider that elaborate complication is required, as if universality were obtained by adding together all things that are not universal. Thus the view arose at one time that the Bahá'í House of Worship when completed would house the shrines and invite the ceremonies and worship of diverse sects and creeds, arguing that tolerance of differences represents the final and utmost victory of divine truth on earth. The Bahá'í

[1] Persian word meaning "Source of the mention of God."

Faith, having no professional clergy, no ritualistic service, but maintaining that one's life is one's practice of faith, preserves the universality which came into being by divine creation in the Revelation of Bahá'u'lláh unadulterated by sectarian influence. The Bahá'í recognizes the sublime truth that revealed religions are fulfilled, not by the perpetuation of creeds and sects, but by transformation into the later and larger Revelation.

UNIVERSALITY OF WORSHIP

The Guardian of the Faith, Shoghi Effendi, has plainly set forth the nature of the Bahá'í House of Worship in this passage of a letter addressed to the American Bahá'ís in 1929.

"It should be borne in mind that the central edifice of the Mashriqu'l-Adhkár, round which in the fullness of time shall cluster such institutions of social service as shall afford relief to the suffering, sustenance to the poor, shelter to the wayfarer, solace to the bereaved, and education to the ignorant, should be regarded, apart from these Dependencies, as a House solely designed and entirely dedicated to the worship of God in accordance with the few yet definitely prescribed principles established by Bahá'u'lláh. . . . It should not be inferred, however, from this general statement that the interior of the central Edifice itself will be converted into a conglomeration of religious services conducted along lines associated with the traditional procedure obtaining in churches, mosques, synagogues, and other temples of worship. Its various avenues of approach, all converging towards the central Hall beneath its dome, will not serve as admittance to those sectarian adherents of rigid formulae and man-made creeds, each bent, according to his way, to observe his rites, recite his prayers, perform his ablutions, and display the particular symbols of his faith, within separately defined sections of Bahá'u'lláh's Universal House of Worship. . . . The central House of Bahá'í worship, enshrined within the Mashriqu'l-Adhkár, will gather within its chastened walls, in a serenely spiritual atmosphere, only those who, dis-

The Bahá'í House of Worship, Symbol of a New Era, Wilmette, Illinois
"... *the ages of darkness have passed away and the century of light has come.*"
—'Abdu'l-Bahá

carding for ever the trappings of elaborate and ostentatious ceremony, are willing worshippers of the one true God, as manifested in this age in the Person of Bahá'u'lláh.

"To them will the Mashriqu'l-Adhkár symbolize the fundamental verity underlying the Bahá'í Faith, that religious truth is not absolute but relative, that Divine Revelation is not final but progressive. Theirs will be the conviction that an all-loving and ever-watchful Father Who, in the past, and at various stages in the evolution of mankind, has sent forth His Prophets as the Bearers of His Message and the Manifestations of His Light to mankind, cannot at this critical period of their civilization withhold from His children the Guidance which they sorely need amid the darkness which has beset them, and which neither the light of science nor that of human intellect and wisdom can succeed in dissipating. And thus having recognized in Bahá'u'lláh the source whence this celestial light proceeds, they will irresistibly feel attracted to seek the shelter of His House, and congregate therein, unhampered by ceremonials and unfettered by creeds, to render homage to the one true God, the Essence and Orb of eternal Truth, and to exalt and magnify the name of His Messengers and Prophets Who, from time immemorial even unto our day, have, under divers circumstances and in varying measure, mirrored forth to a dark and wayward world the light of heavenly Guidance."

FACILITIES FOR SOCIAL SERVICE

In the foregoing explanation the Guardian of the Bahá'í Faith refers to a number of institutions of social service which will be associated with the completed House of Worship. In the Mashriqu'l-Adhkár the modern world has been given an embodiment of spiritual truth in its maturity and power. The Bahá'í House of Worship is to have a direct relation to a number of other buildings which are to be constructed in accordance with the directions clearly set forth by 'Abdu'l-Bahá:

"The Mashriqu'l-Adhkár must have nine sides, doors, fountains, paths, gateways, columns and gardens, with the ground floor, galleries and domes, and in design and construction it must be beautiful. The mystery of the edifice is great and cannot be unveiled yet, but its erection is the most important undertaking of this Day.

"The Ma__sh__riqu'l-A__dh__kar has important accessories, which are accounted of the basic foundations. These are, school for orphan children, hospital and dispensary for the poor, home for the incapacitated, college for higher scientific education, and hospice. . . . When these institutions . . . are built, the doors will be opened to all the nations and religions. There will be absolutely no line of demarcation drawn. Its charities will be dispensed irrespective of colour and race. Its gates will be flung wide open to mankind; prejudice towards none, love for all. The central building will be devoted to the purpose of prayer and worship. Thus . . . religion will become harmonized with science, and science will be the handmaid of religion, both showering their material and spiritual gifts on all humanity."

This is the new, the universal concept of religion which Bahá'u'lláh has revealed today: the source of faith is the Prophet, the Manifestation of God, not the man-made creed, doctrine, rite, ceremony or church, for the will and the love of God are conveyed to humanity in each age by His chosen and inspired Messenger; and the expression of faith is in direct service to human needs, sacrifice for the sake of world peace, and consecration to the cause of the oneness of mankind. Belief in a sectarian creed, and spiritual acceptance of only the fellow members of one's own sect, with indifference for the needs and rights of the souls of all others, no longer meet the need of a world perishing for lack of unity, and are not accepted as real faith by Bahá'u'lláh.

The Bahá'í House of Worship, in this larger ultimate meaning, discloses the coming of the universal truth able to connect, and unify, the world's agencies for religion and its agencies for humanitarian service, now dissociated and incapable of healing human ills. It joins them as one spirit permeating one body.

Without the body, the spirit of religion has no power to act; without the spirit, the body is lifeless. The Bahá'í teachings condemn passive worship on the one hand, and action without spiritual guidance on the other.

THE DOOR OF HOPE

The Bahá'í teachings create a religious society in which all human relations are transformed from social to spiritual problems.

The social problems of the age are predominantly political and economic. They are problems because human society is divided into nations each of which claims to be an end and a law unto itself, and into classes each of which has raised an economic theory to the level of a sovereign and exclusive principle. Nationality has become a condition which overrides the fundamental humanity of all the peoples concerned, asserting the superiority of political considerations over ethical and moral needs. Similarly, economic groups uphold and promote social systems without regard to the quality of human relationships experienced in relation to religion. But when human relationships are held to be political or social problems they are removed from the realm in which rational will can operate under the guidance of divine law. Only spiritual problems can be solved, for only those issues submitted to revealed truth are brought into the arena of unity. In essence, the fatal disruption of international relations arising from war and revolution is the visible sign that the instigator of strife seized a political instrument to express an action contravening spiritual truth and law. Outside that truth and law there is no solution. The result of violent onslaught is eventual ruin.

That is why, when faith weakens and conscience grows blind, the world falls into strife and confusion; for the instigator of violence does not bear the entire responsibility of the war. He could not hope to precipitate overturn for power and profit unless the moral force of the rest of the world was indifferent or divided. At such times, when the way is darkened, the

Prophet returns to mankind, renewing the law and extending the dominion of truth. Those who still believe that the world can attain lasting world order, security and peace, without the unity of conscience produced by mutual faith, fall behind the march of destiny together with those who protest that no social form greater than the nation is needed to safeguard vital interests of the race throughout future time. Spiritual and social evolution have characterized the whole course of human history to this hour. Whoever denies the possibility of one organic religion and one organic social order for humanity, denies the movement of life itself and places his own limitations upon the will of God. For the man of true faith, however, it is enough to recall the ancient prayer which invoked the victory of the divine will on earth as in heaven.

No one can close the door of hope which 'Abdu'l-Bahá flung open in these words addressed to a public audience in America during 1912:

"Religion is the outer expression of the divine reality. Therefore it must be living, vitalized, moving and progressive. If it be without motion and non-progressive it is without the divine life; it is dead. The divine institutes are continuously active and evolutionary; therefore the revelation of them must be progressive and continuous. All things are subject to re-formation. This is a century of life and renewal. Sciences and arts, industry and invention have been reformed. Law and ethics have been reconstituted, reorganized. The world of thought has been regenerated.

"Will the despotism of former governments answer the call for freedom which has risen from the heart of humanity in this cycle of illumination? It is evident that no vital results are now forthcoming from the customs, institutions and standpoints of the past. In view of this, shall blind imitations of ancestral forms and theological interpretations continue to guide and control the religious life and spiritual development of humanity today? Shall man, gifted with the power of reason, unthinkingly follow and adhere to dogma, creeds and hereditary beliefs which will not bear the analysis of reason in this century of effulgent reality?

"From the seed of reality, religion has grown into a tree which has put forth leaves and branches, blossoms and fruit. After a time this tree has fallen into a condition of decay. The leaves and blossoms have withered and perished; the tree has become stricken and fruitless. It is not reasonable that man should hold to the old tree, claiming that its life forces are undiminished, its fruit unequalled, its existence eternal. The seed of reality must be sown again in human hearts in order that a new tree may grow therefrom and new divine fruits refresh the world. By this means the nations and peoples now divergent in religion will be brought into unity, imitations will be forsaken and a universal brotherhood in the reality itself will be established. Warfare and strife will cease among mankind; all will be reconciled as servants of God."

THE MISSION OF PEACE

The final meaning associated with the Bahá'í Temple bears upon the means of attaining world order and universal peace. The location of the House of Worship in the central heart of North America is not less important than its architectural design.

The coming of 'Abdu'l-Bahá to America in 1912 represented the working out of His clear vision of the events and conditions which were to culminate in the establishment of peace on earth. In the process of attainment, North America has been endowed by destiny with the sublime mission of leadership among the nations. On many occasions, and in weighty words, 'Abdu'l-Bahá explained this mission to the American people. The present world outlook, and the constructive social vision, of America proceeds, directly and indirectly, from the truths which He expounded in daily meetings and interviews held for nine months in 1912. He addressed large audiences in churches of many denominations, in synagogues, universities, liberal clubs and peace societies. In these talks He created the

programme and policy which leading individuals and institutions have taken over and are now promoting without full
realization of its spiritual source.

The Bahá'í House of Worship preserves the vital truth
which 'Abdu'l-Bahá conveyed as the most important element
of His message, but which has been neglected by a generation
which came to believe that public policy, if good and helpful,
will prevail by its own impetus. What 'Abdu'l-Bahá pointed
out as the essential condition is the power of the Holy Spirit
flowing through the Manifestation. The Mashriqu'l-Adhkár is
the monument raised by the Bahá'ís to Bahá'u'lláh, and not
merely a public testimonal to a system of liberal truths.

"The body of the human world," 'Abdu'l-Bahá declared,
"is sick. Its remedy and healing will be the oneness of the kingdom of humanity. Its life is the Most Great Peace. Its illumination and quickening is love. Its happiness the attainment of
spiritual perfections. It is My wish and hope that in the bounties
and favours of the Blessed Perfection, i.e. Bahá'u'lláh, we may
find a new life, acquire a new power and attain to a wonderful
and supreme source of energy so that the Most Great Peace of
divine intention shall be established upon the foundations of
the unity of the world of men with God. May the love of God
be spread from this city, from this meeting, to all the surrounding countries. Nay, may America become the distributing
centre of spiritual enlightenment and all the world receive this
heavenly blessing. For America has developed powers and capa-
bilities greater and more wonderful than other nations."

A Temple which is not only the symbol but also a proof of
so many spiritual truths is more than an architectural landmark. The Bahá'ís hope that it will lead a host of seekers to
investigate the teachings of Bahá'u'lláh.

GREATER THAN ANY NATION

IN OUR yet unsuccessful pursuit of universal peace, we have uncovered certain conditions, certain obstacles and requisites far beyond the capacity of the resources which so far have been publicly devoted to the cause of peace to meet. There are five of these conditions or requisites which summarized, provide a rational basis for consideration of the spirit and programme of the Faith of Bahá'u'lláh.

The first condition is that universal peace is not an optional policy nor a deferable ideal. In 1919 when the nations were given their first supreme opportunity to lay the basis of universal peace, a great majority of the peoples of all lands were not yet awakened to the dire menace of the disorder that has since overtaken mankind, and therefore they felt justification in maintaining the attitude that universal peace, while it might be a most desirable and worthy ideal, could be deferred as a practicable policy until some later and more convenient time. The result was, in that prevalent atmosphere, that those who strove for a peace settlement at Versailles created a League of Nations which was expected to be a strong contribution to international peace, but which possessed a structure leaving to each participating nation the right to make its own vital choice at every crucial point. In other words, the majority of peoples considered that world peace was a deferable ideal and an optional policy.

Today we realize that it is rather a question of saving a household given over to a consuming flame or finding the ways and means to prevent a flood from overwhelming the city of man's life. We do not defer action when we realize an emergency of that type. Nor can we defer action in relation to universal peace, when we realize with every faculty of our being that the dislocation of the life of the nations, the races, and the classes has brought about a condition which can lead to even greater destruction than was achieved in the two World Wars.

The second requisite is that peace cannot be a partial or a limited affair. We cannot establish peace for two or three nations or peoples and leave outside that realm another world of darkness while retaining the blessing of peace for those within.

Peace is universal and peace is organic and if, in the world today, we say that such and such a people or nation cannot be permitted to have association as equals with the other nations and peoples of the world, we are like a physician who considers his work is done if seven-eighths of his patient is healthy while one-eighth of the organism is seriously infected, and who thinks that somehow he can isolate the infection so that it will not seep into the rest of the organism. The condition of health for peoples and nations comes into being when there is a true world order in which all the nations and peoples are invited to join.

Any nation which will accept that invitation and endeavour sincerely to live up to the terms of its association with other nations for universal peace, that nation has been forgiven by God Himself for any of its historic errors, sins or crimes; because the determining point is that if we have a sense of suspicion and aloofness which prevents us from co-operating with others on terms of equality, we disclose our unfitness for the association. But if we are ready to participate and make our contribution to the one ideal, then it means that somehow we have attained a condition which others may recognize as one of fitness to work with them.

Therefore, let us not overlook this requisite that universal peace must embrace the peoples and nations of the entire world, and it cannot be a privilege and a superiority of North America or Europe or any other limited area of mankind.

The third condition or requisite is that universal peace cannot be produced by any international body possessing less authority and sovereignty than any or all of the present national states. That was the fatal weakness of the League of Nations. They used the term "peace," but they did not create a world. They retained the separate and exclusive national units. They retained them because none would share the sovereignty of their nation and set up a higher sovereignty for mankind.

The world is greater than any nation and mankind is greater than any nation or people. Therefore, this requisite of peace is of vital consequence because it means that we cannot have in this world any real and valid hope that our ideal of peace has been achieved until the nations and peoples have created a world sovereignty which shall be supreme and from which every nation shall derive a secondary and dependent sovereignty adequate for its domestic affairs. The work done at San Francisco did not produce this fundamental requisite of international peace.

International peace will remain elusive if whatever international body is set up functions only through political channels, for these remain neutral to the fundamental claims of economics, social philosophy, culture and religion. The time has passed when we can isolate aspects of reality, and by giving them separate terminology and organization consider that we have bounded off that realm of reality and made it immune to influences from outside. We cannot have an abiding political structure which is not fully superior to the economic order of the people over which it has jurisdiction.

We cannot have a world sovereignty until we have in that body not only the authority but the power and the capacity to bring together all competitive classes, all diverse philosophies of living, all unrelated claims, from whatever source they arise, and judge them according to the new world standard, approving those things that are of benefit to all humanity and preventing the further operation of those things that exalt one people or nation or class above the others and so make for a new dislocation in the life of mankind. Universal peace implies one standard of truth and justice to which all human affairs

N

can be referred on the practical basis of that which is most useful to world order, and those things that are useful will be the economics or the social philosophy of our future years.

The last requisite is a new spirit in man himself. Whatever type of international structure is raised up to promote and sustain universal peace, no matter how perfect its constitution may be, no matter how complete its statement of functions and purposes, no matter how many and intricate may be its service organizations, it will not have effective life unless there is a regeneration of human beings themselves.

We cannot find a substitute for the qualities and the attributes and the virtues of the human soul. We cannot produce a corporation and endow it with our virtue and become immune, if in the achievement of its corporate purpose that body which we have established contravenes the fundamental moral law. We cannot have universal peace without the conception of a world, a world organism. We cannot have a world organism without world men and women.

Now the world is full of national men and women, and that is why we have strife and war because national men and women are those who are conditioned to that particular social unit and they obey its needs and behests with the fervour of those who would sacrifice themselves for Almighty God.

We need world men and world women, who will have the sustaining force that can take even an imperfect instrument and use it in the name of justice and humanity and lay an enduring basis for universal peace.

Now, where is there in the world any force or combination of forces accessible to the nations and peoples that can realize these conditions of universal peace? Men can make charters, but can they regenerate the human soul?

This is not the first age in which society has undergone disintegration and the spirit of man has lost what it had raised up in the past. This is not the first time that human beings have been divided against themselves and gone down in the great bitterness and sorrow of mutual defeat. That which raised up the world from the depths of the degradation reached by the ancient Roman Empire was the divine and spiritual force that was manifested in Jesus as the prophet of God.

Through Him there came to human beings a truth, which when they accepted it, when they sacrificed themselves for it, raised them up to the level of the truth itself and made a new people, a people that could live according to standards of fellowship and justice in complete contrast to the dishonour and despair around them.

It is vitally important to realize the full meaning of that episode of the Roman Empire and the coming of Christ. Here we know from our own historical experience the Way by which alone the world can save itself.

Bahá'u'lláh came to the world about the middle of the nineteenth century, and He brought a spirit and a truth which identifies itself with the essential purpose of every prophet of the past. But in accordance with the principle of progressive revelation, He unfolded to this age, in addition to the truths that Christ revealed to the people of His day, certain organic principles that pertain to the regeneration and reordering of human affairs. The supreme principle which He revealed was that of the oneness of mankind; and that means that all the scattered peoples and races, all the languages, all the classes, all the denominations and sects, all the diversities of human beings in East and West have attained the full degree of the principle of variety which was the condition of life in the past.

Now therefore the law has gone out summoning these sundered and separated peoples together to form the body of mankind. That is what the spirit of Revelation means for every responsible human being today, that the fruit and the outcome of every teaching and every devotion of the past is fulfilled now as we come together as brothers in humanity, as co-workers to produce the structure of world order and the body of international peace.

Men of the tribes of the past could not attain a higher and farther outlook until the spirit had gathered them up and identified them with the principle of human progress under the guidance of God; nor can we reform ourselves and eliminate those prejudices of nation, of class and creed which tear our hearts to ribbons until we meet with our fellow human beings in worship before the throne of the one God, who is the Father of mankind.

This is the promise; this is the assurance which every prophet of the past gave to his people. This is the day toward which the spiritual souls of the great ones always turn, and so we need not feel that in the new name, Bahá'u'lláh, there is anything alien to the pure truth of our own religious background; particularly when we realize that Bahá'u'lláh, for the capstone, the arch of His teaching, has made it clear to the mind and heart of modern man that in purpose, in aim, in spirit, in consecration, in mission, all the prophets that have come from God are One Being and have given the world one revelation in the successive stages of human evolution.

So it is that *our* prophet cries to us through the lips of Bahá'-u'lláh, and in Bahá'u'lláh we find the prophet of the people to whom, perhaps, we have been alien all our lives. In this identification of the spiritual core of life, the recurrence of the one wonderful phenomenon and agency of truth, we have our relationship not to an exclusive tribal deity, not to a theological. conception that has been invented to give some people a certain advantage, but we have a relationship to the Author of our own being and the Creator of all mankind.

Therefore we may say that peace is in reality a divine creation. It is an order of virtue and truth that has descended into this world from a higher realm. When we step from our doubt, from our selfishness, from our fear, from our ignorance, from the disordered world which men have created, to the universal world which God has created for the human spirit, we enter the realm of universal peace and we touch a power that will realize its purposes through us and through all other human beings and which will bring a blessing to every Government, to every organization on the face of the earth, willing to become a servant and promote the principles of universal peace.

PART IV

THE MAN OF FAITH

THE ROOT OF STRUGGLE

IF WE contemplate the degree to which the principle of struggle has affected human history, and the extent to which that principle controls the world today, it seems impossible to avoid the conclusion that struggle is so deeply rootéd in the very being of man that there is no hope it can ever be extirpated.

The individual struggles to rise or maintain himself in his society, and his society struggles even more fiercely to progress or maintain itself in the world of nations. Our institutions are conditioned by the prevalence of struggle among individuals; and the organized dissension of institutions confirms and augments every type of personal competition. The fact of struggle permeates the whole body of civilization today.

Against that fact what wishful theory can possibly prevail? What large and sonorous formula uttered by the hopeful or naïve few can exert anything beyond a temporary local, restricted, subjective influence?

The fact of struggle has indeed become the basis of determined social philosophies which seek to establish the validity of human hope upon victory, denying the possibility or even desirability of cessation from strife. Thus the chain of causation has become historically complete, from the jungle of primitive man to the jungle of modern civilization.

But the essence of this argument consists in subduing man to the political and economic principles of society in one phase of its development. Its outcome is to make human nature nothing more than the reflex of society. Philosophic reality is established by the nature of the state, and man emerges as its mere instrument. Or the same conclusion is reached by asserting that man's reality consists of the principle of struggle, and the national state hence becomes responsible for organizing this principle for the attainment of the utmost success. The circle closes tightly and completely in whichever direction it is traversed.

Were man a static and predictable organism either argument, or either method of reaching the conclusion, would appear valid, for the fact of struggle is not to be denied.

The more vital truth at issue is that human nature is never static, and its possibilities have never been fulfilled by any form of civilization ever attained upon earth. Consequently the theory that human life must be organized upon the basis of political or economic strife is a betrayal of man. For whenever a civilization has carried such assumptions to an apparently triumphant conclusion; whenever political and economic power has been won by victory in strife, human nature has stirred with irrepressible restlessness, and the children of the conquerors repudiate the spoils or the children of the victims establish envied capacities in higher cultural and subjective fields.

The dynamic quality of human nature, its unhappy dissatisfaction with all that it acquires at the cost of what it might and should have been, is the eternal and unanswerable challenge to the spirit of materialism, however it may be concealed behind the panoply of empire or the fumes of ecclesiastical pomp.

Yet, even if history prove that struggle never attains fulfilment, how are we to deal with the undoubted fact that struggle appears to be so deeply rooted in each individual soul?

The truth only emerges when we grant the fact, but point out that the whole course of human progress clearly indicates that *the energy of personal struggle has been misunderstood and misapplied. The real purpose of that endowment is to equip the individual human being with capacity, not to overcome his fellow, but to transcend himself.*

Here, indeed, is the vital issue raised by religion from age to age: that man comprehend his own being, realize his inherent dynamic quality, and be inspired to direct the precious and holy energy of struggle into the channel of self-conquest and self-development. The fallacy of struggle as competition only arises when the individual repudiates the essence of his own being, abandons the task of true progress, and projects that energy into the negative field of strife, driven by the hounds of unhappiness released whenever a man is untrue to his divinely-created self.

Therefore, the root of struggle in the world today is nothing else than a prevalent self-betrayal on the part of those who have turned away from God. Their betrayal creates these wars and revolutions, establishing their own penalty for losing the path. But no valid philosophy can be constructed from the multiplication of error. The rise and spread of God's religion, the eternal truth of Jesus, Muḥammad and Bahá'u'lláh, will illumine the darkness of the inner life, raise mankind from the pit it has dug, and out of the energy so tragically misapplied create the means of that worldwide co-operation which binds together all who live in the spirit of truth.

THE SPIRITUAL BASIS OF WORLD PEACE

DESPITE its serious mistakes in the realm of ultimate interpretation of values, modern science has made possible one notable advance of at least indirectly a spiritual nature: it has created within the human mind a firm sense of the existence of universal law. The modern man inhabits a world whose processes he is increasingly convinced are understandable and trustworthy, capable of rational perception, and even where not yet known, impossible to be held subject to mere chance and caprice.

By this substantial gain, the modern man stands above and beyond the ancestor whose universe was a superficial appearance concealing forces and powers whose unknown processes continually suggested a variety of conflicting aims and wills, contact with which compelled him to develop elaborate rituals in the nature of a fearful if cunning defence. The modern man, moreover, has won an entirely new sense of courage and integrity not only from his capacity to understand nature rationally but also from his proven power of making mechanical instruments and appliances superior to those with which by nature he was endowed. In the camera he possesses a superior eye; in the radio a superior ear; in the electronic tube a touch infinitely more sensitive than that of the human hand.

But the hour of triumph and conquest in man's age-old struggle with nature has by some mysterious providence coincided with his utter humiliation in his relations with himself and his fellowman. Time surely never witnessed a spectacle more dramatic and more momentous than this tragic contrast between man as scientist and as citizen, between man as mechanic and man as the orphan of life, a lost and bewildered soul.

What wonder that many sensitive and fragile personalities

endeavour, in such a terrible hour, to abandon and repudiate all that so much bitter effort has secured, preferring the passive peace of some irrational and unworldly faith to the active struggle required in order to extend the powers of reason from the scientific to the social domain. By quitting the battlefield, they think to win for themselves some secret treaty, the terms of which will enable them to continue their existence untroubled, even though the continuance be as the dreamless sleep of a child.

For the more heroic, the meaning of life in this age has come to be the supreme obligation, (inevitable, and therefore glorious, because it has been imposed by an historic sequence of events arising from humanity itself), of going forward to the peak of another mountain of achievement, far higher than material science, from which the race can rise above its social ignorance and confusion even as in previous ages man has achieved glory over other problems, which at the time, appeared as desperate as the modern struggle for world peace.

In surveying this supreme obligation in the light of our rational powers, the formidable antagonism of social institutions culminating in the armed national states is clearly no superhuman situation but an antagonism emanating directly from the human will. If we envisage war or economic disaster as overwhelming earthquakes, as all-destroying hurricanes, the symbol cannot be made to transfer responsibility from man to nature, to the universe, from which actual earthquakes and hurricanes proceed. The antagonistic institutions, large and small, are nothing more than groups of people willingly captive to a competitive ideal.

What devastates society is the diversity and conflict of loyalties; in other words the fatal lack of one loyalty embracing mankind. Conscious effort for the attainment of world order must begin here, in an intense and constant realization of the disparity between the organic unity of the external universe and the disunity of the subjective world.

Measured by the diversity of loyalties, human society would

appear to be constituted of members of unrelated species no less essentially committed to strife than the beasts of the jungle or the insects of the swamp. Because the world of nature contains different species which pursue and are pursued, it would appear as though humanity had taken its lesson of life from a lower order, a kingdom of existence bereft of reason, in which nature has implanted the seeds of incessant physical struggle.

But the instinct of self-preservation dominating the animal is adjusted to the attainment of its own goal, while the diverse loyalties of mankind are impossible of realization. Their effect is to undermine the very foundation of human life. Not to instinct, but to spiritual ignorance must be attributed that condition of society in which men's highest loyalties arrive at destruction and death, a self-betrayal rather than a fulfilment of self.

Every loyalty is composed of two elements: an external object which can be rationally grasped and perceived, and a subjective motive which is elusive because identified with the object or goal to be achieved. For this reason, rational comparison of conflicting loyalties is impossible, because the rational power has become adapted to values external to man and is helpless in dealing with the origin and character of motives. The motive is prior to the object, and the motive employs reason as its instrument and justification. Human reason is a searchlight which throws a brilliant light upon scenes outside and beyond the realm of motive, but behind the searchlight all is blackest darkness. We therefore insist upon an unvarying and ever reliable mathematics but tolerate extreme variety and unreliability in religion. We have become rational in relation to all that is below man, but remain pre-rational in relation to all that pertains to the human heart itself.

This chasm in the continuity of rational reality is excused on the assumption that the rational power is inherently limited, can only deal with a restricted area of values, and that consequently, when the profoundest human motives are at issue, reason must give way to faith. This assumption means nothing less than that the searchlight of the rational power cannot, for some reason not explained, be turned in any direction save that external to human nature. It means also that man in himself is not an organic unity but is a dual being, split by the artificial distinction between reason and faith and compelled eternally to act under two irreconcilable laws. The distinction is not removed but rather further complicated by the claim that faith is a "higher" reason, a power having authority to annul, at any time, what ordinary reason holds to be useful, true or necessary. For such a claim establishes more than duality at the heart of human life—it compels a strife between "mind" and "heart" at crucial moments of destiny which constitutes the ultimate source of conflict in society as a whole.

To recapitulate: the civilization in which the very existence of humanity is enmeshed has become the prey of nationalistic, class, racial and also ecclesiastical loyalties. These irreconcilable loyalties have, in our own generation, precipitated international wars and an international economic chaos which have not only released the greatest amount of death and suffering recorded in human history but have impaired the whole structure of civilization. Furthermore, these loyalties, despite the bitterest experience, remain essentially unreconciled and are today more highly armed for destruction than ever before. This is the objective picture of human life today. When we examine these loyalties we find them resting upon motives and flowing from impulses which defy control, rooted as they are in the subjective world of the heart which remains irrational, while rationalizing its wishes and its aims. In this world, blind faith and not reason sits upon the throne. But the demands of that faith no longer correspond to the clear needs of human life. Faith has identified itself not with life but with death. The power of reason, which perceives the crisis, at present cannot deal with motives, but on the contrary is the instrument and tool by which irrational faith forges its own destruction. Every organized loyalty has rationalized itself into a self-contained philosophy beyond the reach of successful attack from without and beyond the reach of suspicion on the part of those remaining within. Society has become a chaos because man is divided against himself. He has become powerful in all realms where he has applied reason; he has become a helpless victim in the realm where he has renounced reason in favour of blind faith. The influence which has made man willing to sacrifice reason for faith, which has convinced him that his deepest motives and highest loyalties are subject to laws outside or beyond reason, is organized religion—the exclusive and dogmatic church.

The next step, therefore, for those who sincerely desire to serve the rational ideal of world order, lies in a re-examination of the claim sponsored by the dogmas of every creed and inculcated into the tender and responsive minds of children, that reason has no concern with the deepest motives of life but is an alien power which must remain outside the holy of holies until given the lesser task of justifying the motives adopted, in some mysterious and irrational way, by faith and also the task of enabling faith to achieve its aim.

The picture of the subjective world corresponding to the insane condition of modern civilization is that man's religion has remained primitive and pre-rational while man's knowledge and capacity for action have miraculously multiplied. The ghost of the savage behind the altar commands the soul of the statesman who instigates war and of the economist who turns industry into a daily and life-long social combat.

The claim that reason cannot deal with the substance of faith is a wholly artificial claim. It rests upon an assumption of human duality directly projecting the conception of warring, antagonistic gods marking the age of the savage. If God is one, and God is the creator of humanity, then the human spirit is one in essence and can achieve an organic unity far beyond this present stage characterized by the assumed irreconcilability of reason and faith. Since progress and achievement have followed upon every determined effort of man to control the forces of life and respond to the rational order of the universe, how can we entertain the impossible and wholly unauthorized claim that the door to the reality of human nature is to reason for ever barred? One-half civilized, one-half primitive savage—this condition of humanity is in itself the most challenging proof that progress, far from being finished and complete, offers today the possibility of advance in the spiritual realm comparable to that already achieved in the field of material science.

'Abdu'l-Bahá carried the power of reason across the chasm which for us still yawns between intelligence and faith. In Him there existed a consciousness fulfilled and organically united, blending perfectly the power of understanding with the quality of faith. His faith had no irrational element, and his reason illumined the dark recesses where faith is born and its quality determined. Against the whole momentum of an age glorifying the savage in its religion, He stood rocklike, immovable in the conviction that these very social disasters are evidence that the time to attain spiritual knowledge has dawned. In place of the traditional conception of man as being for ever divided against himself, He established a reality which reason can accept and faith, true faith, must recognize and extol as the highest privilege of existence. Perceiving that spiritual ignorance has run its course in the organization of armed national states, He spoke with assurance of man's future attainment of world unity and world order to follow this brief period during which the irrational, savage outlook is being finally discredited and left behind.

"God's greatest gift to man is that of intellect, or understanding. Understanding is the power by which man acquires his knowledge of the several kingdoms of creation, and of various stages of existence, as well as of much that is invisible. Possessing this gift he is, in himself, the sum of earlier creations; he is able to get into touch with those kingdoms, and by this gift he frequently, through his scientific knowledge, can reach out with prophetic vision. Intellect is, in truth, the most precious gift bestowed upon man by the divine bounty. Man alone, among created beings, has this wonderful power.

"All creation, preceding man, is bound by the stern law of

nature. The great sun, the multitude of stars, the oceans and seas, the mountains, the rivers, the trees, and all animals, great or small—none are able to evade obedience to nature's law.

"Man alone has freedom, and by his understanding or intellect has been able to gain control of and adapt some of those natural laws to his own needs. . . .

"God gave this power to man that it might be used for the advancement of civilization, for the good of humanity, to increase love and concord and peace. But man prefers to use this gift to destroy instead of to build, for injustice and oppression, for hatred and discord and devastation, for the destruction of his fellow-creatures, whom Christ has commanded that he should love as himself. . . .

"Consider the aim of creation: is it possible that all is created to evolve and develop through countless ages with this small goal in view—a few years of a man's life on earth? Is it not unthinkable that this should be the final aim of existence?

"The mineral evolves until it is absorbed in the life of the plant, the plant progresses until it finally loses its life in that of the animal; the animal, in its turn, forming part of the food of man, is absorbed into human life. Thus, man is shown to be the sum of all creation, the superior of all created beings, the goal to which countless ages of existence have progressed. . . .

"When we speak of the soul we mean the motive power of this physical body which lives under its entire control in accordance with its dictates. If the soul identifies itself with the material world it remains dark, for in the natural world there is corruption, aggression, struggles for existence, greed, darkness, transgression and vice. If the soul remains in this station and moves along these paths it will be the recipient of this darkness; but, if it becomes the recipient of the graces of the world of mind, its darkness will be transformed into light, its tyranny into justice, its ignorance into wisdom, its aggression into loving kindness, until it reach the apex. Man will become free from egotism; he will be released from the material world. . . .

"There is, however, a faculty in man which unfolds to his

vision the secrets of existence. It gives him a power whereby he may investigate the reality of every object. It leads man on and on to the luminous station of divine sublimity and frees him from the fetters of self, causing him to ascend to the pure heaven of sanctity. This is the power of the mind, for the soul is not, of itself, capable of unrolling the mysteries of phenomena; but the mind can accomplish this and therefore it is a power superior to the soul.

"There is still another power which is differentiated from that of the soul and mind. This third power is the spirit which is an emanation from the divine bestower; it is the effulgence of the Sun of Reality, the radiation of the celestial world, the spirit of faith, the spirit Christ refers to when he says: 'Those that are born of the flesh are flesh, and those that are born of the spirit are spirit.'. . .

"If a man reflects he will understand the spiritual significance of the law of progress; how all things move from the inferior to the superior degree. . . .

"The greatest power in the realm and range of human existence is spirit—the divine breath which animates and pervades all things. It is manifested throughout creation in different degrees or kingdoms.

"In the mineral kingdom it manifests itself by the power of cohesion. In the vegetable kingdom it is the spirit augmentative or power of growth, the animus of life and development in plants, trees and organisms of the floral world. In this degree of its manifestation, spirit is unconscious of the powers which qualify the kingdom of the animal. The distinctive virtue or 'plus' of the animal is sense perception; it sees, hears, smells, tastes and feels but in turn is incapable of the conscious ideation or reflection which characterize and differentiate the human kingdom. The animal neither exercises nor apprehends this distinctive human power and gift. From the visible it cannot draw conclusions regarding the invisible whereas the human mind from visible and known premises attains knowledge of the unknown and invisible. . . . Likewise the human spirit has its limitations. It cannot comprehend the phenomena of the kingdom transcending the human station, for it is a captive of powers and life forces which have their operation upon its own plane of existence and it cannot go beyond that boundary. . . .

"The mission of the Prophets, the revelation of the holy books, the manifestation of the heavenly teachers and the purpose of divine philosophy all centre in the training of the human realities so that they may become clear and pure as mirrors and reflect the light and love of the Sun of Reality. . . . . This is the true evolution and progress of humanity."

In this teaching, if we apprehend it correctly, the law of progress is revealed as the action of a higher form of life upon a lower. An element in the mineral kingdom remains in the limitations of that kingdom until it is gathered up and assimilated by the vegetable kingdom, which in turn rises not by its own power but through action of the animal kingdom. Elements in the vegetable kingdom die in that kingdom to be reborn in the animal kingdom, and similarly elements in the realm of the animal, when assimilated by man, die to be reborn as it were on a higher plane.

But how is man to rise above himself? For man there is no higher kingdom of physical existence to extend this principle of development by actual assimilation of the physical type. Of the four degrees of existence in the world of nature, man himself is the apex; wherefore the elements of man's physical being can go no higher, but through his physical death are restored to the lower planes. In this closed circle of physical existence the elements eternally rise and fall, establishing the rhythmic cycle of the world of nature.

In his primitive, savage state, man sought however to extend this cycle from the physical to the conscious realm. He believed that he could acquire the qualities of another man by eating his flesh. This conception, prolonged during nameless ages, assumed an elaborate ritual and formed the basis of his religious beliefs. Little by little the bloody sacrifice became refined;

o

instead of eating the flesh he laid it upon the altar of his tribal god. Eventually the stark savage belief persisted only as a symbol; it became sufficient to sacrifice an animal in place of a human being. By Old Testament times even this more innocent murder was condemned by prophetic leaders. The sacrifice was preferably wholly symbolic, by gifts, by flowers and fruit.

Behind this evolution of belief and religious practice we may feel the burden of a bitter, prolonged struggle for understanding of the spiritual law of evolution: the conception that qualities are obtained by partaking of substance had the apparent sanction of nature itself.

Even today the struggle has not been won. For even today the blind faith is widespread that man draws near God and partakes of divine qualities in mass or communion—by partaking of a physical substance, a consecrated bread and wine.

What wonder, when religion in its most sacred teachings has not left behind the primitive savage who sought to evolve and progress by eating the flesh of his fallen foe—what wonder that mankind has no capacity to arise above loyalties essentially blind, selfish and partisan, loyalties that are tribal in essence, loyalties that can devastate the entire civilized world? For the mirror of rational intelligence, endowed with power to reflect whatever realities it faces, has been given no realm of spiritual truth to substitute for the visible realm of nature—the lower world of insect and of beast.

But 'Abdu'l-Bahá has illumined that lost world of spiritual truth. He has freed the power of reason and intelligence from its servitude to biological fact and disclosed an illimitable universe still to be explored.

The central principle of 'Abdu'l-Bahá's teaching is that the Prophets, human though they are in all that pertains to the body, constitute an order of existence higher than man, a kingdom which acts upon man, purifying his motives and releasing his innate powers, assimilating man and raising him to a plane of consciousness transcending his former nature as truly as the animal transcends the senseless tree. By the spirit that flows through the Prophet, animating his words, man in turning sincerely to that source of reality is saved from the dominance of instincts and motives emanating from the world of nature which is lower in degree because it lacks the quality of mind.

The relation of man to Prophet is not that of flesh sacrificed to a jealous tribal god, not that of slave to a Monarch enthroned upon mysterious magical powers; it is the relation of child to parent, of student to educator, and the true essence of religion consists in attaining knowledge of and rendering devotion to the laws and principles of evolution in the kingdom of spirit. The faithful student of spiritual truth is, in consciousness, assimilated by and into that truth, no less actually than the mineral element which the living root absorbs.

As exemplified by 'Abdu'l-Bahá, religion is clearly a value not merely conforming to reason but the realm which offers reason and understanding its supreme opportunity. The substance of spiritual truth constitutes the real world in which intelligence can function freely and become completely fulfilled. The actual relation of reason to faith arises from consideration of the fact that it is by faith that man has capacity to recognize the Prophet—it is the quality of faith which makes it possible to turn the searchlight of intelligence toward the source of reality; but the knowledge thereby obtained remains a function of the rational mind. Faith, then, is an expression of will and not of intelligence. 'Abdu'l-Bahá has for ever freed man from superstition and imagination. He has interpreted the reality of man in the light of the reality of religion. That religion in its purity conforms to reason is His fundamental claim.

From this higher level of perception one can turn back to the condition of divided and antagonistic loyalties which underlies the sinister turmoil of this period, and apprehend it as evidence of the decay of the inherited religions. The God-given intelligence of humanity is functioning in the darkness of unfaith, and hence the devotion to falsified religions, the hysteria of economic and political movements, the soul-consuming strife of race and class.

In the rise of psychological sciences which explore the "unconscious" and "subconscious" fields in man, we have a valiant, if misdirected, struggle to extend the powers of rational intelligence to control human motives and beliefs. In reality, man has no mysterious "subconscious" self, but rather, in his natural condition, draws upon the instincts and impulses of the animal world. It is the physical organism, directly receptive to and penetrated by the same forces acting upon the animal kingdom, which psychologists actually explore. It is possible to plumb the depths of nature in man's being, but human reality —the direction of man's true progress—lies not backward in that dark abyss but forward toward "rebirth" into the spiritual kingdom.

This age, in its confused struggle of ideals, has but given rational form to the blind feelings of man's physical, therefore animal organism. Our society vainly endeavours, in its most turbulent mass movements, to find outlet for fears, rages and frustrated hopes which in the animal are temporary and harmless, but in a society possessing scientific means of destruction can lead to nothing else than universal conflict. A rational faith —a knowledge of how these motives can be transmuted into forces of co-operation—alone stands between us and this catastrophe. The basis of world order, in short, is a humanity whose mind is not acted upon from the lower kingdoms but is illumined by the light of God.

Until men become imbued with true, rational faith, the supreme goal of world order and peace will never be achieved. For universal peace is a reality only on the plane of spiritual truth. Civilization bereft of any source of reality and guidance is a dead body, prey to the maggots and the worms. Through the power of the Holy Spirit alone can we leave this death behind.

"The Holy Spirit is the light from the Sun of Truth bringing, by its infinite power, life and illumination to all mankind, flooding all souls with divine radiance, conveying the blessings of God's mercy to the whole world. The earth, without the medium of the warmth and light of the rays of the sun, could receive no benefits from the sun. Likewise, the Holy Spirit is the very cause of the life of man; without the Holy Spirit he would have no intellect, he would be unable to acquire his scientific knowledge by which his great influence over the rest of creation is gained. . . . The Holy Spirit it is, which, through the mediation of the Prophets of God, teaches spiritual virtues to man and enables him to acquire eternal life."

In this clear, unflickering light reflected from the mind of 'Abdu'l-Bahá as from a burnished mirror held to the sun, humanity has been granted capacity of vision in the otherwise darkened subjective world. By His insight one can rise above the mass consciousness and apprehend the meaning of the age not as the superficial clash of nations, classes and races, but as the final struggle of the animal nature with the spiritual nature of man. The raging tornado has its central point of perfect calm, and the Faith of Bahá'u'lláh promulgated by 'Abdu'l-Bahá is the universal peace hidden from physical sight behind the desperate movements of the dying civilization in which we live. Entering that Faith, men attain peace within themselves, and by this peace have peace with each other—the Most Great Peace, the Peace of God.

COMMUNION WITH THE INFINITE

Every living thing that exists in the universe is immersed in an ocean of mysterious power. What we call "life" is capacity to transform energy, not capacity to produce it. The world contains no engines of self-contained character; each form of existence is sustained by drawing upon the inexhaustible reservoir of force, and each in turn contributes some share to the mysterious store.

Human beings in their physical nature are bound by the same limitations and conditions as operate upon the animal. Our ignorance may believe that man is independent and free, but the scientist's vision rises above conceit to perceive the successive links by which the power of life is connected from mineral to plant, from plant to animal, from animal to man.

We differ fundamentally from all visible types of life, however, in that men receive and transform energy on many levels. When the body is nourished and sheltered, the feelings, thoughts and aspirations reach out for sustenance, and the consciousness receives the quality of immaterial food, for which it seeks. Within ourselves we are continually developing and altering those elements of the non-physical self by which the mental, ethical and spiritual values are instinctively selected. Man's universe of values is an infinite universe, even though you and I have become aware of only the small area in which our personality has become accustomed to dwell.

No man can transform for his own spiritual uses more than one level of values at a time. If we habitually exclude all save a few interests, our capacity to seek larger values becomes weakened, and by the lack of seeking we end by insisting that the world of the soul is limited, darkened, and devoid of inspiration.

Communion with the Infinite is the most vital gift of human life. It means the opening of windows to the light of truth, to the warmth of love. All men commune daily, but most men commune with objects of finite interest. The miser communes with his material wealth. The self-centred man of affairs communes with the problems and opportunities of his business or profession. The devoted parent communes with his child. The sick man communes with his pain and weakness. The statesman communes with the evolving life of his nation. Communion is a faculty inherent in man; it is the spiritual equivalent to the taking in of nourishment for the physical organism. But how few in this day practise communion as a source of joy, of inner integrity, or renewal for the powers of hope and faith and truth! Why do we live in a darkened corner of the universe, when the heavens of consciousness are flooded always with light from God?

To become conscious of this divine bounty of communion; to practise it day by day as the great musician perfects his power to evoke beauty from a violin—this is the essence of life, for all other gifts and talents become worthless if we fail to commune with God.

There is a mighty saying from the East: "Those who forget God, He causeth to forget themselves." That is, if we commune with lower interests exclusively, we lose the capacity to receive pure Light within the mind and soul. Little by little, our horizon shrinks, little by little the sunlight ceases to shine in the heart. At moments of relaxation from the day's work, we look within, and what we see is frequently depressing.

Our capacity to enter into communion is like the capacity of a mirror to reflect. The mirror reflects only the objects toward which it is turned, and likewise one communes with the interest uppermost in his heart. Freedom of will, potentiality of spiritual development, consist in our power to turn the mirror of meditation upon truth at its source, shutting out the myriad conflicting realities of worldly life for at least a few recreative moments day by day.

What is the Infinite with which man must learn to commune? Is it an infinity of variety, like the universe of space and time? Is it an infinity of knowledge, like a great library full of books? Is it an infinity of emotions, like the possession of a thousand different friends? No, not if we turn to those who illumine history with their power to commune with God. These great souls have found a Revealer of the Infinite—a Prophet whose life and message brings God within our human capacity to know, to love, to obey. Not by extension of knowledge but by singleness of purpose do we enter into that true communion which kindles eternity within the humblest human heart. By rising above our daily habits which degrade our energy to physical levels, by centreing our aspirations upon one point of worship, by transforming our stubborn characters with new capacity to receive truth in terms of enhanced daily life—it is here that we can enter the secret portals of communion and tread the eternal path that leads from the man of flesh to the man of spirit, reborn in the likeness of God. For the Prophet, the Messenger, is the perfect man, and until we have a true standard of perfection we know not where to turn for guidance upon this chaotic earth.

How reassuring are the words of this Commune revealed by Bahá'u'lláh:

"Unto Thee be praise, O Lord my God! I entreat Thee, by Thy signs that have encompassed the entire creation, and by the light of Thy countenance that hath illumined all that are in heaven and on earth, and by Thy mercy that hath surpassed all created things, and by Thy grace that hath suffused the whole universe, to rend asunder the veils that shut me out from Thee, that I may hasten unto the Fountain-Head of Thy mighty inspiration, and to the Day-Spring of Thy Revelation and bountiful favours, and may be immersed beneath the ocean of Thy nearness and pleasure.

"Suffer me not, O my Lord, to be deprived of the knowledge of Thee in Thy days, and divest me not of the robe of Thy guidance. Give me to drink of the river that is life indeed, whose waters have streamed forth from the Paradise in which the throne of Thy Name, the All-Merciful, was established, that mine eyes may be opened, and my soul be illumined, and my steps be made firm.

"Thou art He Who from everlasting was, through the potency of His might, supreme over all things, and, through the operation of His will, was able to ordain all things. Nothing whatsoever, whether in Thy heaven or on earth, can frustrate Thy purpose. Have mercy, then, upon me, O my Lord, through Thy gracious providence and generosity, and incline mine ear to the sweet melodies of the birds that warble their praise of Thee, amidst the branches of the tree of Thy oneness."

CHALLENGE TO CHAOS

Public address delivered in
Bahá'í Temple Foundation Hall, Wilmette, Illinois
August 26, 1954

THE UNITY OF GOD

WHAT DO we mean by the "Unity of God"? Who is God? What is God? Where is God?

We look out into the measureless universe that transcends all our human notions of time and area. God is not there. We examine all the manifold aspects of life in our earthly home—we probe into the psychology, the philosophy of the human heart. God is not there.

God the Omniscient, God the Omnipotent, God the Source of Love, is known by His Creation, through the signs of His wisdom and power, but we human beings do not know God nor shall we ever behold Him in His Essence, because man is a created reality, and the created cannot contain the reality of the Creator.

We have a sign of the Unity of God in that, the scientists tell us, this universe is dominated and controlled by one Will. There is no duality in the universe because it is all under the governance of the one supreme Being. There is no principle of evil, although, through absence of good, people have created within their souls that gloomy vacuum we call evil.

To understand this duality let us think of the distinction between light and darkness.

Any man who has been lost on a dark night feels that darkness is a positive force. It stabs into his eyes, it oppresses his heart, it seems to stretch out hands to seize him as he struggles to find the path. Then! one ray of light and there is no darkness! Darkness is the absence of light. It is not an independent force.

Therefore there are not two principles in the universe—there is but one. But men, having free will, can withhold obedience and understanding, and then life becomes like that of a pilot whose ship suddenly flies through a vacuum. You cannot float an airship on a vacuum, and you cannot rest a human life on the absence of good. The airship crashes, and the evil man goes to ruin.

But the searcher does not find God in the physical universe. There is but one revealer of God to the human heart—His Prophet, His Manifestation.

In majestic words we find this mystery unfolded in the writings of Bahá'u'lláh.

"Praise be to God, the All-Possessing, the King of incomparable glory, a praise which is immeasurably above the understanding of all created things, and is exalted beyond the grasp of the minds of men."

"A sprinkling from the unfathomed deep of His sovereign and all-pervasive Will hath, out of utter nothingness, called into being a creation which is infinite in its range and deathless in its duration. The wonders of His bounty can never cease, and the stream of His merciful grace can never be arrested. The process of His creation hath had no beginning, and can have no end."

UNITY OF THE PROPHETS

"The door of the knowledge of the Ancient Being hath ever been, and will continue for ever to be, closed in the face of men. No man's understanding shall ever gain access unto His holy court. As a token of His mercy, however, and as a proof of His loving-kindness, He hath manifested unto men the Day-Stars of His divine guidance, the symbols of His divine unity, and hath ordained the knowledge of these sanctified Beings to be identical with His own Self. Whoso recognizeth them hath recognized God. Whoso hearkeneth to their call, hath hearkened to the Voice of God, and whoso testifieth to the truth of their Revelation, hath testified to the truth of God Himself. Whoso turneth away from them, hath turned away from God, and whoso disbelieveth in them, hath disbelieved in God. Every one of them is the Way of God that connecteth this world with the realms above, and the Standard of His Truth unto every one in the kingdoms of earth and heaven. They are the manifestations of God amidst men, the evidences of His Truth, and the signs of His glory."

The Prophet or Manifestation of God comes to this earth as the instrument of the Divine Will. He is the instrument of Omniscience and Omnipotence and what He says or what He writes, His message, has the power behind it of the Divine Will. We human beings have betrayed ourselves in thinking that because the physical body of the Manifestation can be tortured, can be exiled, can be crucified, that in human will there is a way to overcome the Will of God. The test is one we impose upon ourselves, because the sign of God in this world is the unique power of the Prophet to rekindle the extinct spirit of Faith in the soul. Faith is not belief in a formula. Faith is a realization of the Will of the Omniscient and the Omnipotent, the realization that there has been made a connection through the Prophets between man and God. And faith, when it quickens the soul, creates a new and higher kind of human being. .

No one can do the work of the Prophet of God in quickening the soul and no one but the Prophet can be a point of unity to bring together into reconciliation and fellowship the hosts of the peoples of the world. We have had many forms of unity aside from faith, although every form of unity began, no doubt, as an aspect of faith, in the beginning. We have unity of race, unity of class, unity of nations and unity of creeds, and if you look at the world in which we live today I think you will honestly agree with me that these forms of limited unity which operate outside faith in the universal Will of God, are actually instruments of disunity and violence. The only unity is the common experience of faith, in which man sees himself as the child of God and sees all other men as the children of God and therefore could not lift his hand against them because it would be against the will of God.

Why are there so many diverse religious systems each derived from a Prophet of the past?

The first generations of believers believe in God. They believe in the power of the Divine Will. They feel themselves caught up in a spiritual world and they give their lives and their fortunes because nothing that they have as human beings is commensurate with what they have been given by the Grace of God—immortality and joy. But as time goes on and the person of the Prophet recedes, the values begin to change. 'Abdu'l-Bahá described this as the succession of the seasons: the Prophet is the springtime, the Renewer of life, the Germinator of all the seeds of the past; and then you have your fruitful summer, and your harvest; and then the winter of unfaith. And therefore if we seek the reason for the diversity of systems in the world today we can only find it here in that, to the degree that any religious system differs from the original teachings of its own prophet, it will necessarily differ from other religious systems which also have repudiated much of the value of their own Manifestation. They differ from each other because they differ from the standard of truth that was given them by God Himself. The prophetic teachings are not the foundation of human life today—their values, their truths, their principles, their devotion, their ardour—and therefore human life today is menaced with destruction.

Now, Bahá'u'lláh brings us a new teaching. It is the teaching that the Prophet returns to this earth at intervals of approximately one thousand years, more or less—returns to this world in order to revive the extinct spirit of faith. And therefore the history of religion is the coming of many great Prophets. But alas! their followers have all said that their own Prophet was different and superior and therefore there could be no reconciliation with the people who were equally loyal to some other Prophet.

Bahá'u'lláh proclaimed this majestic truth—that in their inmost being, in their functions as Manifestations of God, in their powers and attributes—the Prophets are one! So that when Jesus came, He was Moses, and the people who did not accept Him did not accept Moses, because their idea of Moses was not Moses. It was their conception. And when the western world refused to accept Muḥammad, the Bahá'ís say that in His inmost being He was also Christ. That is the test that God imposes—it is not ours. No human power could devise a test like that—that a great Being comes into this world at intervals, different in body, different in family name, different in circumstances, but with the same inner spirit. So that in reality there is but one continuous, eternal faith of God in this world, but it goes through stages of evolution; because with this teaching of oneness the Bahá'ís also say religion is progressive.

That is to say, the human race is evolving; new powers and capacities unfold from age to age. There was a childhood of primitive man; there was youth; and now we enter the great age of maturity. So we say that the Bahá'í message has revealed God more fully than the Prophets of the past because the age requires and has capacity for a greater revelation. Today religion is for humanity—not for one isolated race. At the time that Jesus walked upon this earth they did not even know that North and South America existed. Marco Polo made his journey to China and back, from Italy, in the thirteenth century. So you see the limited world that those people around the Mediterranean Sea were aware of, and Christ gave them all of the truth that those peoples had capacity to receive. He was not limited. He sacrificed Himself to raise the people from that degree to a higher degree, so that this eternal process of spiritual evolution can go forward age after age, world without end.

We must also realize that with the evolution of man from stage to stage, from immaturity to maturity, his problems become more complicated with every successive cycle and the reason for the confusion in the world today is that so many people are trying to solve today's problems with the truths that were adapted to the past. I do not mean a truth like "Love thy neighbour as thyself" except that the word "neighbour" does not mean what it did a thousand years ago. But the social complications, the intricate relationships of human beings to politics, economics and culture, these raise problems which human beings can only solve by the teachings of their own day. So Bahá'u'lláh has come with a teaching for humanity, and a social order. The Prophets before Him could have brought the teachings for humanity, but there was no humanity. There were races, classes, nations and creeds. Humanity has just been born. And have we ever stopped to think that the unity of mankind is demonstrated by its present condition of interdependence? We cannot get away. We are completely interdependent, and the first sign—the tragic sign—of man's capacity to enter one common faith is that we have already had one great emotional experience together—the whole human race. You say "What experience?" and I say "anguish." Anguish is the experience that has sought out and taken hold of people everywhere. It may not be the anguish of the American family who had sons in this war or that war; it may not be the anguish of Europe; but it is anguish, and anguish is the first sign of the purification of the human spirit.

We do not think deeply enough about religion. We bring religion down to human nature. Religion is not human nature. Religion is God's Will, but God's Will so offered to human beings that that Will can penetrate and reinforce their will and raise them up into a new condition; unfold latent powers and attributes. That is religion.

THE UNITY OF MANKIND

From outer evidence nothing could be more impossible. Mankind is divided all the ways there are to divide. If there are any new ways we will find them out tomorrow morning. They are not only divided in feeling, in thought, in habits, in actions, political interests, economic interests, and even in worship—people are not merely divided, they are armed! So

our repudiation of the prophetic law, carried forward generation after generation, has come to its climax in the two great
armed camps into which humanity is divided in this hour—
each capable of manipulating the laws of science and techno-
logy, to invent new and better ways of slaying multitudes of
people with the pressure of one button. *That is our world*, and
collectively all are responsible for it—we and our fathers.
Because it did not happen in a decade; it did not happen in
twenty or fifty or a hundred years—it slowly developed until
the opportunity for this violence was handed to the spirit of
unfaith in the human heart.

How, then, can one speak of the unity of mankind?

You remember, perhaps, that in the Qur'án, Muḥammad
spoke of Himself as the Seal of the Prophets. Among the people
of Islám that is taken to mean that therefore He is the last of
the Prophets. There will be no Prophet ever again, because He
is the "Seal" of the Prophets.

The Bahá'í teachings throw that concept into a better perspective. We have lived through what is termed the "Prophetic
Era," the era of preparation, the preliminary development of
man's spiritual being, and each Prophet of the past gave a sign
of assurance that the day would come when the Will of God
would prevail over the entire earth, but not in His own day.
He gave assurance that the day would come but not now, that
is, the "now" of the Prophet. So those days of preparation,
those ages, are called "The Prophetic Era." What Muḥammad
accomplished was to end the Prophetic Era and the Prophet
after Him inaugurated the Dispensation of Reality; of understanding. Things are no longer veiled and symbolized; things
are no longer kept secret among the occult few; truth is poured
out for the whole world, and any man who climbs the ladder
of truth can become an angel. He may be blacking your boots
today and an angel tomorrow. Don't despise any man because
of his economic condition, because God loves us all and He
knows the qualities within the heart and He can use some very,
very odd people that you and I would never select.

In this day of maturity, the problem of survival is the problem of co-operation and peace. That is where we stand. We cannot survive economically, politically nor physically with an extension of the present crisis many, many years more. What is the starting point toward unity? The starting point toward unity is unity with God; obedience to Divine Will; recognition of His Messenger; love for His Message and understanding of His sublime truth. That is the beginning. You say it is impossible?

Now, if we turn to the physical sciences we find that no matter how hard and resisting a material may be, the scientists can always find a way to overcome its resistance. Perhaps they find an element that will eat it away or a degree of heat that can melt it. Nothing is impossible any longer in the world of substance.

In the world of the soul, forces operate which are far beyond our understanding. All social movements are working toward the victory of a universal Faith. God employs the good and the evil alike as instruments for the victory of His plan of unity. Not what the press acclaims as important from day to day, but the release of the Holy Spirit is the transcendent matter with which we are all concerned.

The longer we resist its imperative call to unity, the more we will devise means of suffering for mankind, but we cannot turn back the Holy Spirit nor deny its ultimate achievement. God has expressed His Will through Bahá'u'lláh. His omnipotence and omniscience are its assurance.

The starting point of unity is unity with God. But every man who turns to God turns with new eyes to his fellow-men.

And there is a nucleus of people forming all around the world who love humanity; who understand that we are going through a new stage of development and they are prepared to accept the principle of a new order. As 'Abdu'l-Bahá said, the great principle today is to extend the American principle of federation until it embraces the nations of the world. He said that in 1912 in the United States.

P

What is the obstacle? Many people say, "Oh, these great powerful institutions with vested interests!" But there's nothing weaker than institutions. The only thing that has any strength is human beings. The obstacle, my friends, is simply this. Every child is born with a spirit from God, with a soul, latent, undeveloped, feeble; he may not even be aware of it, but it is there, because it is God's gift to every human being. That little child, growing up, then comes under a racial culture, family influence, all kinds of indoctrination, the fanciful sociological notions of his particular day, or a theology. And then what happens is that around those God-given powers we have a thin but hard cover that prevents that child from reaching out to God. And that child's infinite spiritual treasure is wasted on secondary matters that have no reference to God whatsoever. They are human schemes and devices.

God is giving us an experience that is going to crack through the hard shell of indoctrination and reduce every human being to the degree of his elemental human self; then those gifts will be released and as the trend toward peace begins to be recognized, many, many thousands and millions will say "Oh, thank God, it has *come*!" because God has given us a hunger for righteousness and peace.

"O kings of the earth! He who is the sovereign Lord of all is come. The Kingdom is God's, the omnipotent Protector, the Self-subsisting. Worship none but God, and, with radiant hearts, lift up your faces unto your Lord, the Lord of all Names. This is a Revelation to which, whatever ye possess, can never be compared, could ye but know it."

"Wash from your hearts all earthly defilements, and hasten to enter the Kingdom of your Lord, the Creator of earth and heaven, Who caused the world to tremble and all its peoples to wail except them that have renounced all things and clung to that which the Hidden Tablet hath ordained."[1]

While the fundamental mission of the Bahá'í Faith is to reverse the human trend toward violence and inspire mankind

[1] Bahá'u'lláh, *Tablet to the Kings.*

with the spirit of universal peace, the teachings establish land-marks along the path to spiritual understanding. One landmark is the application of Divine Law to rulers and governments as well as to the mass of human beings. One is the command that no follower of Bahá'u'lláh is to engage in political affairs nor take part in any seditious movement. Obedience to govern-ment is incumbent upon Bahá'ís, including the civil authorities of countries where they may travel or reside, in addition to their native land.

Already there are Bahá'ís in more than two hundred and forty-five countries and territorial divisions, the actual demon-stration of the power and unity manifested through the Prophet by the Divine Will.

All doors to security and progress are closed except that which opens upon the new world of Revelation. Truth has become law, and the power of Law is Omnipotence.

This last passage from the Writings of Bahá'u'lláh is ad-dressed to every human soul. It strips the veils of superstition and self-interest from all people.

"Tear asunder, in My Name, the veils that have grievously blinded your vision, and through the power born of your belief in the unity of God, scatter the idols of vain imitation. Enter, then, the holy paradise of the good pleasure of the All-Merciful. Sanctify your souls from whatsoever is not of God, and taste ye the sweetness of rest within the pale of His vast and mighty Revelation, and beneath the shadow of His supreme and infallible authority. Suffer not yourselves to be wrapped in the dense veils of your selfish desires, inasmuch as I have per-fected in every one of you My creation, so that the excellence of My handiwork may be fully revealed unto men. It follows, therefore, that every man hath been, and will continue to be, able of himself to appreciate the beauty of God, the Glorified. Had he not been endowed with such a capacity, how could he be called to account for his failure? . . . For the faith of no man can be conditioned by any one except himself."

PART V

THE CENTRE OF THE COVENANT

THE VICTORY OF FAITH

THOSE who live in the depths of a small, narrow valley, and make no effort to climb the lofty mountains by which they are beset—such people never behold the landscape stretching beyond the hills; they know not what the mountains may conceal.

But he who makes the mighty effort, leaving behind him the narrow valley of human selfishness and ease; he who has the supreme courage and strength to gain the summit, for him the invisible becomes visible; for him the infinite divine horizons are unfolded, and that which was hidden behind the mountains is revealed.

One of those recurrent visions that come again and again, whenever selfishness and greed and fear are truly overcome— that landscape which ever greets with its beauty the soul who reaches the highest hill—is the vision of a united humanity, a single faith, one worship, one law, one God. To this every traveller in the world of spirit has testified, and their testimony ever agrees. We find this vision singing in the words of Isaiah; Augustine, in his great work *The City of God* rediscovered it; its perception haunted the great souls in the Middle Ages; today once more the people of magnanimity like Emerson have testified eloquently that the same spiritual landscape still exists. You may search the records of the vision of every people, East and West, North and South—wherever the soul has become articulate, its speech is the praise of that which it beholds before it, beyond the hills.

To these witnesses, that vision is reality, and the world's division, suffering and pain is an unreality they have for ever left behind. By and for and in that reality they have lived and died.

But their witness is incredible to the people in the darkness of the valley. In the valley, the description of the landscape beyond the hills seems no more than an empty dream, a denial of the plainest facts confronting one on every hand. Here, reality is the struggle for existence, the survival of those who are "fit," a constant and painful effort to gather fruit from trees on which the sun too seldom shines. That such a fruitful landscape lies on the other side of death, many in the valley will agree; but that it lies on the other side of sacrifice here and now, this they repudiate, this they vehemently deny. And their repudiation and their denial are sanctified by those to whom they are accustomed to turn for authority in matters that pertain to the life of the soul.

That faith has had no visible victory in any era of recorded time, is all too evident; that the vision of human brotherhood never seemed so dim, so unreal, so legendary as in this troubled age, is no less apparent.

Nevertheless, it is well to recall that some hundreds of years ago Leonardo da Vinci drew plans for the construction of a machine that would fly. In his day, even the thought of aviation was inconceivable. The failure of his efforts appeared to his neighbours like the judgment of an offended Providence against one who had attempted to contravene the divine law.

But now that aviation has become a commonplace occurrence in this age of scientific progress, what are we to say of da Vinci?

In the world of thought, da Vinci achieved aviation—in the world of thought he stood abreast of the people of today. It was in the world of material fact, and in this world only, that da Vinci failed. He failed only because certain material conditions had not yet been fulfilled. He had no suitable motive power, no suitable structural elements such as we now have. But the principle of flight was certainly his—and time itself has worked to vindicate his aspiration.

Therefore we see that there are two worlds—the world of vision and the world of outward fact. Vision ever precedes fact

—vision creates fact. For the world of vision is the world of causes; the world of outward fact is the world of effects. That which exists in the world of vision must eventually come to existence also in the world of fact. The world of fact cannot resist the world of vision, any more than the earth can resist the growth of the seeds that are sown. For the earth is composed of the very substance of vegetation—and in like manner, the world of effects is composed of the substance of vision. Where the earth is too scanty for vegetation—where the earth resists the growth of the seed, there the stunted vegetation rots and goes back to the earth; and when this has happened season after season, the earth is fertilized by the very vegetation it seemed to resist. So humanity, denying the spiritual world, resisting the growth and development of the life of spirit, is gradually spiritualized by the influences it destroys, or rather seems to destroy.

Thus if we consider once more the recurrent vision of human brotherhood, righteousness and unified faith: since this reality has ever existed in the world of perception, the world of causes, it must also come to existence in the world of outer fact. For the separation of these two worlds is not the eternal separation of life and death, or good and evil, or light and darkness; rather their separation is that of cause and effect. It is a separation which lies in time, and lying in time, is also joined by time. As the tree is the effect of the seed, but the tree and the seed are separated by time, yet connected in time; so also human brotherhood is the effect of the soul, the fruit of the soul, and the long agony of the soul's sacrifice is not only the measure of the duration of time, but also the measure of time's meaning.

For there must needs be concurrent conditions for the realization of brotherhood, just as there had to be concurrent conditions for the realization of mechanical flight. Just as the thought of flight remained perfect, unchanging in the world of causes until certain conditions had been established in the material world, so the vision of peace on earth has existed perfect and unchanging, a landscape beyond the hills of sacrifice and endeavour, until little by little, those outer conditions might be established of which peace and righteousness are the consummation, the purpose, the motive, the fruit. Never has the man of faith denied the reality of human brotherhood, but in all ages his concern has been to further the inner and outer preparations for its eventual victory.

Let us not be deceived by the apparent predominance of hatred, suspicion and the desire for material conquest in this age.

In 1913 a child might have travelled from Berlin to Paris in a few hours, without danger, without annoyance. A year later, in 1914, more than a million men attempted to make that journey, and not one man arrived. Why was this? Not one man arrived because they came on conquest, and coming on conquest they raised up forces of opposition that proved mightier than they.

This is a new condition in the world of humanity. Hitherto, no power has existed strong enough to resist empire except the mysterious power of time. Rome was overthrown, overthrown at last, but Rome was overthrown so slowly that people did not perceive the seeds of Rome's downfall were sown by the first legions Rome sent forth to conquer the world. Hence arose, in all past ages, the apparent justification of conquest and the apparent unreality of love; the effects of ambition and greed were so separated from their causes that the people could not realize that cause and effect are actually one.

But today, cause and effect are no longer mysteriously separated by time, or place, or personality. The material unity of all races and all countries, and their complete interdependence upon one and the same economic organization, has created a condition wherein spiritual motive and material consequence are as inseparable as the heart and the mind of the same man.

There is an old saying about "those who fish in troubled waters" which we can complete by adding the words "*must stand on dry land.*" That is, to profit by others' domination one must stand beyond the consequences of their domination.

Today no immunity exists or is possible for any individual or group. For men are no longer associated together as self-sustaining groups, but each community has become an essential wheel or lever in the one world machine—an essential organ or limb in the one body of humanity.

In the light of this new condition let us perceive the sequences in which vision, as cause, becomes reality, as effect.

The origin of love, in evolving humanity, is sympathy, and sympathy is the sharing of the same danger, or suffering, or pain. So long as humanity stood divided from itself, in separate races, and religions, so long was sympathy confined in its action to the separate community, and the result of sympathy, love, expressed itself as loyalty to the one nation and the one creed. Therefore love ever resisted and overthrew its own desire, since loyalty to the one nation and the one creed involved opposition to other nations and other creeds. Just as injury to one part of a body is injury to all parts, so injury to any portion of humanity has today its effects upon all other portions. The very universality of suffering in this age has overthrown the foundations of limited loyalty, and the mutual danger we face through warfare or economic disaster is the pledge of a common sympathy as inevitable as the rising of tomorrow's sun.

If we seek for confirmation of this in one another's spiritual limitations, however, we may seek in vain. For just as an imperfect mirror exaggerates every image, so in our imperfection of thought and love do we tend to confirm each other in our selfishness rather than in our aspiration for the common good. Without some source wherein each may find his own perfection steadfastly set forth, we shall continue as it were in the narrow and endless valley of self, increasing the crisis of modern existence until another and greater war engulfs us all.

'Abdu'l-Bahá's spiritual influence alone can overcome the bitterness of suspicion and the habit of hate.

'Abdu'l-Bahá has brought back in its fullness the ancient, the timeless vision of brotherhood, righteousness, peace and love. 'Abdu'l-Bahá has given this vision an expression in word and deed which transcends every limitation of race, of class, of nation, and of creed. No community can claim 'Abdu'l-Bahá for their own spiritual leader, and make His inspiration the justification of separateness, as men have done with every spiritual leader of the past. In the divisions of humanity He has arisen as the true centre and point of unity, a mirror reflecting the light of one love and one teaching to every horizon. As each community, seeking relief from its own restrictions and its sufferings, turns to 'Abdu'l-Bahá for guidance, it finds all other communities illumined in the same compassionate love.

When a reporter of the New York *Globe* visited 'Abdu'l-Bahá at Haifa in the course of an investigation of the Zionist movement in Palestine, 'Abdu'l-Bahá gave her this message: "Tell my followers that they have no enemies to fear, no foes to hate. Man's only enemy is himself."

It means nothing how many or how few 'Abdu'l-Bahá's followers may be at this moment here or in other parts of the world. That message was the expression of the reality emerging from the present era of confusion, of trouble, of unrest, of universal change. To receive that message from the lips of 'Abdu'l-Bahá at the time it was uttered is to be forewarned and forearmed; but the message is inescapable, soon or late, by reason of the actual conditions of the world. 'Abdu'l-Bahá recorded the spiritual evolution that went on behind and within the material evolution of this age. He witnessed for us the victory of faith.

As one considers the strife that is taking place everywhere today, one recalls the ancient story of Atman the king.

One day Atman summoned his four sons to his presence and said:

"My sons, because you expect to share this mighty kingdom after my departure, you are making no effort to develop in yourselves any capacity or any worthiness. As you are my sons I love you, but I also have a duty to my people. Therefore go forth, each of you, into the world, and to him who best proves his worthiness I shall leave the kingdom."

So the four sons went forth, one to the East, one to the West, one to the South, one to the North. And as each had inherited of the father's capacity, so each made a mighty effort to develop worthiness, and each rose to leadership in the country where he lived.

Then having become a leader in his country, each of the four sons remembered his father's promise, and set forth to return to Atman's capital and claim the right of inheritance. So each set forth on the way, bringing with him a mighty following of soldiers and servants that Atman his father might realize how worthy he had become.

Now arriving on the great plain before the gates of the city, each brother beheld the army of the other also arriving, the army of the East with the banner of the dragon, the army of the West with the banner of the eagle, the army of the North with the banner of the bear, and the army of the South with the banner of the palm. But seeing these other banners, each brother thought that hostile armies had gathered to destroy the kingdom of his father Atman, and to defend his father each brother led his army against the other armies on the plain.

By reason of their courage, the four brothers fought at the head of their armies, where the banner was upheld, and in the course of a few hours all the banners were thrown down and the four leaders wounded.

Then the armies, the banners thrown down and the ranks hopelessly intermingled, ceased to fight, and around the four brothers as they lay wounded a circle of mourning soldiers stood in silence.

Then the oldest brother, feeling his heart's blood ebb away, raised his voice in a mighty cry of grief and lamentation:

"O Atman, my father! O my father, Atman the king! Bitter enemies surround thy city, and they shall lay it waste and slay thee in the midst. Gladly have I given life for thee, O my father —alas, that the enemies were too strong and I have died in vain."

So lamented the eldest brother. And when the other brothers

heard him lamenting their father Atman, the king, then they lamented also, and more bitterly even than he, for now they knew that it was no enemy they had fought, but their own brothers they had so blindly attacked and so unwittingly harmed.

Even so the strife in which we are all engaged, even now—strife political, strife economic, strife social, strife religious. This is not an ordinary strife; like the battle of the four brothers, it is the universal combat which precedes mutual recognition and prepares for the Most Great Peace in the *hearts* of men. For there is no recognition possible between the strangeness of our customs and the intensity of our desires, but recognition is in and through the common fatherhood of God, reconciliation is in and through obedience to the one universal Will.

Let us not be dismayed by this frantic confusion of strife. It is the final and complete expression of divine love, compelling humanity to destroy the foundations of its own injustice and greed. Were there to be no such universally disastrous consequences of age-long injustice, the divine compassion would be entirely absent from the arena of human affairs. This period of universally disastrous consequences is that of which they, the witnesses of God from age to age, have ever warned humanity. All the spiritual witnesses return in this age of fulfilment. They speak in the voice of 'Abdu'l-Bahá.

THE MASTER

A Pilgrimage to Thonon

"'Abdu'l-Bahá at Thonon, on Lake Leman!" This unexpected news, telegraphed through the courtesy of M. Dreyfus, brought my wife and me to the determination we had long agreed upon of making a pilgrimage to the Master at our earliest opportunity. With only a few days intervening before His journey to London, we set out immediately from our home in Siena, and arrived at Thonon in the afternoon of August 29. Prepared in some measure for the meeting by the noble mountain scenery through which we had passed, we approached the hotel feeling ourselves strangely aloof from the tourist world. If I could but look upon 'Abdu'l-Bahá from a distance I considered that I should fulfil a pilgrim's most earnest desire.

The *Hotel du Parc* lies in the midst of sweeping lawns. Groups of people were walking quietly about under the trees or seated at small tables in the open air. An orchestra played from a near-by pavilion. My wife caught sight of M. Dreyfus conversing with others, and pressed my arm. I looked up quickly. M. Dreyfus had recognized us at the same time, and as the party rose I saw among them a stately old man, robed in a cream-coloured gown, his white hair and beard shining in the sun. He displayed a beauty of stature, an inevitable harmony of attitude and dress I had never seen nor thought of in men. Without having ever visualized the Master, I knew that this was He. My whole body underwent a shock. My heart leaped, my knees weakened, a thrill of acute, receptive feeling flowed from head to foot. I seemed to have turned into some most sensitive sense-organ, as if eyes and ears were not enough for this sublime impression. In every part of me I stood aware of 'Abdu'l-Bahá's presence. From sheer happiness I wanted to cry—it seemed the most suitable form of self-expression at my command. While my own personality was flowing away, a new being, not my own assumed its place. A glory, as it were from the summits of human nature poured into me, and I was conscious of a most intense impulse to admire. In 'Abdu'l-Bahá I felt the awful presence of Bahá'u'lláh, and, as my thoughts returned to activity, I realized that I had thus drawn as near as man now may to pure spirit and pure being. This wonderful experience came to me beyond my own volition. I had entered the Master's presence and become the servant of a higher will for its own purpose. Even my memory of that temporary change of being bears strange authority over me. I *know* what men can become; and that single overcharged moment, shining out from the dark mountain-mass of all past time, reflects like a mirror I can turn upon all circumstances to consider their worth by an intelligence purer than my own.

After what seemed a cycle of existence, this state passed with a deep sigh, and I advanced to accept 'Abdu'l-Bahá's hearty welcome. During our two days' visit, we were given unusual opportunity of questioning the Master, but I soon realized that such was not the highest or most productive plane on which I could meet Him. My questions answered themselves. I yielded to a feeling of reverence which contained more than the solution of intellectual or moral problems. To look upon so wonderful a human being, to respond utterly to the charm of His presence—this brought me continual happiness. I had no fear that its effects would pass away and leave me unchanged. I was content to remain in the background. The tribute which poets have offered our human nature in its noblest manifestations came naturally to mind as I watched His gestures and listened to His stately, rhythmic speech; and every ideal environment which philosophers have dreamed to solicit and confirm those manifestations in him seemed realized. Patriarchal, majestic, strong, yet infinitely kind, he appeared like some just king that very moment descended from his throne to mingle with a devoted people. How fortunate the nation that had such a ruler ! My personal reverence, a mood unfortunately rare for a Western man, revealed to me as by an inspiration what even now could be wrought for justice and peace, were reverence made a general virtue; for among us many possess the attributes of government would only the electors recognize and summon them to their rightful station.

At dinner I had further opportunity of observing 'Abdu'l-Bahá in His relation to our civilization. The test which the Orient passes upon the servant of a Prophet is spiritual wisdom; we concern ourselves more with questions of power and effectiveness. From their alliance—from wisdom made effectual, from power grown wise—we must derive the future cosmopolitan virtue. Only now, while the East and West are exchanging their ideals, is this consummation becoming possible. Filled with these ideas, I followed the party of Bahá'ís through the crowded dining-room. 'Abdu'l-Bahá, even more impressive walking than seated, led the way. I studied the other guests as we passed. On no face did I observe idle curiosity or amusement; on the contrary, every glance turned respectfully upon the Master, and not a few bowed their heads. Our party at this time included eighteen, of whom some were Orientals. I could not help remarking the bearing of these splendid men. A sense of well-being, of keen zest in the various activities of life—without doubt the effect of their manly faith emanated from all. With this superiority, moreover, they combined a rare grace and social ease. All were natives of countries in which Bahá'ísm has not only been a capital offence in the eyes of the law, but the object of constant popular hatred and persecution; yet not one by the slightest trace of weariness or bitterness, showed the effects of hardship and wrong upon the soul. Toward 'Abdu'l-Bahá their attitude was beautifully reverent. It was the relationship of disciple to master, that association more truly educative than any relationship our civilization possesses, since it educates the spirit as well as the intelligence, the heart as well as the mind. Our party took seats at two adjoining tables. The dinner was throughout cheerful and animated. 'Abdu'l-Bahá answered questions and made frequent observations on religion in the West. He laughed heartily from time to time—indeed, the idea of asceticism or useless misery of any kind cannot attach itself to this fully-developed personality, The divine element in Him does not feed at the expense of the human element, but appears rather to vitalize and enrich the human element by its own abundance, as if He had attained His spiritual development by fulfilling His social relations with the utmost ardour. Yet, as He paused in profound meditation, or raised His right hand in that compelling gesture with which He emphasizes speech, I thought vividly once more of Bahá'u'lláh, whose servant He is, and could not refrain from comparing this with that other table at which a Prophet broke bread. A deep awe fell upon me, and I looked with a sudden pang of compassion at my fellow-Bahá'ís, for only a few hours before 'Abdu'l-Bahá had said that even in the West martyrs will be found for the Cause.

After dinner we gathered in the drawing-room. The Master's approaching visit to London was mentioned. I recoiled momentarily as I pictured him surrounded by the terrible dehumanizing machinery of a modern city. Nevertheless, I am confident that nowhere else will Bahá'u'lláh's presence in Him, as well as the principle of Bahá'ísm, so conspicuously triumph. Precisely where our scientific industry has organized a mechnism so powerful that we have become its slaves; precisely where *men* have become less than *things*, and in so dwarfing ourselves have lost a certain spiritual insistence, a certain necessity *to be*, without which our slavery stands lamentably confirmed—precisely there will the essential contrast between spirit and matter strike the observer most sharply. The true explanation of our unjust social arrangement does not consist in the subjection of poor to rich, but the subjection of all men alike to a pitiless mechanism; for to become rich, at least in America, implies merely a readier adaptation to the workings of the machine, a completer adjustment to the revolving wheel. But 'Abdu'l-Bahá rises superior to every aggregation of

Q

material particles. He is greater than railroads, than skyscrapers, than trusts; He dominates finance in its most brutal manifestation. His spiritual sufficiency, by which our human nature feels itself vindicated in its acutest agony, convinces one that the West can free itself from materialism without a social cataclysm, without civil war, without jealous and intrusive legislation, by that simplest, most ancient of revolutions, a change of heart. When by the influx of a new ideal we withdraw our obedience from the machine, its demoniac energy will frighten no more, like a whirlwind that passes into the open sea. 'Abdu'l-Bahá restores man to his state a little lower than the angels. Through Him we recover the soul's eternal triumphchant *I Am*.

Next day the Bahá'ís, increased by other pilgrims from various parts of Europe, met again at tea. On this occasion we new-comers were presented with a Bahá'í stone marked with Bahá'u'lláh's name. Rightly considered, such objects contain a spiritual influence quite apart from the belief of superstition—a suggestive value, which, recalling the circumstances under which the objects are given and received, actually retain and set free something of the holy man's personality. Superstition errs in reckoning their power apart from the receiver's worth or his power of receptivity. At my request, 'Abdu'l-Bahá graciously took back the stone I had received, and returned it with a blessing for my baby girl who thus, as it were, accompanied us on our pilgrimage and shares its benefits. I had spent the morning walking about Thonon. Following so closely upon my first meeting with the Master and the unique impression this made upon me, my walk invested the commonplace of our community life with a new significance. So much that we accept as inevitable, both in people and their surroundings, is not only avoidable, but to the believer even unendurable! Yet while inwardly rebelling against the idle and vicious types, the disgusting conditions in which our cities abound, I was conscious of a new sympathy for individuals and a new series of ties by which all men are joined in one common destiny.

Perhaps the most enduring advantage humanity derives from its Prophets is that in their vision the broken and misapplied fragments of society are gathered into one harmony and design. What the historian ignores, what the economist gives up, the Prophet both interprets and employs. The least of those who enter into a Prophet's vision become thereafter for ever conscious of the invincible unity of men. Not himself only, but all men seem to undergo a new birth, a spiritual regenesis.

I have not yet mentioned the presence of Mírzá Assad'u'lláh. I suffered the good fortune to be seated beside him at dinner, and was irresistibly attracted by his gentle and tender spirit. Clothed in the same beautiful Persian style of garments as 'Abdu'l-Bahá, he represented a striking contrast with the Master, as if two wines of different fragrance had been poured into similar glasses. Without 'Abdu'l-Bahá's majestic qualities, his nature is nevertheless infinitely sweet and lovable, inspiring a regard not exalted into impersonal awe, but full of that devotion which unites the members of a happy family. As we parted from the Bahá'ís on this last evening, after an impressive benedictory farewell by 'Abdu'l-Bahá, Mírzá Assad'u'lláh, with the most touching sweetness, approached my wife and said that he wanted to be her father; that if she ever needed a father's help she must turn to him. Of all the heart-renewing incidents with which our little pilgrimage was brimmed, this was the most affecting, the most significant; for it is an example of that religious fellowship, deeper than race, broader than language, which Bahá'ísm has awakened in both hemispheres, and a prophecy for the earnest days when 'Abdu'l-Bahá is no more, and we men and women, heirs of Bahá'u'lláh's manifestation, labour to erect the House of Justice amid the increasing charity and enthusiasm of the world.

Quattro Torri, Siena.

September 3, 1911.

BAHÁ'Í ASSEMBLIES

WHEN EVENING twilight falls upon the world, and shadows cast from the western mountains fill the home, then the servant goes from room to room, lighting the lamps, in order that darkness may not oppress the people of the household.

And, in the same way, when the evening of civilization approaches; when the light of custom and tradition dies; when the mind stumbles, the heart fails and the soul is enshrouded with sudden fear; when the works of shadow and darkness are done—by wars, by strife, by confusion; and the prescience of universal ruin flies like a bat of ill omen over the uplifted heads and staring eyes; then the Divine Servant passes silently from room to room of the household of the world, lighting the lamps of hearts with the flame of spirit, whose illumination, for those who are severed from all save spirit, is as the rising of the True Dawn after the overcoming of that besetting inner twilight which the world mis-calls truth, mis-terms reality, mis-conceives as *life*.

But when the lamps of the hearts are lighted, then silently, then mysteriously, even as the Divine Servant came, so He departs; and in that departing we know Him by the glory of the illumination whose rays have penetrated the heart; or we know Him not at all.

This is the first solemnity of the hush of that hour when it is realized that 'Abdu'l-Bahá, the Divine Servant, having lighted the lamps throughout the household of the East and West, departs unto that Source of Light whence He came.

The shining of the lamps of hearts lighted by the hand of the Divine Servant is the mystery whose outward manifestation stands visible in the life of the world as *Bahá'í Assemblies*, lamps that shone unseen in the last flickering moments of that false illumination of the material age; lamps that shine the more brightly as material daylight ebbs from the life of men.

For the believers, this is the mystery to be considered, the task to be realized, the worthiness to be attained: that from their unity and by their unity the fulfilment of the coming of the Divine Servant may be established in the foundations of the New Age throughout the world. The unity of the believers one with another is as the rays of light from the lamp. If unity does not exist—unity in the depths of spirit—then the lamp burns only to itself; for the world it would be as though the lamp had not been lighted, and as though the Divine Servant had not come.

For the lamp burns not to itself, but to the world, through the manifold rays which the believers are: each believer a ray, all the believers the visible shining of the lamp. The lamp shines not through one ray, but through the infinity of rays; not upon one object, but upon all objects; not for one horizon, but unto all the horizons. Through the personal unlikeness of the believers, the glory of the lamp is manifested. No believer can be spared, lest the lamp be shorn of its rays.

Therefore, in a Bahá'í Assembly, all the aspects of personal unlikeness exist. The believers are not of one kind, not of one sort, not of one character, not of one training, not of one capacity; which unlikeness is essential to the full shining of the lamp. But the believers are alike in this, that each is a ray of light shining forth from the lamp, whereby the lamp illumines one particular object, one special horizon, revealing itself to that horizon through that one ray which the believer, by reason of his faithfulness, his devotion, his selflessness, has become. The lamp shines through all its rays, and no ray is more important than any other ray shining from the lamp.

Each of the believers has two aspects and two stations. He has the aspect and station of his personality, which is the aspect and station of difference; and he has the aspect and station of the ray, which is the aspect and station of oneness. The oneness of the believers is the lamp lighted by the hand of the Divine Servant; the difference of the believers is the work of the world of nature and of mankind, in whose activity we evolve and by whose influence we are conditioned.

In the life of mankind there have been many lamps, each lamp shining unto one room, one community, one horizon; and the rays of these lamps could not overcome the darkness beyond the one room where the lamp shone. Now there is but one lamp, the Sun of Truth, whose shining is for all the rooms of the household of humanity, all the horizons of experience, all the objects of thought and activity.

Therefore, that the oneness of the Sun of Truth may be manifested, it has become necessary in this New Age that the rays shall have no confinement; that all the distinctions shall be burned away; that reality shall be perceived by one light and known of one spirit. Wherefore, in every Bahá'í Assembly, all the conditions of humanity—all the separateness, all the differences, all the degrees, all the capacities, all the kinds, all the influences built up during the evolution that has gone before— must needs, by the providential law of this New Age, be made one gathering, manifesting the oneness of the Sun of Truth even despite the testimony and evidence of all the differences of personality which emanate from the influence of the world.

This is the mystery of a Bahá'í Assembly: not that its members readily agree, but that they can overcome their differences; not that they are one in personality, in instinctive sympathy, in ambition, in desire, in training, in influence; but that they can penetrate to the foundation of oneness revealed by the glory of the Sun.

Every Bahá'í Assembly is the world in miniature, containing the differences and personal problems of the world, even intensified to the utmost degree. This is our glory, our privilege, our attainment, our distinction; not our weakness, not our shame. No other power save the power of the Sun of Truth could have revealed the oneness in so much difference. It is the spirit of this oneness overcoming our manifold differences, that makes a Bahá'í Assembly a divine foundation, a healing for the world, an inspiration for those who turn from darkness and seek light. Elsewhere differences are organized, but here is unity; elsewhere darkness is worshipped, but here the light shines; elsewhere activity is the pursuit of shadows and reflections, but here activity has one end and aim: that each of the believers may attain to selflessness, and become a ray emanating from the Sun of Truth.

May the friends of the Divine Servant continually assist one another to arise from the station of personality to the station of selflessness which is the station of the ray. May we become infinitely considerate one of another, having cast out pride, ambition, thought and desire, which are veils of the personal self. May we be ever conscious that the unity of each Bahá'í Assembly in itself, and the unity of all the Bahá'í Assemblies one with another, is the preliminary condition to that world unity for which the Divine became Servant in this age. May we be ever conscious that the ray is nothing in itself, but is an emanation from the Sun; that the Sun manifests its power through the ray, and the Sun is all in all.

Then, as the personalities diminish, and the world weakens its secret hold upon the hearts, the Sun will assert its predominant power, having rays unto all the horizons. Then even the consciousness of yielding up self will flee as the ultimate shadow before the Dawn, and the meeting of this selflessness, the community of this faithfulness, will penetrate humanity with a new spirit and a new life.

Now is the work of becoming selfless; but the work of the Sun is at hand.

OUR COVENANT WITH 'ABDU'L-BAHÁ

THE HUMAN race is immersed in the ocean of the spirit. Bahá'u'lláh is universal, and He has surrounded humanity with all the blessings of the Day of God. You and I are aware of the fact that we are immersed in the ocean of the spirit, but the majority of the people are not yet aware, and when we are not aware of the spirit that surrounds and penetrates us, and tries to act upon a reluctant heart and a mind that is full of the shadows of the past, the individual encased in this unawareness is fearful of the spirit because the spirit, to him, is something that threatens what he thinks is the basis of his human personality. It is as though he were constantly being threatened by death—not physical death—but the extinction of what he considers to be his security. Those who *are* aware of the spirit, and know it can do nothing but bless those who become aware of it, have laid upon themselves the mission of the ages, to remove the obstacles from human personality which shut people out from the Spirit of Bahá'u'lláh.

In this great Day of God there is no *one* way to free all souls. The number of ways is exactly the number of the Bahá'ís themselves, which means that every Bahá'í has a mission, and if any of us fail to do our part in the quickening of souls, it means we have left certain people in the prison of their human personality, because we have thrown away the keys that would open the doors and make them Bahá'ís.

When Bahá'ís meet together—and they always meet, whatever the intention of the programme—they meet on three levels of experience. Bahá'ís *meet*—but other people in a room or gathering do not meet because the meeting of human beings today is only possible on the basis of the worship of the One True God. It is in the world of Prayer and Devotion that human beings meet. Otherwise they encounter one another, and make some kind of a partial impression, but they really do not *meet*. Bahá'ís meet on the level of *prayer and devotion*, and therefore it is a true meeting. Bahá'ís meet also on the level of *consultation*, because we are all not merely interested in the activities of the Faith, but each of us is charged with his particular concern. Finally, we meet in the spirit of *action*, because no matter how illumined we feel we are, or how pleased we are with the beauty of the Teachings, if we do not give them action, the spirit does not flow through us, and that portion of the spirit which has entered us becomes stagnant, and the Holy Spirit itself can be our doom if it is not always renewed. This is a mystical experience, the meeting of Bahá'ís on the three great levels of human experience.

Since entering this hall, it has been close to my heart to try and speak of a certain attitude of the creative nature of this Faith and I turn my heart to the time when Bahá'u'lláh, in the flesh, manifested the bounty of God. Bahá'u'lláh came to connect man with God. He delivered His message to mankind whether He was in meditation in the prison, or whether He was speaking to those with whom He walked in the garden, or by the bank of the river, or whether He was revealing a Tablet to an individual Bahá'í or to one of the kings of the earth. Bahá'u'lláh was addressing Mankind, but *there was no mankind to hear*. There were the people of Persia, but they were not "mankind"; they were a race, or a nation. There were the people of 'Iráq, and Turkey, but they did not constitute "mankind." They were separated from mankind, and therefore we have this illimitable mystery of God's comprehension of the human race and speaking with the utterance of the Infinite to mankind before mankind had become one being.

Now a message from God must be delivered, and there was no mankind to hear this message. Therefore, God gave the world 'Abdu'l-Bahá. 'Abdu'l-Bahá received the message of Bahá'u'lláh on behalf of the human race. He heard the voice of God; He was inspired by the spirit; He attained complete consciousness and awareness of the meaning of this message, and He pledged the human race to respond to the voice of God. My friends, to me *that* is the Covenant—that there was on this earth some one who could be a representative of an as yet uncreated race. There were only tribes, families, creeds, classes, etc., but there was no man except 'Abdu'l-Bahá, and 'Abdu'l-Bahá, as man, took to Himself the message of Bahá'u'lláh and promised God that He would bring the people into the *oneness of mankind*, and create a humanity that could be the vehicle for the laws of God. It is because 'Abdu'l-Bahá was 'Abdu'l-Bahá, and because He could be this Hearing Ear, this Answering Heart, this Consecrated Will, that an Eternal Covenant was made, and because of 'Abdu'l-Bahá you and I are here as Bahá'ís. You and I are here as parts of the Mankind that has to be, because man is not man until he is imbued with the qualities and life of the Merciful, and there is no humanity until this one Spirit of Truth, and the guidance of the Divine Will, enters into the consciousness of all human beings to such an extent that each individual is not only drawn nearer to God, but he becomes *one* with all other men.

This process has begun. 'Abdu'l-Bahá came to this very city in pursuance of his sacred mission to create the soul and mind of man, and you who are here are the servants of the Divine Covenant. When 'Abdu'l-Bahá left this earth He laid upon the Bahá'ís the mission of fulfilling His promise to God, and He did not charge us with anything beyond the capacity of faith. He charged us with something that is impossible without faith; something that could not be attained, or something if attempted could not be carried out by division and fear, but gave to us the capacity to fulfil the promise He made to Bahá'u'-lláh, and He told us the way to enter into this capacity is to *serve*.

'Abdu'l-Bahá never turned to any Bahá'í and said, "My son, or daughter, I want you to study fifty-eight volumes of psychology, or thirty-three volumes of history and science." He said: "I charge you to serve—to be active." And with every step you take on the path of the Covenant, the qualities you need will be given you.

Faith is the basic characteristic of the Bahá'í in that it is not "I" nor "you" but that it is the Faith we have in God through the Covenant that will give us the capacity to do the thing that is impossible, so that the unlettered Bahá'í can be a servant of God to a degree that the greatest ecclesiastical dignitary on earth does not possess.

It seems to me that we have to continually draw back into that experience of the mysterious meeting with 'Abdu'l-Bahá and the renewal of the Covenant, because I know, perhaps as well as any one here, the feeling of utter incapacity, of complete discouragement and bewilderment that overtakes the souls of men if even for a moment they turn away from the Covenant. We are given that which is impossible for human beings to do, but *not* that which is impossible for faith, and we will not be measured in the Kingdom in accordance with any human standard of failure or success, but I think the Master will face each one of us as we walk over the threshold on the other side of the wall, and He will just simply ask one question: "Did you help *Me* fulfil My promise to Almighty God?"

Now that is something that should raise us up out of the very gutter of discouragement, from the feeling of personal inadequacy, and charge us with a conviction that despite ourselves, we are qualified to serve *if we serve*, but that no matter what remarkable human qualities we may have, if we do not serve, we will lose them, one by one.

You and I are members of a World Faith, and from day to day that World Faith is growing more and more potent and decisive in the destiny of the human race. O, if we could but increase our *service—do* things—*dare* things! Is there a man with whom we are seated on a train? Is there some one we meet in the normal daily experiences of life? We have been too hesitant. I do not mean we can assail another soul.

I wonder if it would not be a good teaching technique for

the individual Bahá'í to begin to figure two or three very simple questions about world conditions, or about certain spiritual attitudes reflected by the present, with a view to testing the response from the individual we meet for the first time? Try such questions out. We are making an effort to contact the *inner* man. If we do that and fail nine or ninety-nine times, do not let us be discouraged, because our one task is to learn how to meet the *inner spirit* of the people, and not just revolve around and around their outer personality. The person in this room who may feel the least qualified, may prove to be, on the actual field of service, the most brilliant and successful exponent of the power of the Covenant. The only Bahá'í who need really worry is the Bahá'í who is vain—not the Bahá'í who is humble. But humility can be a screen if we use it as a reason for not serving, so remember the dividing line is not *how much* we know—not how many books we have studied— but whether we passed from *inaction* to *action*, because we are pledged to serve, and 'Abdu'l-Bahá has pledged to serve us if we serve Him.

—*Talk at Los Angeles Bahá'í Centre, October 23, 1948.*

WHAT ABOUT ME?

Excerpts from a Talk given
at Area Teaching Conference, Temple Foundation Hall,
June 11, 1955

ALL HUMAN action and thought—all our feelings—spring from the mysterious depths of our being.

Most of us are unconscious of the nature and possibilities of this area of our self. We are conscious of *what* we say and do, and *how* we feel, but not *why* we act and talk and feel in particular ways.

Somewhere in those mysterious depths of the unconscious lies our supreme endowment as human beings—capacity to know, to love and obey God, which is also capacity to reject and deny God. Always and ever, whether we realize it or not, we draw nearer to the divine Wisdom or we are turning away. The world can give us no sure test to determine which direction we are taking. This the individual must learn for himself.

We do not and cannot serve the Cause of God with the thoughts, feelings and actions of the natural man. The activities of the man of nature have corrupted and destroyed every revealed religion of the past. They made religion a mode of self-worship, an arena in which the physical, mental and psychic powers could be fulfilled. Capacity to serve God is from the Word, for the Word transforms man from attachment to the secret springs of instinct by connecting him with the life of the heavenly world.

If the first step is devotion to the Word of God, each for himself, with no substitute for the Word in minister, priest or teacher, the second step is the establishment of the true relationship with others. No man acquires true self-respect until

he loves the Word of God; and no man can truly respect others
until he has attained respect for the divine creation within himself. As the Bahá'í Teachings state, we do not know ourselves
until we have knowledge of God.

Bahá'u'lláh calls for consecrated individuals to speed the
"glad tidings" throughout the earth. But this is not all. The
Faith of Bahá'u'lláh also requires a unified world community
composed of many unified national and local communities, all
centred in harmony upon the redemption of mankind and the
establishment of a new world order. The community of the
Greatest Name can only unify *believers*—souls which, in their
varying degrees, are become a mirror reflecting the light of the
Word—and its pillars are consultation and kindness, those
germinating powers which evoke new and nobler attributes
within mankind.

Therefore, it can be said: *First*, continuous individual devotion to the creative Word, *second*, continuous regard for that
unity which is God's special and wondrous blessing for this
age. Out of these two conditions will spring our particular
services to the Cause of Bahá'u'lláh.